GOOD GUYS,
WISEGUYS,
and
Putting Up
Buildings

ALSO BY SAMUEL C. FLORMAN

Engineering and the Liberal Arts (1968)

The Existential Pleasures of Engineering (1976)
SECOND EDITION (1994)

Blaming Technology (1981)

The Civilized Engineer (1987)

The Introspective Engineer (1996)

The Aftermath: A Novel of Survival (2001)

GOOD GUYS,
WISEGUYS,
and
Putting Up
Buildings

A Life in Construction

Samuel C. Florman

Thomas Dunne Books
St. Martin's Press
New York

THOMAS DUNNE BOOKS.
An imprint of St. Martin's Press.

GOOD GUYS, WISEGUYS, AND PUTTING UP BUILDINGS. Copyright © 2012 by Samuel
C. Florman. All rights reserved. Printed in the United States of America. For
information, address St. Martin's Press, 175 Fifth Avenue, New York, N.Y. 10010.

www.thomasdunnebooks.com
www.stmartins.com

In Chapter Two, the description of work performed by Japanese personnel under
the supervision of Seabees on the atoll of Truk is adapted from "The Pacific Campaign, Dam Division," an op-ed article by Samuel C. Florman that appeared in
The New York Times, September 4, 2010.

Library of Congress Cataloging-in-Publication Data

Florman, Samuel C.
    Good guys, wiseguys, and putting up buildings : a life in construction /
Samuel C. Florman.—1st ed.
        p.   cm.
    ISBN 978-0-312-64167-2 (hardcover)
    ISBN 978-1-4299-4108-2 (e-book)
    1. Civil engineers—United States—Biography.   2. Contractors—United
States—Biography.   3. Construction industry—New York (State)—
New York—History.   4. New York (N.Y.)—Buildings, structures,
etc.—History.   I. Title.
    TH140.F59A3 2012
    624.092—dc23
    [B]   2011041332

First Edition: March 2012

10   9   8   7   6   5   4   3   2   1

FOR: JUDY
DAVID, CINDY, JULIA, RACHEL
JONATHAN, LISSA, HANNAH, LUCY, SYLVIE
with much love

Contents

GOOD GUYS,
WISEGUYS,
and
Putting Up
Buildings

ONE | *I Can Have You Killed for Fifty*

THE CRIME TOOK PLACE in the Bronx on the northeast corner of Claflin Avenue and 195th Street. The perpetrators stood on the sidewalk adjoining a nearly completed six-story apartment house that my construction firm was building. When I arrived on the scene, three men were engaged in animated conversation. The masonry subcontractor, Lou, was pleading with a city inspector to grant him "just a few more minutes," and our construction superintendent, Norman, was saying something like "jeez, give the guy a break." I joined the group just in time to see the inspector shake his head and then say loudly, "No way, no how!" It seemed that a small forklift was being used to transport concrete blocks from a parked truck into the building, and a problem had arisen when no updated building permit could be produced. The discussion grew more and more heated, and for a moment I thought that the mason and the inspector were going to come to blows.

But suddenly the shouting stopped, and very quietly the inspector said, "OK." Pause. "It'll cost you a hundred bucks." Norman and I glanced at each other and cautiously backed away. But not before we heard Lou say softly, "Oh yeah? A hundred bucks." Then even more softly, "You gotta be kidding." Finally, almost in a whisper: "I can have you killed for fifty."

There was silence as the two men studied each other. After a moment, the inspector turned around, walked swiftly to his car, and drove away.

I refer to a crime, yet what had actually happened? On the face of it, a bribe was solicited and murder threatened while two witnesses— one of them me—stood by in stunned silence. But what if the verbal exchange was not meant to be taken literally? What if it was merely a ritualistic expression of intimidating bluster like two athletes talking trash on a basketball court? On the other hand, what if . . . ?

Clearly the inspector took Lou's words seriously. Very seriously. And as I recall the scene, the atmosphere was charged with menace.

Whenever I tell the story it gets a laugh, or at least a smile. Partly this is because the tale contains a surprise punch line. But there is something else that entertains my audience—the shiver of fear, to- gether with the comfort of personal safety, the very same *frisson* that makes it a special pleasure to view *The Godfather* or *The Sopranos* in the comfort and security of a theater or one's living room.

I start to write about my career as a builder and find myself leading with murder and intimidation. A touch of swagger and bravado? I suppose so. But not idle fantasy. In the words of the New York State Organized Crime Task Force (1990): "Historical and contemporary evidence, including our own criminal investigations, establish be- yond any doubt that corruption and racketeering pervade New York City's construction industry." And, further, bearing on the incident just described: "The presence of so many known organized crime figures in the industry makes the explicit threat of violence credible and the implicit threat of violence sufficient." The implicit threat of violence was clearly enough to send one veteran building inspector quickly on his way.

The Mafia and construction are joined in the public's imagination— and, as amply documented—literally in the real world. But estab- lished criminal organizations have no monopoly on malfeasance in the industry. Society is not that neatly organized, corruption not so circumscribed. Wherever construction contracts are awarded and buildings erected, skulduggery seems endemic—among contractors, developers, tradesmen, politicians, purchasing agents, inspectors, and union delegates. The media report almost daily on every conceivable sort of misdeed—bribes, kickbacks, extortion, bid rigging, inflated claims, use of inferior materials, and more. Transparency International, the global coalition founded in 1993 by an array of highly respected individuals, cites construction as the single most corrupt industry that exists on the face of the earth. The contract award process appears to lend itself to underhanded dealings, stratagems that even competitive bidding cannot eliminate. The very activity of building is linked historically with cheating. Paradoxically, the many layers of supervision intended to monitor construction projects and guarantee propriety—the permits, change orders, regulations, approvals—provide unique opportunities for wrongdoing.

Adding to these time-honored problems, we find violence on the job sites, the belligerence of rugged men sometimes getting in one another's way, the perpetual conflict of union versus nonunion workers, and occasionally one trade fighting for its very existence, such as when, in the 1950s, drywall began to replace plaster. The Civil Rights Movement saw minority workers battling for their rightful share of employment and then, in some cities, falling prey to labor racketeers. In New York in the 1980s aggressive gangs swept down on building sites in yellow school buses, demanding jobs but seeking payoffs and kickbacks, often two or more mobs competing, sometimes with gunplay involved.

Beyond crime, corruption, and violent intimidation, building construction, in its very nature, is rough and tough and turbulent. Visit any job site. Motion and noise. Monstrous machines, enormous beams, cables swaying, concrete hoisted aloft in buckets. The weather—sometimes frigid, sometimes sweltering—adds to the feeling of adventure. Observe the men, the hardhats: boisterous, seeming as strong and hardy as the tools they wield; rugged, macho, toiling deep in the earth and high into the sky, as much a part of American mythology as the cowboys of earlier days. (There are a few women on the jobs, but very few.)

In a busy city most citizens walk by construction sites with hardly a glance. And even sidewalk superintendents may idle away the time wrapped in their own thoughts. Yet alert observers cannot help but feel the pulse-quickening excitement infused with a sense of danger.

And the danger is real, independent of crime and conflict. In the United States there are more workers killed in construction than in any other single industry. The death rate per capita may be slightly higher in a few other occupations—notably logging, ranching, fishing, and mining—but the 1,000 to 1,300 annual construction fatalities is the largest number for any industry sector and represents approximately one in every five recorded in the nation. As might be expected, the number of nonfatal injuries is also extremely high. Nor are the perils limited to workers on the job. Frequently a passerby—or even a citizen hundreds of yards distant from a building site—is injured or even killed in a freak accident.

After the construction process ends, the hazards associated with man-made structures do not disappear. Buildings, new and old, shed bricks and stone, sometimes with deadly consequence, or even collapse, explode, or spew steam from broken pipes. Physical perils naturally have financial consequence, as evidenced by the extremely high insurance rates associated with the activity of building.

THIS litany of menace brings us inevitably to the phenomenon of financial disaster. Physical mishap is only one of the many dangers that confront the builder. Business risk has burrowed into the very marrow of the construction industry, making it America's most perilous enterprise, except for restaurants, as a percentage of company failures. In any given two-year period almost a quarter of the nation's non-single-family construction firms close their doors. Half of new firms fail within four years, three-quarters within ten years. Part of this stems from the ease with which the adventurous can enter the field—all it takes is a few tools, a few dollars, and some guts.

But, while a large majority of the nation's 7.2 million salaried construction workers are employed by very small companies—five employees and fewer—financial ruin stalks firms of every size. The top 400 contractors—those whose annual volume runs from the $150 million range to several billion—do more than 20 percent of the nation's $1–1.25 trillion building and take a sizeable share of the financial setbacks. Every year sees large, long-established firms incur devastating losses.

According to a report prepared by FMI Corp., a top management consultant, the typical contractor is "numb to risk," exhibiting "a heroic audacity." There is probably some truth to this view, but I think it underestimates the treacherous nature of the business and the role of bad luck. Be this as it may, to quote an often heard maxim, in the construction industry financial ruin is "just one bad job away."

SO, how did I get into this business? Quiet by nature; devoted to family; a lover of books, opera, and the New York baseball Giants—I was a high-achieving student who once thought of becoming a mathematician or possibly a physicist. I never liked riding my bike too fast, much less doing the reckless things that appeal to so many thrill seekers. I don't much care for heights or for gambling, even when I win. Not that I'm totally immune to the attractions of risk. None of us is. Scientists tell us we enjoy the charge of dopamine that accompanies danger because taking chances helped early humans find food and mates, hence the genes that favor daring are within us all. It's a question of degree, however, and, though I enjoy adventure stories and cowboy movies, watching sports on TV, even—once upon a time—playing a rugged game of soccer, I don't fancy that my quota of peril-loving genes is very high. Also, assuming that we are shaped by nurture as well as nature, there was little about my childhood environment that would have contributed to making me a daredevil. As a city kid I occasionally dashed between moving cars, rode the subways alone, and even shared forbidden ventures into the West Side railroad yards. But each time I left home, my parents' parting admonition was, "Watch your crossings!" and to a certain extent I always have.

As for corruption—jeepers! For twelve years, in the 1930s and 1940s, I attended the Ethical Culture Fieldston School in New York City, taking an ethics class at least once a week. Not that a few hundred ethics classes make for a good person; but the school was serious in its purpose and, in good measure I believe, effective. Also, like many kids of my time and place, I was taught to "behave," certainly to respect authority and obey the law. Pranks and a few white lies— well, that was to be expected; but criminal malfeasance, action that might bring shame on the family—that was, and is, a horror beyond imagining.

And yet I've made my career in the construction industry, which is renowned for crime, corruption, violence, physical danger, and chronic risk of financial catastrophe.

I look back on this career with relish, not, I hasten to say, because I engaged in crime, corruption, and the rest, but because of the challenges met, the rousing adventures encountered. Also there have been satisfactions of a different sort: the enchantment of seeing architecture made real; the pleasure of solving complex technical problems; the pride of creating housing, hospitals, schools, places of worship— shelter for the body and nourishment for the spirit. And wonderful people met on the journey—along with a challenging assortment of knaves.

TWO | *Can Do*

"WHAT DO YOU WANT to be when you grow up?"

Every child encounters this question, early and often, annoying when asked by adults, but engrossing when thought of in solitude. A fireman? A baseball player? A movie actor? President? More realistically, if a boy, do what your father does?

I knew from an early age that heroic visions were, well, just visions. I also knew that I didn't want to do what my father did. He was in the millinery business. Having come to this country in his teens from Russia, he worked as a traveling salesman, mostly in the South, and from this set up a small office in New York City representing many of the merchants he had visited. New York was at the time a manufacturing center for the garment industry, and the specialty of ladies' hats was an important part of that bustling scene. My father would buy hats from New York manufacturers on behalf of stores in faraway places. Many of the store owners visited New York in the early spring, and I recall big men with booming voices, some of them wearing boots and cowboy hats, coming to our home, often bearing gifts. Easter was the time, traditionally, when women in small-town America would buy a new hat—assuming they could afford it, for those were lean years.

Let me put this in context: I grew up in the heart of the Great Depression. Luckily, since many Southern women regarded the new Easter bonnet as one of life's fundamentals, my father's business survived. In this we were more fortunate than many. Yet one didn't have to be destitute to feel the effects of that terrible time. I particularly recall the poor souls who came to the courtyard of our apartment house and sang or played musical instruments, picking up the coins tossed down from the windows by tenants like us. At that bedroom window, overlooking the courtyard, I felt pity and fear and also, thinking about my own future, a resolve not to end up singing for charity. At the same time, I hoped it would be possible to make my way without having to deal in millinery. I don't know why I had those negative feelings about my father's trade, but it's just as well that I did. By the time I reached adulthood, American women had almost totally given up wearing hats.

There was a second window in my bedroom at a right angle to the first, and this one overlooked an empty lot. Through that window, for a two-year period, I was treated to a close-up view of an apartment house under construction. The new structure rose into the sky, just twenty feet away from my private viewing site. A highlight of that theatrical production was the erection of the steel frame. What excitement! Rivets, heated to a glowing red state, were tossed through the air—sometimes long distances—caught in a metal basket, placed with tongs into holes in the steel beams, and then hammered into final shape with a pneumatic gun. Today we use high-tension bolts, efficient but not nearly as dramatic.

It would make a neat story to say that between the poverty viewed through one window and the flying rivets viewed through the other, I decided to make a career in construction. But that's not the way it was. The construction was thrilling indeed, not only as seen from my window, but wherever I encountered it in the city. Yet, like a circus or a ball game, that was excitement for observing, not something in which I could envision myself playing a part.

My father once mentioned that I might want to build subways, although I don't think he was entirely serious. On Sunday mornings he used to go horseback riding in Central Park—as did many people in those days—and on several occasions he rode with Sam Rosoff, the renowned constructor of subways. Rosoff's multimillion-

GOOD GUYS, WISEGUYS, AND PUTTING UP BUILDINGS

dollar subterranean projects were exciting to consider, and perhaps if I had been older and could have become acquainted with Mr. Rosoff, talking business on horseback—but, no, that was just idle fantasizing.

ALTHOUGH I toyed with the idea of becoming a mathematician or a physicist, from what I could tell these were not fields in which one could make a living, except perhaps as a teacher. Somehow—based on I know not what evidence—I concluded that if one liked math and science, and also wanted to be employable, the solution lay in the profession of engineering. I didn't have a clear idea of what engineers did, but I formulated my own definition—math and science with a paycheck. Also, after a fashion, engineers were cultural heroes. The newsreels that I saw every weekend between two movies at Loews 83rd Street often featured the dedication of a new TVA dam or some other impressive public work. There was much cutting of ribbons and drinking of toasts, each event celebrating a counterattack against rural dust bowls or urban slums. And when the movies themselves depicted engineers—usually in the B film, to be sure—they were stalwart men in high-laced boots engaged in heroic endeavors such as building railroads or prospecting for oil. Intellectually challenging, financially sensible, and withal a touch of romance and adventure—engineering seemed like an ideal calling.

So, when it came time to look at colleges, I kept in mind the option of pursuing an engineering degree. As for admissions, today's population pressures lay far in the future. Any accomplished student—and I did well—coming from a quality school—which mine was—with a family willing to pay full tuition—my parents would make any sacrifice on the altar of education—could be cautiously optimistic. So when I fell in love with Dartmouth College, my advisers encouraged me to apply. It was not only the beauty of the New Hampshire campus and the spirit of the place that I found beguiling. The engineering school at Dartmouth, the Thayer School, featured a five-year program leading to a BA degree at the end of the fourth year and a Civil Engineer degree, equivalent to a masters, at the end of the fifth. This unique program sought to enrich engineering with a wholesome experience in the liberal arts, a concept that I found appealing and that I value ever more to this day. As a final attraction, I learned that Dartmouth's Tuck School, traditionally ranked as one of the elite graduate business institutions in the world, offered a joint program with Thayer. I was excited by the possibility of becoming a liberally educated engineer with superior training in business as well. The best of all possible worlds—and good insurance against ever having to sing for coins in the courtyard of an apartment house.

I recall the weekend visit to Hanover during which I decided to make Dartmouth my first choice. It ended on a Sunday in December—by happenstance the day that the Japanese bombed Pearl Harbor. Just as I was thinking about college, the United States entered a world war. Although I didn't know it at the time, the fates determined that day that my path to the future lay through Dartmouth College to the United States Navy, and ultimately to a career in the construction industry.

ONE doesn't instinctively think of the navy and building construction having much to do with each other. Indeed, before World War II, construction of naval shore facilities was performed exclusively by civilian contractors. The U.S. Navy Civil Engineer Corps, which provided oversight, consisted of fewer than three hundred officers and zero enlisted men. However, looking at a theater of war that stretched across the Pacific, navy officials realized that a militarized naval construction force would be a necessity. Within weeks of the Japanese attack a decision was made to recruit men from the construction trades for assignment to newly created naval construction battalions—CBs—the Seabees. To obtain men with the necessary qualifications, physical standards were relaxed and the age range for enlistment was extended to fifty. America's hardhats proved that their loudly proclaimed patriotism was more than talk.

During the early days of the war, the average age of Seabees was thirty-seven, and rumor had it that some of the enlistees were over sixty. After December 1942 these voluntary enlistments were halted by orders of the president, and men for the construction battalions were obtained mainly through the Selective Service System. As a result the average age of the Seabees declined, and many young men came into the service with only rudimentary construction skills. Still, the accomplishments of the Seabees—"Can Do"—were legendary. Eventually this newly created force consisted of more than eleven thousand officers and three hundred thousand enlisted personnel. It was into this remarkable body of men that serendipitously I made my way, although by the time I joined their ranks the war was in its final days.

TO those of us who were young when the war began—I was sixteen on Pearl Harbor Day, seventeen when I graduated high school in June of 1942—life continued in oddly familiar ways. The conflict was faraway, and for many months little seemed to be happening. There was no such thing as television, and whatever military news appeared in the press was heavily censored. The draft law that had recently been passed by Congress set age limits of twenty-one to thirty-six. Armed-forces recruiters manned booths in Times Square, but nobody came knocking at my door in patriotic fervor. Maybe the war would be short. So my classmates and I continued with our schoolwork and applied to colleges in accordance with existing schedules. In due course I was accepted at Dartmouth and looked forward to a new chapter in my life.

There was no summer break after high school graduation. Because of the war, most colleges instituted a year-round schedule. Strange as it seems in retrospect, for an entire year I—and many thousands of freshmen throughout the nation—lived a relatively normal college life: regular classes, football weekends, freshman hijinks, and all the rest. Gradually, however, the real world intruded. As it became clear that the war would not end quickly, the draft age was lowered, standards for deferment were tightened, and recruiters from the several military services made frequent visits to our campus. They offered a variety of enlistment opportunities tailored to college students, most plans featuring continued time in school, then military training leading to a commission. No promises were made, and I saw many of my contemporaries sign up for great-sounding programs, only to be swept off to basic training as progress on the battlefields required.

For those Dartmouth students who were committed to engineering, the navy offered a program that would leave us in Hanover to complete our course of study, obtain our degree, and then be sent to officers training school and commissioned as ensigns in the Civil Engineer Corps. No guarantees, of course, but that was the plan. It sounded good but contained no provision for my dream of combining engineering and business in the Tuck-Thayer program. When I mentioned this concept to the recruiting personnel, the response was, to say the least, negative. The option being offered was meant to prepare officers for the Seabees. If I was interested in economics and business administration, I could look elsewhere—and good luck. Perhaps I would end up with a commission in the Supply Corps. More likely I would end up as a seaman apprentice sent to join the fleet.

So this was the moment. Not that most young people let their military service determine their life's occupation. But for me this is exactly what happened. Set on a particular road, I found that it suited me well, and I followed it all the way. Not a career in the navy, to be sure, but a career in construction that started in the navy.

I signed the fateful enlistment papers in December 1942, and seven months later—one year after arriving on campus—was called to active duty. It was a strange fusion of roles: I put on a sailor's uniform and learned to march in formation, shout out orders lustily, salute sharply, and say yes, sir. (At least one classmate was sent off to boot camp for failing to give marching orders with enough authority.) Yet I remained on campus, and my main occupation was taking classes. The engineering school was a long distance from the gymnasium, and on certain mornings I had just a few minutes to race from the classroom to the swimming pool, where I was taught to leap from a high tower—as from a ship—and then, rising to the surface of the water, swing my arms about as if keeping clear of burning oil on the surface. A half hour later I was in a laboratory testing concrete or in the library studying for an exam.

Our curriculum included a few of the standard liberal arts courses but was weighted toward the sciences and gradually evolved into the study of civil engineering. The work was hard, but I took to it: the design of structures, the nature of materials, hydraulics, water supply and sanitation, highways and railways, soil mechanics, electricity and electronics—and, most fun of all, surveying. It was great sport taking the measure of the New Hampshire countryside and, for directional orientation, sighting the North Star by transit at midnight.

In February of 1945, two and a half years after my arrival at Dartmouth, the navy decided that my classmates and I were engineers and ready to move on. We had in fact earned four and a half years' worth of credits, more than enough to qualify for a bachelor's degree, which we were awarded, but not quite enough to earn the Thayer School five-year degree, which I was able to obtain in later years.

At the time, niceties of academic status were not a priority in anyone's thinking. Allied troops were moving toward victory in Europe, and plans were being developed for an invasion of Japan. As part of the projected attack force, Seabee battalions were assembling in the Philippines, and we Sailor-students were told that our turn to serve had come. We said good-bye to the campus, and, after two months of officers training school in Rhode Island, received our commissions. There followed another two months of "military training"—an odd mix of hiking, crawling, shooting the newest antiaircraft guns, and waving traditional signal flags—then a final leave and a cross-country train ride. By the time we were transferred to pre-embarkation barracks at Camp Parks in Shoemaker,

California, the date was August 7, 1945. During the hectic preparations for boarding ship, I overheard the latest news. The previous day some special sort of bomb had been dropped on a Japanese city—Hiroshima.

The significance of this event was not at first made clear to us. We sailed on schedule, and only as we voyaged across the Pacific did we begin to realize that the war was coming to an end. We were relieved, certainly, but also struck by a feeling of anticlimax. Several in our group kept watch for hostile submarines or lurking enemies in the jungles of Eniwetok and Ulithi, islands where we stopped, hoping to lay claim to having experienced combat. As it turned out, on September 2, the day after our arrival in Leyte Gulf, a surrender agreement was signed aboard the battleship *Missouri* in Tokyo Bay.

The war was over. But the occupation of Japan—and many of its island bases—required the continued participation of American forces. Since the Seabee heroes who had been in the forefront of numerous island invasions were anxious to go home, we newcomers were welcomed as replacements. And becoming a Seabee—for me, joining the Twenty-ninth Naval Construction Battalion on Samar Island in the Philippines—was a thrill. The "Can Do" motto of this branch of the service applied not only to construction skills but also to cleverness in general, somehow acquiring choice food, for example, finding or creating special comforts for their living quarters, and managing to cope with navy regulations while not taking them any more seriously than seemed necessary.

My first assignment was oversight of road maintenance, mostly dirt roads that had to be continually regraded, reshaped, and compacted. The enlisted men, who were skilled operators of the equipment, delighted in teaching newly arrived officers the tricks of their trades. This wasn't strictly in accord with regulations, but in the somewhat giddy atmosphere that stemmed from knowing the war was over, military discipline was loosened a bit. Suddenly I, who had barely learned to drive a car at home, found myself double clutching behind the wheel of an enormous truck and experimentally operating bulldozers, road graders, backhoes, and cranes. What a thrill it was to be in the seat of a monstrous, powerful bulldozer and actually to control its actions. In addition to running equipment, I laid brick, troweled concrete, and wielded a variety of tools, an introduction to construction that I cannot imagine encountering under any other circumstance. Such experience can't be bought in engineering school and would never be available on any construction job that I have ever seen.

AFTER two months on Samar, the battalion received word that we were moving on. The destination was Truk (now called Chuuk), an atoll in the Caroline Islands that had served as headquarters for the Japanese fleet. Protected by a circle of coral reefs, this formidable base had been bypassed during the American advance across the Pacific and then bombed into rubble from Guam, Saipan, and other nearby islands. At war's end the U.S. Navy decided that the main airstrip should be rebuilt along with a basic military camp. According to a unique provision in the surrender agreement, three thousand Japanese were to remain on Truk for a year to perform the necessary construction, working under the direction of an American force. Our battalion was selected to be that American force, and so, after a marine unit was sent ahead to assure security, we assembled an assortment of basic construction equipment and prepared to be on our way.

But how, exactly was this journey to be made? Since most shipping was committed to returning troops and equipment to the United States, the Twenty-ninth Seabees traveled from the Philippines to Truk in three LCIs and an LST. An unimposing flotilla if ever there was one. The LCIs—landing-craft infantry—were just what their name implied, flat-bottom vessels designed for beaching and discharging troops. At 158 feet long and 23 feet wide at the middle, they were not intended to travel across open ocean, and during our journey they seemed to lurch upward and slam down with every wave. The LST, landing-ship tank, also designed to support amphibious operations, was a large, lumbering vessel, 330 feet long, able to carry 18 Sherman tanks (or in our case, the equivalent in construction equipment) on its lower deck and a number of lighter vehicles on its upper. It didn't skip and toss as did the LCIs, but it rolled uncomfortably at its cruising speed of 8.75 knots. For a group of men nominally part of the navy but used to service on shore, our ten-day voyage through rough seas was somewhat unnerving.

UPON arrival at Truk, we found ourselves surrounded by a horde of the erstwhile enemy—approximately forty thousand warriors noted for their ferocity in battle. Marines had preceded us, but their presence and surrender agreement notwithstanding, one could not help feeling a bit edgy. In discussions among ourselves we agreed that it would take years—perhaps a generation—before our hatred of this enemy would diminish. How the Japanese felt in defeat we could only guess. Whatever the sentiments on either side, tranquility prevailed. The Japanese remained within designated areas strictly policed by their officers, the majority of them preparing for their journey home on such ships as they could muster. The cadre selected to work with the Americans moved into special quarters they were to occupy and awaited instructions.

Our men hastily erected a tent camp, and the officers held a series of meetings to plan and schedule our assigned work. The major objective was to restore the airstrip, and for this our most experienced engineer officers undertook the design and oversight. They decided to accomplish the task with coral dredged from the sea, a method unfamiliar to most American engineers, and one that prompted much debate. The doubters took a lot of convincing; but in the end, both in execution and results, the enterprise was eminently successful.

Once the airstrip operation was under way, electric generators were assembled and a basic power system established. A concrete mixing plant was built and permanent structures commenced. A well-equipped field hospital received special attention.

As the youngest and newest officer, I was put in charge of one of the less imposing projects: building a small earth-fill dam on a mountain stream for our water-supply system. I had no experience with earth-fill dams, but parameters were available in handbooks, and ample guidance was provided by senior engineer colleagues. So within a few days rudimentary plans were prepared and the work was scheduled to begin. The structure, as I gauge it now from recollection and faded photographs, was about fifty feet long at the top and rose approximately twenty-five feet from the bottom of a small gorge. It had to be thick enough to prevent failure by seepage, which by our cautious calculation made it bulky rather than graceful. Not exactly Grand Coulee, but for me at that time and place it loomed as quite a challenge. For work in the field, I was given three enlisted men from our battalion—men experienced in excavation work, one in particular, Frenchy, a take-over kind of guy, whom I designated as foreman. I was also assigned a Japanese crew, about two dozen men under the command of one of their lieutenants.

On the appointed day, the two teams gathered at the construction site and for what seemed like a long time simply stared at one another. Was there hostility or fear? I cannot say for sure. Friendly feelings? Certainly not.

It was up to me to make the first move. I walked over to my Japanese counterpart and ceremoniously unrolled the drawings that I had prepared, showing him the outlines of the job we were to undertake. I then set up a basic surveyor's transit, and within minutes my men were driving pointed stakes at designated spots and stretching cord between them. Soon the Japanese soldier-workers were attacking the earth with shovels and picks.

My men, with Frenchy in the lead, provided supervision, first hesitantly, then with increased zest. To my amazement, they and the Japanese workers were soon engaged in attempts at banter and boisterous pantomime. I had arranged for a claylike soil to be brought to the site by truck and wheelbarrow, and the Japanese devised a wooden pounding tool with which to compact the material. Within a few days the two groups had settled into an efficiently rhythmic working routine interspersed with episodes of playfulness. Efforts to learn words in one another's languages added to the spirit of affability.

The Japanese lieutenant and I, inhibited by notions of military protocol, did not warm up to each other right away. But enthusiasm for the task at hand, and pride in the progress made, led first to mutual respect and eventually to friendship. I knew that there had been a breakthrough when he encouraged me to call him Moe, an abbreviation of a name that I had difficulty pronouncing.

The anticipated generation-long era of fear and hatred seemed to have been reduced to mere days.

After about two months the project was deemed complete. Frenchy had often exhorted the workers by calling them, in an aggressive but friendly way, "a bunch of characters," and at the end he suggested that the structure be given the name Characters' Dam. I approved, nobody countermanded the order, and accordingly an ornate sign was prepared and placed in a prominent spot.

We planned a dedication ceremony, and for the occasion Moe surprised me with the gift of a small ceramic statue. It was accompanied by a message that had been translated by one of Moe's fellow officers and transcribed painstakingly onto a white kerchief. The message read:

> April 2, 1946. The souvenir of the water plant completion. This is a statue of Admiral of the Fleet Count Hehachiro Togo, I.J.N. He was born at Kagoshima in Kyushu about a hundred years ago. He won the great victory in the Naval Battle of the Japan Sea. Namely he defeated the great Russian fleet (the Barutic Fleet). But some years ago he had a natural death. The world people say that he is the Nelson of the east. I pray that you may be able to make a great work as well as his achievement.
>
> Lt. Moe

Today the statue stands on a shelf in my office, and the kerchief, framed, hangs on the wall beside it. Perhaps one shouldn't generalize from this somewhat idyllic tale, but I do. It is one example, I believe, of the camaraderie that seems universally to spring up among people who work together creatively.

*   *   *

I look back fondly on the nine months I spent on Truk. The construction work was exciting, and the opportunities I had—the responsibilities—were quite remarkable, especially considering my youth and lack of experience. However, when I think of the feeling of accomplishment, the unmitigated fun of it all, I have to remind myself that money was not involved, at least not at my level. We had tasks, objectives, and the pressures that go with any job one wants to "do well." But we didn't have to think about making a profit, much less about losing money or going broke. My introduction to building was free of the anxieties that accompany construction in the "real world."

Truk Lagoon is a gorgeous place with spectacular beaches, and today it has become a popular tourist destination. It is particularly appealing to scuba divers, attracted by the remarkable underwater world that has evolved around the numerous sunken Japanese ships— beauty born of the horrors of war. There were moments—after our primitive camp of tents was converted into a relatively comfortable abode—when I almost felt like a vacationer myself. I visited, touristlike, the islands of Guam, Saipan, and Tinian, traveling as an "officer courier," a pleasant perk that our commanding officer distributed as widely as possible.

OF course, I was not on holiday; I was serving in the military. The two professions, engineering and the military, have a historical connection much closer than is generally recognized. In fact, engineering evolved from a trade into a profession as governments, starting in France in the seventeenth century, provided formal schooling for military engineers. The founding fathers of the United States, Washington, Adams, and particularly Jefferson, impressed by the effectiveness of the French engineers and officers who helped train the Colonial Army, advocated a national university to be based on the French model. In 1802, by act of Congress, President Jefferson created

CAN DO

19

the military academy at West Point, and subsequently, in 1817, Major Sylvanus Thayer, having studied at France's École Polytechnique, became the academy's superintendent, adapting much of the school's general approach to learning. (Yes, that was the same Thayer, popularly known as "the father of West Point," who in his later years helped found my alma mater, the Thayer School of Engineering, at Dartmouth College.) Well into the middle of the nineteenth century, most of America's engineers and engineering professors were retired army officers. And until fairly recently, the army approach—severity and strict discipline—were strong influences in engineering schools and throughout the profession.

Yet the spirit of the hardhat, the "Can Do" attitude of the Seabees and of construction people in general, is in many ways at odds with the military temperament. Leafing through my own thin service record, I come upon a "report of violation" sent from the provost marshal of the occupation forces, Truk, to the island's commanding general. My violation? Defiance of military regulations. One day I was "apprehended" by the military police and "warned." The offense was parking my weapons carrier in the middle of the road. The arresting MP was a marine second lieutenant, officer of the day, and I suppose we must have exchanged some unfriendly words since just twenty minutes later I was again "apprehended," this time for driving in excess of the thirty-mile-per-hour speed limit—and also for carrying a passenger on the running board. I escaped a court-martial by writing a report explaining that I had been picking up a couple of my men and transporting them from one job site to another, that I was in a hurry to get necessary work accomplished, and that I meant no disrespect toward the officer of the day—even though I had called him a meddling SOB. and maybe worse. Just a minor, mildly diverting example of what can happen when the forces of military order run counter to the forces of hurry-up construction spontaneity.

BY midsummer of 1946 I was back home in New York, parting company with the navy and beginning to wonder about getting a job in the construction industry. I've often thought of returning to the Pacific Islands, particularly Truk, but have never done so. It's probably just as well. In my imagination Truk Lagoon remains a tropical paradise, a place where Characters' Dam still stands.

THREE | *Explorations*

THE SUMMER OF 1946. Our nation: victorious, at peace. And everyone home. Not everyone, of course. More than three hundred thousand Americans killed in battle, and double that number wounded. Just the lucky ones returned unscathed. Most of my friends and high school classmates were in this category, safeguarded, as was I, first by age, and then by education. As college freshmen they had been recruited by the military and then sent to study all sorts of things—Japanese, Italian, meteorology, nuclear physics, statistics, cryptography—and were eventually assigned to a variety of behind-the-lines duties, some fascinating and useful, but not especially hazardous. There were exceptions, to be sure: two good friends who were under fire in the Battle of the Bulge, and a high school classmate who spent more than a year in a German prison camp. But they also came through unharmed. This was good news; and the past was quickly put aside. After greetings and celebrations, everyone I knew seemed to have one thing in mind: getting back to school.

Unlike most of the others, I already had a degree and was resolved to get on with my career, which meant going out to get a job. Yet the swarming movement of my compatriots back to campus gave me pause. Was I really ready to move on? The words of Chappie Lindquist, chaplain of the Twenty-ninth Seabees, returned to haunt me. As the only nonengineer officer in the battalion, he was constantly chiding us for our lack of interest in art, politics, religion, literature—anything that wasn't strictly technical. "Dear Lord," he intoned after dinner one evening on Truk: "I know that I am unworthy, I confess that I have sinned; but why did you have to abandon me on this island with nobody for company but these boring engineers." Was I truly finished with schooling, ready to go to work? I had managed to avoid most of the humanities component of the Dartmouth program, an evasion that was permitted only because of the war. Had I shortchanged myself? What if study in the liberal arts, in addition to enriching one's broad life experience, made for a better engineer, a better builder? Besides, what was my rush? Why did I need to get a head start on my contemporaries? And, argued a friend, don't forget who pays the tuition—as if I had to be reminded of the GI Bill.

So I changed my mind. One September morning I took a bus uptown to Columbia University and signed up for a master's program in English literature. With only two semesters of English to my credit—freshman English at that—I was surely one of the least qualified candidates ever to apply for that particular degree. But my intentions appeared honorable, and the spirit of the day favored giving veterans a break.

This is not the place to recount the details of that remarkable academic year. But remarkable it was, since I was privileged to take courses with two of the great professors of the age, Lionel Trilling and Jacques Barzun. My written thesis—the topic suggested by Professor Trilling—was entitled "American Criticism of Franz Kafka," and the required research brought me into touch with Freudianism, Marxism, existentialism, and all the other *isms* of the day. Most of my fellow students seeking an MA in literature were preparing for careers in academe, and their conversations often took me into fields far removed from engineering. A decade was to pass before C. P. Snow would call attention to the issue of "the two cultures." But the gulf between the humanities and the sciences is as old as civilization, and the benefits of bridging this gulf have long been discussed and debated. For me, the time spent at Columbia led to a heightened interest in the humanities. I should say—giving proper credit to my earlier schooling—led me back to this interest.

In the years that followed, research and writing—particularly about the relation of engineering to the general culture—became for me a serious avocation. But I never second-guessed my commitment to a career in construction. This was practical, a question of how best to make a living, but also philosophical. It was all very well for Plato to say that art and abstract thinking is better than "doing"; but that seems ironic when one considers that the glory of Athens rested on the marvels of Greek technology. Most important, it was a matter of my personal vision of the future. Did I want to spend my working life in a classroom, in an office, or alone with a typewriter? Did I want to teach or write or buy and sell? Or be a lawyer or a doctor?—it was a bit late for that. Or I did I want to return to the life for which I had studied and that I had found so exciting in the Seabees?

IN any event, I wasted no time in getting on with my chosen career. The ink was hardly dry on my Columbia diploma when I found a job with a builder of houses. At the same time I enrolled in the engineering program at New York University, taking evening courses in soil mechanics and structural design.

The job that I found, I should confess, was a job that found me. My brother-in-law at the time was Edward Benenson, a Realtor, and he had agreed to finance the building of a half dozen houses in Cedarhurst, New York. The builder with whom he invested needed a helping hand, and I was anxious to get to work, so agreement on a modest salary was readily reached.

I was an extra pair of eyes on-site, and my surveying skills proved useful. But probably my greatest contribution was as provider of transportation. I had a car—a small gray Plymouth that was a coming-home present from my parents—and early each morning I would pick up my new boss at his residence in Manhattan and drive to the job site on Long Island, passing by Idlewild Airport (later JFK), then under construction. After driving alongside the huge machines that were clangorously working on that enormous enterprise, the job on which I worked seemed awfully puny. The building of one-family houses, sometimes called "stick construction," basically consists of erecting a framework of two-by-four wooden studs (today often made of lightweight steel tubes or channels). These studs support wooden rafters of various sizes, topped by a roof of plywood and asphalt shingles. It is in many respects a different industry from "construction," and while I found the experience engaging, I don't know that I would have been thrilled to repeat it over and over again. It was an hors d'oeuvre, not the main course for which I hungered.

While the project might not have been very impressive technically, I did receive an eye-opening introduction to the business end of a building venture. I was fascinated to hear my boss negotiating on price with the subcontractors and then grumbling about their imperfect workmanship, shouting profanities when they did not provide manpower as promised, and answering their complaints about lack of timely payment. I saw building-department inspectors come and go and, as the job advanced, real estate brokers and potential home buyers going through their routines. The workers were not unionized, so there were no delegates or accredited foremen, and I overheard occasional arguments about pay rates, overtime, and the like. The disputes were carried on in several languages and at various levels of passion. But, in general, high spirits prevailed, the good-natured give-and-take that I have found typical of construction jobs everywhere. Physically, the perpetual motion and exposure to the elements was invigorating.

At day's end I left the dusty, clamorous job site and returned to my home, which at the time happened to be in one of the swankier places in the city, the Carlyle Hotel. During the war, my parents had given up our apartment on the West Side and opted for this totally different sort of residence, renting a one-bedroom unit with a small kitchen. I never did understand why they did this, except that my mother had apparently tired of "keeping house." So, a corner of the spacious living room, furnished with a pull-out couch bed, became my domicile. Not ideal by any means, but serviceable for an interim period.

While I was a student at Columbia, I came to feel comfortable at the elegant hotel, at ease in the lobby and the dining rooms, often enjoying a room service dinner before settling down with my books. But when I started my construction job, I discovered a whole new world. Leaving in the early morning, dressed in blue jeans and carrying a lunchbox, I shared friendly chatter with the cleaning ladies who were polishing up the ornate marble lobby. I returned in the early evening, just as the beautiful people were arriving for cocktails. Those doormen who didn't know me tried to send me around to the service entrance, and those who knew me well tried to hustle me along unnoticed. I had always understood that construction was thought of as a blue collar occupation; but the early morning departures and evening arrivals were a vivid demonstration of social reality. In later years I learned to dress in button-down shirts, but I have never forgotten those blue-jeaned passages through the Carlyle lobby.

MY housebuilding career lasted from the spring of 1947 to year's end, when the houses were substantially complete—and, fortunately, sold. The project was a financial success, but no follow-up was planned, which was fine with me. I was ready for a change.

As a matter of fact, I was restless and ready for a substantial change. The corner of the hotel living room was beginning to feel confining, and I couldn't find affordable quarters of my own. In the realm of romance, skies were cloudy. And, thinking back to my sojourn in the Philippines and the Pacific Islands—while thinking ahead to a wholesome bourgeois life of work and family (which I wanted but viewed with trepidation)—I developed a serious case of wanderlust. Having heard tales of well-paid construction jobs in exotic lands, I decided that this was what I wanted and assumed that it was something I could readily find. After several weeks of answering ads and scheduling interviews, I discovered something that I should have known from the start: there were indeed good jobs to be had, but only for someone willing to sign a two-year contract. I was gung ho for adventure but not ready to make that sort of commitment. So, nothing daunted, I resolved to go abroad and seek a job on my own in the country of my choice. But here, too, I was cautioned by knowledgeable people that finding work abroad entailed all sorts of complications—getting working papers, for starters—and that I would be well advised to seek employment with an American company with offices abroad. All right, so be it.

Through the friend of a friend I was introduced to one of the top people at the Hegeman-Harris Company, a fine old firm with much experience in foreign work. Their big undertaking at the time was in Venezuela, where huge oil reserves had been discovered and were being exploited. Go to our office in Caracas, I was told, and if you can sell our people on your education and abilities, and assure them that you are willing to stay on a job for, say, a minimum of six months, your chances of getting work should be fairly good. They're terrifically busy. And, here, this letter of introduction should help. Armed with that friendly epistle and a bundle of confidence, I arranged to take passage to Venezuela on a freighter that sailed from Baltimore.

It was just a few days by sea to the port of La Guaira and a long haul by bus up into the mountains to Caracas. After settling into a rather seedy hotel—since my funds for this venture were limited—I splurged on a taxi ride to the Hegeman-Harris office. Luckily, the interview went well, as indicated by a letter in my file dated April 1, 1948, signed by the manager of the Hegeman-Harris Caracas office:

> *Dear Mr. Florman:*
> *This confirms our verbal agreement to employ you on our works in Paraguana as Engineer Surveyor for a probationary period of 60 days at $400.00 monthly, mess and quarters found.*
> *You will be expected to lay out buildings, run levels, measure quantities, collect and present such information as should be*

required for an adequate system of costing and such other related
duties as instructed in the field.

At the end of the probationary period, you will be confirmed in
your appointment or not, as circumstances should warrant.

Obviously I wasn't going to make my fortune earning $400 a month, but "mess and quarters found" meant that all my living expenses would be paid; so after six months—the "probationary period" was just a formality—I would have accumulated close to $2,400, which in 1948 sounded like a lot of money.

AH, Venezuela. Someday I must set aside time to study that nation's rather feverish history. It is replete with revolutions, including in 1948, the year I was there, a bloodless coup, the leader of which was kidnapped and murdered two years later.

But none of this seemed to have any effect on the world in which I found myself, the world of oil that was Lake Maracaibo. Hegeman-Harris's contract was to build housing for the Creole Petroleum Corporation, a subsidiary of the Esso Standard Oil Company. Between Creole, Shell, and Gulf there were more than a thousand active wells on and about the lake, one of the centers of the world's oil production. Oil taken from under the lake was transported on specially manufactured "lake tankers" since the channel from the lake to the sea was not large enough to accommodate ocean-going vessels. (A channel was dredged in 1953 to permit the huge tankers to pass, but that was five years into the future.) On the coast adjoining that channel is the Paraguana Peninsula, which served as a stopping point where oil could be transferred from small tankers to large. Paraguana was also destined to have its own huge refinery and miles of pipelines running in every direction.

The housing project to which I was assigned had been planned to accommodate workers in this industrial maelstrom—nothing fancy, single-story barracks really, and our job was to build them fast. In some respects I felt that I was back on Truk with the Seabees. But there were significant differences between the two environments. For one thing, the landscape itself. The Pacific Islands were lush with vegetation. Paraguana was arid, dominated by wind-blown sand. More important was the difference in the men. The Seabees were basically the same people one would find on a construction job in the United States, engineers and tradesmen, socially a cross section, possibly a notch above average, having been qualified and trained by the navy. The men with whom I worked in Venezuela could have been cast for a movie. Many were adventurers, oddballs, loners, losers, heavy drinkers. Of course, eccentrics can be very good company— great guys with whom to have a beer.

It is important to note that all these years later, in a global economy, a career spent in foreign climes can attract not losers and oddballs, but many men and women of high quality and laudable ambition. In fact, even back then, the few oil-company people I met were different from the construction executives. The Esso men had serious long-term careers that required some work abroad; but this work represented steps up the ladder instead of adventuring in the wilderness. Many of them had their families with them.

And those families made quite a difference for me personally. Shortly after I started work in April, the college students began to arrive for summer break, and their presence during most of my contract term provided a delightful campus community into which I was welcomed. My coworkers had introduced me to the nightlife in nearby towns, colorful frontier stuff—guitars, tequila, and women— great for the memory books, but not exactly a milieu in which I wanted to spend all my leisure time. Many of the oil families hailed from Texas, and my invitation to their social circle started with barbecue parties given in grand style. But the barbecues, however festive, soon paled in comparison to the pleasures of getting to know pretty Texas girls.

THE cadre to which I belonged on the Paraguana Peninsula was composed of Americans, recruited and supervised by an American construction firm. The men who performed the actual fieldwork—digging into the earth, mixing and pouring concrete, laying brick, installing pipes and conduits and so forth—were Venezuelans, supplemented by many workers from other countries, most, as I recall, from Portugal.

At Paraguana, although the plans had been drawn by American architects and our entire supervisory staff spoke English the predominant language used in the field was Spanish. Languages have never been my strong suit, but necessity is a great teacher, and after a few weeks my Spanish was serviceable.

The work I performed was varied and challenging, and for the most part fun. I handled a transit better than anyone else around and so was on call from all corners of the site at all times. I was also given responsibility for overseeing a cost-control system, and this entailed taking a four-day trip, by ferry, bus, and car, to an office in the city of Maracaibo. There I was given instruction by the accounting gurus. The system—or at least the element of it relating to our work in the field—was fairly basic and involved no arduous study on my part. What I remember best about that brief journey was the sightseeing opportunity, particularly the ferry ride, where I shared the deck with a pig, numerous chickens, and a variety of colorfully garbed men and women bringing produce to market.

When I think back to that long-ago experience, the incident that I recall most vividly—both amusing and instructive—related to the cost system that I brought from Maracaibo. A discrepancy had been found in the masonry cost data that we simply couldn't understand. The masonry foreman had told us how many concrete blocks could be laid in a day by a mason and his assistant; yet the actual figures showed the production rate to be exactly half of what was projected. I resolved to spend one entire day watching the operation. I did this, and at the end of the morning shift my observations confirmed that the projected rate was being maintained by each team. Puzzled, I reviewed the figures as the men went to a shady spot behind the building to have their lunch. After the lunch break, work resumed, and again it appeared as if each crew was producing at the appropriate pace. But wait! The men I was now watching didn't seem to be the same men I had observed in the morning. Suddenly I heard loud talk and laughter coming from behind the building. The mystery was solved. Half the gang had been working in the morning and the other half in the afternoon. The group that wasn't working hung out in the shady space behind the building, conversing jovially and smoking their small cigars.

The foreman, confronted with my discovery, was unfazed. He explained, *senor*, that it was simply too hot to work continuously in the sun at the established pace and that the men needed to spend part of the day resting in the shade. I reported these findings to my superiors, and negotiations ensued. In the end, reasonable rest periods were agreed to and a supply of cool drinking water provided. The half-day respite became a thing of the past—gone but not forgotten, certainly never to be forgotten by me.

MY agreed six-month work period ended the last day of September, and despite the offer of a considerable salary increase—it was gratifying to be wanted, but no—it was time to move on.

Move on to where and what? Home, of course, and to a real life. But in the same mood that had preceded this escapade, I argued with myself. Here I am in Venezuela, $2,400 in my pocket, and free of all obligations, absolutely free. When will such an opportunity ever be mine again? While I'm at it, why don't I see the rest of the world? Or at least some part of it. Wander, say, until the end of the year—or at least until my money runs out.

Learning that Curaçao was a great center for shipping, I made my way to that nearby island and spent several days checking the comings and goings of freighters that had quarters for a few paying passengers. The choices were abundant and the temptation great to take off to distant romantic-sounding places. But, opting for a more conventional goal—western Europe—I took passage on the SS *Brasil,* heading for Antwerp, with a final destination of Gothenburg, Sweden. It was a pleasant crossing with an interesting assortment of fellow passengers, although disaster befell on the last night. Incredibly, in the North Sea the ship ran into a floating mine left over from the war. A large hole was blown in the hull, the ship listed precariously, and high waves added to the sense of drama. I was looking for adventure, but this was ridiculous. In the best Hollywood tradition the ship limped safely into port, newspaper reporters rushed aboard, and we had our few moments of local celebrity.

FOR several weeks I wended my way from Sweden down to Italy, responding to invitations from a few family friends, joining up with young travelers along the way, and being guided mostly by whim. Occasionally, when I passed a construction site, I would stop to observe, trying to convince myself that my travels had some slight professional value. Often the construction featured repairs to war-ravaged city blocks. Conserving old buildings, as they have done for centuries in Europe, is quite wonderful. But rebuilding structures that have been blasted apart by bombing and artillery fire is something very different. Watching such work was a sobering part of the travel experience.

In general, the days passed enjoyably and my allotted time went quickly by. To maintain my self-determined schedule of arriving back in New York by the end of the year, I spent my last few dollars on an airplane ticket. No more tramp steamers; air travel was now the thing, convenient, increasingly affordable, and, most important, time-saving.

Well, sort of. My handsome TWA airliner, with its four magnificent propeller-driven engines, spent six hours getting about halfway across the Atlantic and then turned back because of headwinds and concern about fuel. We landed in the Canary Islands and found that a number of other planes had done the same thing. The airlines put everybody up at a nice hotel, and, in a partylike atmosphere, most people decided to make the best of the unanticipated delay. I still had time to make it to a New Year's Eve party long planned by friends.

Except that a snowstorm in New York diverted us to a landing in Philadelphia. Even this was OK since the trains were running and it was still early evening. Yet one more crisis loomed. At the behest of my Uncle Jimmy, I had purchased an assortment of French perfumes, and bringing them into the country apparently violated certain tariff regulations. My crafty uncle had been relying on his good friends in the customs service; but they were in New York and I was in Philadelphia. I phoned Jimmy, and he solved the problem by having me leave the offending bottles in bond. Sensing my anger, not only at the delay but at the apparent illegality, he laughed and said: "Sorry about this. It's no big-time smuggling, you know, just a few small bottles of perfume for my lady friends."

Then, to change the subject, he said: "Welcome home. And get ready to meet the president of one of America's top construction companies. He's a new buddy of mine, and I've told him all about you. If you can stop complaining about my perfume, I think he's almost ready to offer you a job."

With this, the phone conversation ended, and I dashed off to the train station. All the way to New York I couldn't help thinking about the prospective meeting with "the president of one of America's top construction companies."

I arrived just barely in time to make it to the party. And when midnight chimed, I exchanged a toast with my someday-to-be wife.

1949 showed promise of being a good year.

FOUR | *The Stupendous Builder*

THOMPSON-STARRETT COMPANY—the firm to which my Uncle Jimmy had referred—was indeed one of America's top construction organizations. *Time* magazine, in 1926, referred to the company as a "stupendous builder" that had constructed six of the eight "hugest" buildings in the nation. "New York's Skyline is Thompson-Starrett's Byline." Thus read the banner headline on the brochure I was handed by the firm's president when I first met him, and the photos bore out the proud text: the Woolworth Building (the world's tallest building from 1913 to 1930), the fabled Waldorf-Astoria Hotel, the Equitable Building, the Municipal Building, Gimbels Department Store, the *New York Herald Tribune* building, the Downtown Athletic Club, and another two dozen of the city's landmark buildings. As the brochure further demonstrated, the firm had contributed substantially to the skylines of Chicago, Baltimore, Washington, San Francisco, Cleveland, and Pittsburgh.

Uncle Jimmy also spoke truly when he told me he had become pals with the firm's president. It seemed likely that a job might be in the offing for a young chap like myself, who had education and some experience, especially with a supportive introduction.

However, the year of this introduction was 1949, and as I was to discover in due course, the company was entering a time of transition. The president, my uncle's new friend, was Jules Van Raalte, not an experienced builder but an investor who, with financial associates, had recently taken control.

How I would have relished meeting Louis J. Horowitz, the fabled president of the company in its glory days. Horowitz, who retired in 1934, had lived the classic American saga of success, coming to the United States as a teenager, working his way up from errand boy and shoe salesman to small-time real estate operator and achieving recognition for brilliance and initiative. He was recommended to Theodore Starrett, head of Thompson-Starrett, "a genius builder," as Horowitz later described him, but a man who detested the details of finance and was pleased to hire a commercially savvy young man. All five Starrett brothers, as noted by Horowitz in his autobiography, "were strangely gifted by blood inheritance as builders." In various combinations they founded not only Thompson-Starrett but also Starrett Brothers and Eken, builders of the Empire State Building. The brothers didn't always see eye to eye: in fact Paul, the second oldest, was for a time president of George A. Fuller Company, a major competitor of the Starrett firms.

Horowitz's financial genius fit well with the technical talents of Thompson-Starrett's staff. He was named vice president and general manager in 1905 at the age of thirty, and president five years later. Remarkably, given his background, he formed close relationships with Du Ponts, Woolworths, and other prominent industrialists, including the Rockefellers, for whom he built not only commercial properties but also the family residence at Pocantico Hills. His memoirs are filled with tales of handshake agreements, magnanimous gestures, and just-plain-friendly dealings with storied tycoons. He had retired fifteen years before my arrival on the scene, but the company name still glowed in the aura of his genius.

Jules Van Raalte was a simpler sort, a pleasant fellow, clearly not familiar with the financial operation of a construction company, much less with the technical side of the activity. He had no special relationships with industrial barons, nor was he even acquainted with many of the employees in the company of which he had assumed leadership.

But he was energetic and filled with optimism. After all, the firm had work on hand; a large, experienced staff; and a fabulous reputation.

On the day of my interview, Mr. Van Raalte greeted me heartily, chatted a while, then took me on a tour of the company's spacious offices at 444 Madison Avenue. He left me with Rodney Smith, the leader of field operations, and I assumed that a job offer was forthcoming. To my surprise and dismay, Mr. Smith told me—gruffly, that was his way—that, Van Raalte's endorsement notwithstanding, there was no place for me on any of the company's job sites. In fact, within the next few days he was faced with the unpleasant task of letting some people go. Seeing my crestfallen expression, he softened a bit, and said, "Let me take you over to see Henry Buschen; he heads up our office operation, and he may have an opening."

A half hour later I left the office, hired as an assistant estimator. This meant that I was designated to "take off" quantities from plans, that is, measure and calculate amounts of materials required for particular buildings—cubic yards of concrete, pounds of reinforcing steel, numbers of bricks, square yards of plaster, square feet of tile— and so forth. I wanted a job of course. But taking off quantities? What about my experience in the field, my talents with a transit, my experience in scheduling deliveries, overseeing work crews, dealing with subcontractor foremen? And, I thought somewhat glumly, what about being out in the open air, sharing the excitement of the building operation? I was assured that my work in the field was excellent experience and that perhaps through estimating I might work my way into project management, the ideal combination of office authority and field activity. "Let me tell you a secret," said Henry Buschen, quietly as if he didn't want anyone else to hear. "It's fun to be out on the job site; but essentially that's blue collar stuff. The money is made in the office." I was impressed by this, but not convinced. And to this day I believe that Buschen's Law—because that's how I've always thought of it—is a half truth at best.

*　*　*

FEBRUARY 1, 1949, exactly one month after my return from overseas, I started work at Thompson-Starrett. My salary was $400 a month, coincidentally the same as I had earned in Venezuela. But abroad I had no expense for rent and food, so this represented a reduction. A step backward? No, everyone knew that work in foreign lands paid more. In any event, cash income was not my main concern. I was living with my parents again, this time in a two-bedroom apartment. The chance to work with one of the world's great construction companies—and to be on friendly speaking terms with the firm's president—that counted for more than any misgivings about salary.

My first day at the office I was given a stool and a place at an enormous table, a table big enough for eight men, four on one side facing four on the other, each of us with room to spread out a set of blueprints. In addition to a spacious working area, we were provided with calculating machines, pads and pencils, and small metal measuring tapes scaled on one side 1/4 inch equals a foot, on the other side 1/8 inch equals a foot, these being the two scales most commonly used by architects and engineers. (I quickly internalized the figures $1/8 = 0.125$, $3/8 = 0.375$, $5/8 = 0.625$, and $7/8 = 0.875$: these were the elements of my new basic language.) Our assignment was to measure and compute, working on whatever plans were given to us. For the most part, we calculated quantities for cost estimates, mainly for jobs being bid competitively. Also, on jobs already under contract, we provided detailed figures to assist those in the office who negotiated with suppliers and subcontractors. We also worked on "change orders" whenever contract documents were revised. Sometimes we were handed "shop drawings" or schedules submitted by subcontractors: these had to be checked carefully for quantities, dimensions, and manufacturing details. We were a great precision machine, measuring everything, counting everything, and checking everything with a specificity that in retrospect seems incredible. I recall reviewing hardware schedules, analyzing each lockset—the term "right hand reverse bevel" sticks in my mind—and counting structural glazed block, which we used a lot for hospitals—how many with cove base, how many with right bullnose corner, how many with both? Today we place great reliance on subcontractors and suppliers and on the architects and design engineers who review shop drawings and material details. We are careful but not fanatical. At the Thompson-Starrett I remember everything was checked and then checked again. Nothing was trivial enough to be taken for granted. And our table of eight was just part of a larger operation. There were mechanical experts to check mechanical items. There were specialists who read thick specification books and seemed to learn them by heart. There were even two men whose job it was to travel the country checking on factories where materials were being manufactured.

Looking back, I can see that the company was living in the past. Once upon a time Mr. Horowitz promised John D. Rockefeller, Jr. that Thompson-Starrett attended in-house to every detail, and in the field performed masonry, carpentry, and other key trades with its own forces, "without resorting to subcontractors." That might have been the way things were done in an earlier age, but by 1949 subcontracting was standard—at Thompson-Starrett and everywhere else—the natural consequence of the industrial quest for efficiency, and of course economy. Growth of labor unions also contributed to the change. This didn't mean that general contractors had become "brokers." There was—and is—much professional skill required to plan, schedule, and oversee erection of ever more complex structures. And a talent for estimating costs, without blind reliance on subcontractors, is still one mark of an effective builder. But the need for the general contractor to measure and record every widget in every corner of every job was giving way to a more streamlined approach. A company where that was not recognized had fallen behind the times.

Thinking of that large table at Thompson-Starrett I envision a scene from Dickens: scriveners hunched over their books, with green eyeshades and quill pens. Yet I didn't find the work onerous. There was camaraderie, and we were free to chat, tell stories, and compare notes. Also, I found that the world of diagrams and numbers had a certain hypnotic appeal. Every engineer—especially every construction engineer—is beguiled by the charms of geometry.

All of our work product was submitted to Mr. Buschen. He took it into his office and there did his magic—applying dollar figures to our areas, volumes, weights, and other bare numbers. This operation took place behind closed doors. I found this frustrating, and one day, mustering up my courage, I told Mr. Buschen that I didn't want to forever measure quantities without learning something about pricing those quantities. Also, I hoped that he hadn't forgotten his implied promise that I could work my way out of the world of quantity take-off into the world of project management. He replied first of all by delivering a lecture on the virtues of patience. But he took my point, and soon afterward introduced me to the head of the company's cost department, which was the source of many of his magic dollar figures. He also steered me to several publications where methods of deriving costs were discussed and where current costs were reported. As for project management, he said, make your mark by concentrating on the work at hand. Let us see that you're smart and hardworking. Right now we're concentrating on getting new projects. When we land a couple of jobs you'll get your chance to make a move.

EVEN though our takeoff work was fairly routine, it was exciting to be part of the estimating process. When an estimate was being submitted in competition, especially to public agencies where the bid openings were public and the time of the opening precisely established, the feeling in the office was electric. The usual routine was for one person to go to the place where bids were received, taking along the bid form, all filled out except for price, and then be in telephone contact with the office. Mr. Buschen would be huddled in his inner sanctum, conferring with his key people, analyzing our in-house figures and reviewing the latest prices being phoned in from subcontractors. Just moments before the scheduled opening, a decision was made and the bid figure was recited to our man at the bid site. He would write the dollar amount on the bid form and submit it in a sealed envelope. The experience was tension-filled, and I remember well the time that one of our young men, Eddie Mulcahey, was the designated courier. The bid amount was $2,700,000—not a huge job, but this was at a time when a million dollars was a lot of money. The figure was told to Eddie over the phone and there followed a moment of silence. "Eddie, do you have that?" Mr. Buschen asked. Another pause. Finally Eddie, his voice quavering, asked, "How do you spell 'two'?" The incident became a staple of office legend. We all had a feeling for the stress it revealed.

Before long, a few of our bids bore fruit, and sure enough I was given the opportunity to take on some project-management duties. I attended job meetings and discussed daily activities and long-term schedules with our superintendents and subcontractors. I came to recognize the importance of expediting, of planning material deliveries and manpower assignments so that steady progress could be maintained. Even when the scheduling was precise, the fates of the "real world" could wreak havoc. Deliveries could be carefully planned, but then manufacturing plants could fall behind schedule, or be hit by a strike. A pivotal subcontractor might suddenly become busy—or go broke—at the same time he was expected on one of our jobs. Critical equipment—a truck, a crane, a hoist—could malfunction. Weather was an ever-perfidious hazard.

As time went by, I had my first personal contacts with architects and design engineers, and—a real eye-opener—with inspectors. I had always known that inspection was part of the construction process. Quality control was essential to guarantee structural integrity and, overall, compliance with building codes. Such control was overseen by building departments, either through their own personnel or certification of professionals retained by the owner. However, there are many aspects of a building that do not relate to codes or public safety but rather to "quality," standards that are sometimes difficult to define. Here, the owner, whether an individual, a public agency, or a private institution, usually relies on the design professionals, and more specifically on the individuals given responsibility to judge whether the work is "acceptable." How smooth is smooth? What tolerances are allowable? The possibility of differences of opinion, indeed for conflict, are manifold.

Since my apprenticeship with Thompson-Starrett in 1949, I have had countless discussions with inspectors, mostly calm, reasonable exchanges leading to agreement; sometimes testy but ultimately resolving in compromise; and on rare occasions—happily very rare—leading to a battle of some sort. However, my earliest experience in this arena was absolutely unique, and nothing in subsequent years has dimmed the feelings of wonderment it evoked.

The first building for which I was given project-management assignments was the Convent of Saint Paul, built for the Paulist Fathers on West Fifty-ninth Street in New York City. John Steinmuller, a vice president at Thompson-Starrett, was the executive in charge, and it was through his good offices that the firm had been put on the bidders list and subsequently negotiated the contract. It was not a large structure—only five stories tall—and progress had been largely trouble-free. However, when completion was at hand, and final inspections under way, an extraordinary problem arose. Mr. Steinmuller, quite agitated, called me into his office to be present as he discussed the matter on the telephone. I knew that there was trouble when I heard him say loudly, "Father, please! You can't be serious! You're about to turn me into a Methodist!"

It seemed that the owner's inspector had summarily ordered us to remove and replace large portions of the front facade. Some of the bricks were excessively dark, he explained, a sign that they had been overburned in the kiln. He not only deemed the color range unacceptable but also feared that the overburning had affected the strength and porosity of the brick, making it liable to disintegrate or absorb water. The demand seemed totally unreasonable and if pursued would have entailed tremendous cost, confusion, and delay. But the inspector was adamant.

I was charged with investigating the matter, which entailed conferences with chemical engineers, one working for the brick manufacturer, one representing the manufacturer's trade association, and one retained by the architect; then we met with engineers from two testing laboratories. Eventually all the professionals concluded that the installation was safe, durable, and watertight. The architect expressed willingness to accept the variations in color. Still, the inspector was not satisfied, citing the issue of permissible variation. He argued that if the bricks were accepted, the contractor would "get away" with something. At the very least, some penalty ought to be assessed.

Tempers flared, diplomacy failed, and the matter was referred to "the authorities." What this meant was a hearing before a church official representing the Catholic Archdiocese of New York. The hearing took place in a splendidly decorated ecclesiastical chamber, and the decision was rendered in the form of a sermon. The lesson of the day, complete with biblical references, was that in the nature of things, bricks should be expected to come out of the kiln with slight variations. The inspector was looking for a degree of perfection found only in heaven.

"A degree of perfection found only in heaven." In the ensuing years I've quoted that memorable line to many inspectors—with, I must admit, varying degrees of success.

A happy ending for the convent job earned me credit that I really didn't deserve but was pleased to modestly accept. What followed was, first, a permanent release from the estimating table. I have mentioned the hypnotic appeal that I found in the world of diagrams and numbers; but I also yearned for action and a degree of authority. So I was delighted to be assigned to the project-management team of the Owl's Head Wastewater Treatment Plant in Brooklyn. What a change. What a project. This was no simple building with rooms and doors and windows. Not at all. There were huge mechanically raked bar screens designed to remove solid objects from the influent; the sedimentation tanks where sludge settled and grease and oils were skimmed off; the aeration machinery and lord knows what else, designed to yield an end product of relatively clear liquid and relatively harmless sludge that was taken away by barge. Today it makes me dizzy to think of the intricate machinery, the oddly shaped concrete and steel contours. But at the time I reveled in the complexity of it all.

The complexity, the enormity—and the danger. Yes, danger. There were no great heights, but in a way that was the source of the problem. In building an apartment house or a hospital there are flat floors accessed by stairs, elevators, or screened-in hoists. Occasionally there are ladders, safe enough if you don't look down. In a sewage plant, however, there are many pits and pools, and during construction one is liable to find beams and planks across these various craters—beams and planks that provide walkways for the daring. The safety codes of the day, even if observed, provided little protection. (The Occupational Safety and Health Administration—OSHA—wasn't founded until 1970.) As a "guy from the office" I had come to expect challenge—indeed a form of hazing—in every visit to the field. I tried to measure up; but there were limits. One day an assistant superintendent led me across a plank spanning a pit. I looked down—six feet, maybe ten feet to a soft surface—a potential sprained ankle, well, all right, macho was the way to go. But there followed a narrow walkway across an abyss—twenty feet deep or more—let them call me what they would: there were limits to my bravado. It was a game of chicken we played, and on that occasion I felt that I "won" by acting totally unfazed while refusing to take a reckless dare.

AS I moved steadily higher on the ladder of responsibility, I found myself looking more critically at the company with which I had cast my lot. The people at Thompson-Starrett were competent, diligent, and decent; but when it came to money they seemed curiously apathetic. Surely Mr. Van Raalte and his associates were anxious for the firm to make a profit. But that zeal, that appetite, that passion hadn't been transmitted. Even the people who negotiated prices with subcontractors and suppliers didn't seem to have the vigor, the drive, that one would expect. Nobody had the instinct or incentive of ownership. Nobody's compensation seemed connected to corporate profit. I recognized the attitude within myself. I rarely thought about whether the firm was making money. I did my job, did it well enough, and recognition seemed to follow. The beginning of my second year, my salary was increased from $400 to $450 a month; a year later it was $500. I rented my own apartment and started to think about getting married. All seemed right with the world.

Yet when I looked to the future, when I wondered about what might be in store for me at this organization of nice people, I felt vaguely uneasy. I had practically no experience with the world of "business." Yet I was not blind to the existence of competition, free enterprise, and survival of the fittest. If in a company there is a lack of concern about making money; if there is a surplus of people doing superfluous work, as I had sensed at the large estimating table; and if there is a lack of intensity—well, isn't that a recipe for trouble?

And, sure enough, trouble came knocking at the door. Without warning, in July 1951, more than a dozen people were let go, including the top administrators: Buschen, Smith, and Steinmuller. Nobody said that it was a cutback to save money. I was told it was "a major reorganization" and that new leaders were being brought in, recruited from some company in California. I myself was not affected. In fact, I was promoted to "Change Order Engineer: In charge of all change orders and related matters" and given a midyear pay raise of 10 percent, to $550 monthly. Still, I felt the shock almost as if I had been among the suddenly jobless.

I happened to have wedding plans for mid-August, which I wasn't about to change. Also a three-week honeymoon, which I suppose could have been cut short in an emergency. But I was reassured by Mr. Van Raalte himself, congratulated on the forthcoming nuptials, indeed, introduced to one of the new people as a future president of the firm. So, off I went, somewhat bewildered, saying sad farewells to those who would be gone upon my return.

Actually, my melancholy was short-lived. As Winston Churchill says at the end of his memoir, *My Early Life*: "I got married and lived happily ever afterwards."

WHEN I returned to the office in September it was like entering a different world. I was introduced to a Mr. Jim Tripp, a veteran of the international construction scene, and told I was to help him on the Sariyar Dam project in Turkey. Turkey? A dam in Turkey? That's what they said and that's what they meant. I found myself studying plans of a hydropower plant to be built in a town eighty miles west of Ankara, featuring a concrete dam three hundred feet high and a third of a mile across at the crest. I was soon back in the world of quantity takeoff, although in categories that were, to say the least, unfamiliar: cubic meters of concrete for the intake tunnel and spillway piers, linear meters of exploratory drilling holes and grout holes for consolidation grouting, square meters of chipping and roughening concrete surfaces of diversion tunnel plugs, and so forth. I sent my work sheets off to Mr. Tripp, who had taken up residence at the Ankara Palace Hotel. A week later this energetic buccaneer of a man returned to New York, and, much to my amazement, through some mysterious process of bidding, negotiating, and legerdemain he brought with him a consulting contract for our firm. This put me to work at a drafting table, designing and drawing a concrete batching plant and a cableway that would be used to carry buckets of concrete across the river for pouring the body of the dam. I had very little idea of what was to be done, but Mr. Tripp worked with me and taught me much, including a prodigious new lexicon of profanity. To keep pace with some impossible schedule, another man was brought in to work at night on the drawing over which I labored during the day.

In early April 1952—having worked half a year on the project—I was named supervising schedule engineer of the Sariyar Dam with a salary increased from $550 to $750 a month. I never got to see that dam, although I learned that it was indeed built. I don't know what, if anything, Thompson-Starrett contributed to its construction beyond the estimates and drawings for the concrete batching plant and its cableway. Mr. Tripp—he finally insisted I call him Jim—Jim, then, directed my efforts from afar. Such efforts had nothing to do with the dam but consisted mainly of preparing qualification brochures for other projects on which our firm hoped to bid. We sought these projects first in Turkey, then in Greece, Spain, Iceland, Ecuador, and other places I do not recall. Needless to say, such brochures were required to contain lists of available experienced personnel, and these I was told to garner willy-nilly from Jim Tripp's personal address book. As for the rest, pictures of past projects came from ancient Thompson-Starrett literature, and lists of equipment, cost estimates, proposed schedules, and the like, these sprang from Tripp's off-the-cuff comments, embellished by my somewhat-vivid imagination. I was informed from time to time that these documents had earned us entrée to interviews and bidders' lists. But no new contracts were forthcoming.

One day I realized that I hadn't received a communique from Jim in almost a month. I sought out Mr. Van Raalte and was told that there was no longer any formal connection between the company and Jim, although "if something turns up" he'll be in touch.

So, at the start of 1953, my fifth year with the firm, I found myself administrative assistant to the latest of several imported chief operating officers. We were still preparing estimates and seeking new work of all sorts all over the world. But the new work seemed elusive, and increasingly I found myself involved in jobs that were in the finishing stages, several of them bogged down in claims and counterclaims, and even unpleasant legal disputes. It was impossible not to feel that the ship was sinking.

Sure enough, soon there was another reduction of the office force, this time including secretaries, bookkeepers, and all of my old friends at the estimating table. Most of the people who were not terminated saw their salaries reduced by 20 percent. I was part of a select group who were cut only by 10 percent.

Mr. Van Raalte sought me out to say that he still had hopes for the company—and for me. But when I pursued the topic of corporate survival, this normally ebullient man gave me a grim look that I took as a sympathetic warning.

THUS did one of the great construction companies approach its final days. The end did not come with a catastrophic accident or a cataclysmic miscalculation or an ugly lawsuit. If I had to characterize it, I would say that the patient died of too much niceness.

Perhaps "died" is not the appropriate word. Thompson-Starrett, the "stupendous builder," stopped building. But the company stock had a life of its own. A September 1, 1967, article in *The New York Times* reported that the corporation had entered the field of scientific instrumentation through the purchase of the Federal Scientific Corp. The following year Thompson-Starrett merged into Elgin National Watch Company to become part of Elgin National Industries.

By that time, my five years with the "stupendous builder"—pleasant and instructive years—were just a long-ago memory.

FIVE   *Nice Guys Finish Last*

IN LATE 1953 Thompson-Starrett was no longer a likely place for a young man to seek his future. I conferred with the few of my contemporaries who remained on the payroll, and we concluded it was high time to start checking out the job market. Our friends among the subcontractors were a dependable source of both gossip and solid information, so we sought out a few for confidential discussions. Those talks gave us a shared sense of optimism. Employment prospects seemed good. After a few introductions and interviews we felt even better. There were jobs to be had.

In a way we were competitors—albeit friendly competitors—seeking the same type of work in the same locale. But I was surprised to find how different our ideas were about the sorts of career paths we wanted to follow. Much as I appreciated my experience with Thompson-Starrett—a large, established organization—I was determined now to try something very different. I felt a stirring of ambition, for exactly what I couldn't say, but definitely for a change from the placidity that I felt around me. I spoke of seeking out an energetic go-getter, of hitching my wagon to a star, to a comet, to a new entity blazing into the unknown. Others were more conservative, in particular my good friend, Ed Stoessel, who was unnerved by such fervent talk. He had just received a job offer from William Zeckendorf, and it made him anxious even to mention it.

Zeckendorf. Big Bill! One of the nation's most prominent real estate developers. Just recently, in the biggest office-building transaction in real estate history, he had purchased the Chrysler Building. Several years earlier he had gained instant fame by selling to the Rockefellers a site along the East River that was subsequently donated for the building of the United Nations Headquarters. The embodiment of glamorous real-estate deal making, Zeckendorf was now branching out into construction, planning, among many projects, the gigantic Roosevelt Field Mall on Long Island. Who could resist such a dazzling opportunity?

But Ed Stoessel was put off by the glamour and excitement. He also had offers from George A. Fuller and Turner Construction, two of the biggest, most respected construction firms in the nation, and he thought that their stolid professionalism was more suited to his nature. Zeckendorf was out of the question—too risky said Ed—and in what seemed to me to be a coin flip, he chose to join Fuller.

It appeared to be a good decision. When, in 1958, *Engineering News-Record* began ranking U.S. building contractors by volume of work completed, Fuller was number two. The firm flourished, and Ed Stoessel flourished with it. In 1967 he was named a vice president, an event deemed worthy of announcement in a *New York Times* article.

By way of contrast, Zeckendorf's company, after experiencing a number of crises, underwent a spectacular bankruptcy in 1965. Ed Stoessel thanked his lucky stars that he had made the conservative choice. But—speaking of stars, lucky and unlucky—on January 6, 1970, Ed visited a job site and stepped into a trailer to study a set of plans. At that moment a bucket of concrete—or was it a load of steel?—dropped from above, crushing the trailer and killing Ed instantly. I recall the funeral in a church in Connecticut, the casket wrapped in an American flag, a token of Ed's military service years earlier. Indeed, his death, sudden and violent, reminded one of the perils of a battlefield. Family members were grieving of course. They were also stunned and disbelieving. I am still disbelieving; and many is the time when, entering a construction shanty, I think of Ed and of that tragic event.

It is small solace to think that Ed was spared experiencing the decline of the Fuller company in subsequent years.

Turner, in the first decade of the twenty-first century, continues to prosper, a perennial leader, in volume and reputation, among American contractors (although in 1997 the firm was purchased by Hochtief AG of Germany).

AS for me, when in 1953 a group of us, young and eager, took our leave of Thompson-Starrett, I was fortunate enough to find exactly what I was looking for. This was a start-up operation headed by an individual who was smart, ambitious, apparently well financed, and who, so I was told by knowledgeable people, had every prospect of forging a successful future. Joe Blitz—Joseph P. Blitz—a construction engineer in his midforties, a shining light with the Tishman Construction Corporation, had just founded a new firm and been the successful bidder on two projects. He had taken with him from Tishman a secretary, a bookkeeper, and an experienced estimator, and now he had need of a project manager. Just as he personified the energetic go-getter I sought, so was I the answer to his needs: a young construction engineer, highly recommended by a mutual friend, and willing to work for a modest salary. I was soon to learn just how important this last qualification was in the thinking of my prospective employer.

What was I earning in those days? $750 per month at Thompson-Starrett, reduced by 10 percent because of the firm's financial crisis, translates into about $155 a week, and whatever the exact figure, that was my starting pay at Joseph P. Blitz, Inc. I had to "prove myself" to earn a penny more. It doesn't sound like much, and it wasn't, even though the cost of living now, more than fifty years later, has increased by a factor of about eight. But it was enough. My wife and I were paying $93 per month for a nice one-bedroom apartment at Peter Cooper Village, a pleasant campuslike development built after the war in Manhattan's east 20s. Contemplating the start of a family, we were on the waiting list for a two-bedroom unit listed for $103. Indeed, the two-bedroom apartment became available shortly after our first child arrived in the middle of 1954. Although my wife wasn't working at that time, we managed nicely on the amount that Joe Blitz saw fit to pay. Everyone was content: I wanted that job on almost any terms, and Blitz wanted an enterprising young man at a bargain price.

In fact, Joe Blitz wanted most things at a bargain price. When I sat in on his negotiations with a subcontractor I felt that I was learning from a maestro. Only I quickly discovered that some skills are not readily transferrable. One could watch the virtuoso at work and still not be able to do what he did. To this day I have not mastered the techniques of sharp dealing. Buying as Blitz did entails seducing, charming, bewitching, but also threatening. His implication: if you don't take this job at the price I'm offering, you'll regret it. And how patient he was. He could make an offer and then outwait his quarry, feigning nonchalance even when there was desperate pressure to have the subcontractor on the job.

Joe relied upon a rough-and-ready mathematical formula, and this I learned quickly enough: any price quoted could be discounted by at least 10 percent, and one should not hesitate to offer 20 percent below what was asked, or even less.

In bidding for new work this translated into adding up the subcontractor bids, arbitrarily cutting the total by 10 percent, and then adding back about 5 percent for his firm's gross profit. In other words, he prepared a bid with a 5 percent loss built in, a loss that had to be made up in the buying; and then additional buying was expected to generate the profit—gross profit that had to cover office overhead before yielding a net. On the day of a bid, after applying this formula, Joe would start to study the figures intently, then flip through the plans and stare out the window. Eventually he would get what he called a "feeling." This often resulted in an additional cut accompanied by muttering about the state of the market or the greed of the subs. The firm's estimator, Gus Forsell, invariably had developed some figures, representing his idea of what each trade was worth; but this was back-of-the-envelope stuff compared with the detailed analyses prepared by the estimating teams at Thompson-Starrett. Joe would glance at Gus's figures, and I suppose they would somehow enter into his "feeling." But he seemed to be mainly interested in the names of the subcontractors who had submitted the lowest bid in each trade, and he studied the difference between the low bids and the bids above, assuring himself that no obvious errors had been made. He would go through the list one by one and mutter, "that bastard will be broke by the time this job starts" or "that son of a bitch doesn't know what time of the day it is" or "that wiseguy expects to make his fortune with that bid." He told me once that it was the practice for some of his competitors to negotiate with one or more subs before the bid was submitted, obtaining a favorable price in exchange for a commitment—if I get the job, you get the job at our agreed price. But Joe preferred to take his chances. If he got the job, he wanted to be totally free to deal with anyone. Finally, with reluctance, he would add a small figure for contingency or, if the spirit so moved him, make an additional cut. And that was it. He was not superstitious, as I later found others to be, and he didn't fiddle with the final figure, thinking to settle on a "lucky" number. The figure was what it was.

At the time of bidding, Joe's attitude was icy calm. And if we were unsuccessful, he could be complacently philosophical. However, if we were the successful bidder a startling surliness took over. Not for owners and architects, of course, with whom he radiated considerable charm. But for his own people, with the start of a new project he turned abruptly severe. For those of us in the office he would growl about our failure to "get off our butts." When he visited the job site he would hurl complaints rapid fire at the superintendent. I can't say that he was a mean-spirited person or even, away from his work, anything other than civil or often amiable. He simply believed that building construction was something one did best in a nasty mood. "Nice guys finish last," said the baseball manager Leo Durocher in those days, and the phrase had caught on. "No more Mr. Nice Guy" wouldn't become widely used until the 1970s. But, however expressed, the idea has been around forever, and, come to think of it, the concept is perhaps more widespread in our industry than in many others.

I was given ample responsibility—project management for an elementary school in Levittown and at the same time a high school in Rockville Centre. The jobs went well. As I look back I realize how short of experience I was—and how lucky. Sometimes it just happens that way. You wake up in the morning expecting troubles to appear, but suddenly it's quitting time and nothing bad has happened. I received little praise—actually no praise. But at that time and place, absence of complaint was praise enough.

Blitz proceeded to take on additional jobs—adding estimating tasks to my increasingly heavy workload. He controlled the buying operation himself, but had me assist with analysis of the plans and specifications, making detailed lists of each subcontractor's scope of work. I was often called to sit in on negotiating sessions, mainly to nod affirmatively when he told subcontractors that their prices were not competitive. I was overworked, but pleased to feel like an insider and to learn a bit about the financial side of the business.

Eventually it became clear that more help was needed, and Joe reluctantly hired another project manager. This time it was an older man nearing the end of his working years. It occurred to me that Joe found an advantage in employing men at both ends of the age spectrum, the advantage, of course, being meager salary demands. He also hired a young woman to help with office chores. She sat in a chair and wrote in shorthand as I dictated, something that I had never done before and in fact never got used to. I was relieved when dictating machines became the norm.

Most of my work was performed in the office, talking on the telephone, attending meetings, drafting letters, studying plans, calculating and recording prices and schedules. Yet I visited the jobs as often as I could find a reason to do so. Being on a construction site invariably brought a charge of excitement. Not that work in the field was all fun and games. When one of our superintendents went on vacation and I was assigned to take his place for two weeks, I learned to appreciate the demands of field supervision. The various foremen, playing the time-honored game of hassling the young guy from the office, barraged me with problems—"You're holding me up here," "It's impossible to do what the plan shows," and so forth—coming at me aggressively, several at one time. When each subcontractor has a problem to be solved, and a crew standing by idly awaiting an answer, the pressure can build intensely. I tried to keep my poise, not always successfully. One afternoon, adding to the chaos, I charged out of the trailer, stepped awkwardly on a concrete block, and tumbled to the ground with a sprained ankle. Happily, this is the most serious physical damage I've suffered in an industry noted for its high rate of job-related injury; but that fact didn't ease my pain and embarrassment at the time.

When working in the office I came to know many of the owners of the subcontracting firms who were such a critical part of the construction operation. But meeting them again in the field, along with their tradesmen, I got a deeper understanding of how things worked in the world of the hardhats. One man in particular stood out as the ultimate builder—rough and tough and boisterous—and smart, indeed brilliant, in the ways of erecting structures. Joseph DePaola was his name, and he was destined to become one of the preeminent figures in the New York construction industry. I first met him as a subcontractor doing concrete foundations for a school, a hardworking, loud-yelling fellow, likable and good to have on the job, but not an individual who seemed destined for great things. Yet, although I didn't know it, in the early 1950s Joe was already embarked on the innovation that was to make him famous and wealthy, and that was to be a key to the remarkable chronicle of the high-rise apartment house—a phenomenon known as "the two-day cycle." According to the oft-told story, an opportunity arose when a Manhattan developer encountered a lengthy delay in obtaining the structural steel required for a planned fifteen-story building. Joe told the owners that, in the absence of a framework of steel beams and columns, he could build the structure out of reinforced concrete—round steel bars (readily available) embedded in poured concrete—and save money as well as time. The developer took advantage of the challenge, had an engineering firm, Farkas & Baron, perform the necessary redesign, and the rest is history.

Amazing. The erection of wooden forms, installation of reinforcing bars and electrical conduit, and the pouring of concrete is so coordinated that every other day a new floor is in place. Even when the cycle is paced at one floor every third day, the structure rises with magical speed. Most office buildings, because of their need for large open spans and flexibility for tenant layouts, are still built using steel-beam structures. But most high-rise apartment houses are designed for reinforced concrete, and on projects across the land, the DePaola method, essentially unchanged after more than half a century, dominates the workday.

Just as I never dreamed that Joe DePaola was destined for great things in the construction industry, neither did I consider the possibility that our paths would cross again in the future. But ten years down the road, in the early 1960s, our paths did indeed cross again. It was my good fortune that, just as I remembered him as a good guy and a good subcontractor, he remembered me as a young fellow who hadn't given him a hard time and incidentally had seen that his bills were paid on time.

WHILE I was involved in building schools on Long Island, however, the Joe most on my mind was Joe Blitz. As the holiday season approached in 1955, my tenure with the firm was approaching two years, and I thought that, all in all, I had done well. I also had reason to believe that the firm had done well. In other words, I was expecting recognition by way of a bonus and a meaningful raise. At the end of my first year, my salary had been increased by 10 percent, from about $155 to $170, and the bonus had been perhaps two weeks' pay, certainly not more. Now, after two years of good work, and making money for the boss, my hopes were high. High, but soon dashed.

"No raise right now," said the boss; "maybe something a few months down the road." "But Joe," I protested, "the jobs I worked on made money, good money, I know they did." "That may be," came the reply. "But would you have shared in the loss if there had been one?" Silence. "Were you at risk?"

Struck dumb, I can't recall what I said, if anything. But I decided on the spot, without an instant's hesitation, that I was going to quit. I also decided that I was not going to quit until I had another job in hand. There was a baby at home and rent that had to be paid.

MY future lay elsewhere, but let me say a final word about Joe Blitz. He was not Mr. Sweetie Pie; but neither do I think of him with dislike or resentment. When I told him I was leaving he smiled faintly and nodded with what I took to be understanding and approval. He knew that I was looking for something he was not willing to give, some share in his achievement. And achieve he did, running his company successfully—quite successfully as far as I could tell—for many years. As time passed, I would meet Joe occasionally, at a restaurant or in the theater, and I always had the feeling that he took some pride in my successes, such as they were. Indeed, he had taught me a lot in a short time, not as a tutor—that was not his way—but by letting me see how he operated. When he reached the age of eighty, he simply closed his business down, showing that not every construction company has to perish cataclysmically in flames.

IN moving ahead, I turned again to subcontractor friends for help and was rewarded with an introduction to Carl Morse, a high-profile individual who had recently joined the Diesel Construction Company. In subsequent years Mr. Morse, having formed Morse Diesel Inc., constructed many notable Manhattan edifices, including the Pan Am Building, in its time the largest commercial building in the world. This titan in the making offered me a job, but for very little money and with no mention of future prospects. According to a newspaper profile, he took pride in being called "an S.O.B.," and during the time I spent in his office, in every phone call he took, he seemed determined to demonstrate this self-characterization. Carl Morse was to become a heroic figure in the industry, but I left his office having decided to look elsewhere.

I tried a new source, unlikely yet obvious: the help-wanted ads. Timing, good luck, destiny, I know not how to characterize it—but they provided the answer I sought and set me on the road I have traveled for over fifty years. I don't have a copy of the particular ad that first captured my attention, but I do have the letter, dated November 23, 1955, written by Jack Kreisler, president of the newly formed firm of Kreisler Borg Construction Company. He acknowledges receipt of my résumé and suggests that an interview be scheduled. "We are a young organization," writes Kreisler, "with young ideas, and there is an unusual, once-in-a-lifetime opportunity here for the right man."

I met with Kreisler and his partner, Bob Borg, in December, and by January of 1956 we had agreed on the terms of my employment.

BETWEEN leaving Blitz and starting with the new firm, my wife and I determined to take a two-week vacation. With our not-quite-two-year-old son, we retreated to a motel room on the beach at St. Petersburg, Florida, where our typical day consisted of wading, splashing, calling to seagulls, and taking afternoon naps.

Early in our stay, our son and a little girl about his age took to playing together at the water's edge, and the little girl's grandfather and I took to chatting about this and that, as adults overseeing young children are likely to do. The man seemed very old to me at the time, but he was still quite active in some manufacturing business, and he expressed interest in my own occupation, past, present, and future. We became friendly, and after the passing of a few days we had shared in some detail the stories of our careers. One morning he greeted me in a particularly paternal way, and said, as I can best recall the words, "Sam, it may not be any of my business, but I've been thinking about what you've told me, and I can't resist offering you a bit of advice. You don't want to just take a job with the two young fellows you've told me about. You want to become their partner. I'm going to say one word, and I want you to remember it. The word is: partnership."

Years later, when I saw the movie, *The Graduate,* with Dustin Hoffman, I was particularly struck by the scene in which Ben, the young hero, receives advice from a friend of his parents. The exchange has become famous in movie lore. "I just want to say one word to you," says the older man, "just one word." "Yes, sir," says Ben. "Are you listening?" "Yes, I am." "Plastics." "How do you mean?" "There's a great future in plastics. Think about it. Will you think about it?" "Yes, I will." "Shh! Enough said. That's a deal."

The word vouchsafed to me was "partnership," and I didn't take to it any more than Ben took to "plastics." I had this vague concept of joining people on the upswing, contributing to their ascent, and sharing in their success. But partnership implied investment, and investment meant financial hazard. For starters, I didn't have money to invest, and, if I did, I wasn't sure that I would want to put it at risk.

Yet as we returned from St. Petersburg to New York, I found that I was carrying "partnership" in my beach bag.

SIX

A New Beginning, Treacherous Tides,
and a Bit of Luck

ON MARCH 1, 1955, Jacques Kreisler, Jr., and Robert F. Borg founded
Kreisler Borg Construction Company and opened a small office in
White Plains, New York. Borg was thirty-two, a graduate engineer
with a law degree working for a large construction firm. He had
long nursed an ambition to be the owner of such a firm. Kreisler, a
year or so younger, was employed by his father's company, Kreisler
Manufacturing Corp., makers of expandable metal watchbands. I
don't think that Jack had any special interest in construction. He
simply wanted to escape from the family business and be on his
own. The tale of how Kreisler and Borg got together, retold frequently through the years, had mixed elements of destiny and comic
relief. Their respective mothers-in-law, sitting side by side in a
beauty parlor, chatting about family, decided that the two young
men—alike in their restlessness and ambition—ought to be introduced. That's all it took. A couple of meetings, a handshake, a lawyer, an accountant, an insurance broker, and, since they both lived
in southern Westchester, a decision to lease cheap space on the second floor of an unpretentious building on Mamaroneck Avenue in
White Plains. And the opening of a bank account. I never did inquire
about the financial details of the founding, but since Kreisler senior
held the position of chairman of the board—an informal group of
four that included Borg's brother and met occasionally in a coffee
shop—I assume that he, the father, had put up some of the money.

As best I could piece it together after my arrival, the original capital must have been in the $20,000 to $30,000 range. (In all that follows we have to remember that the dollar was worth about one-eighth of what it is today.)

After purchasing stationery and basic office supplies and hiring a woman to type and answer the phone, the first order of business was to submit bids in an effort to "land a job." Borg had worked in the field of heavy construction—with Spencer, White & Prentice, one of the many large, highly esteemed firms destined for decline in later years—and it was Bob's idea that there might be a niche for a firm to undertake small contracts in the heavy-construction field. He reasoned that large companies, builders of dams and highways and tunnels, might not bother to compete for the small stuff—such as repairing a slightly damaged radio tower, restoring a cracked retaining wall, or replacing broken railings on a bridge. Not worth bothering about. As for regular building contractors, such jobs would be out of their realm of interest. It was a good idea, and it served to get the company started. Eventually the concept was abandoned, as the niche was found to be small, the few available jobs tended to entail high risk, and, as the 1950s advanced, Westchester experienced a population explosion that presented attractive opportunities in the construction of schools.

But when I arrived in 1956, one year after the company's founding, Kreisler Borg had already completed its first two jobs in the small-heavy category, a $12,210 repair of a wooden railroad bridge in Yonkers and and a $62,275 contract for shoring up sagging floors in the Consumers Union Building in Mount Vernon. Contracts were signed for repairs to equipment in a sewage-treatment plant and for building small concrete storage structures for the Nuclear Development Corporation in Pawling. In addition, a separate small company had been established for the building of swimming pools. The two young entrepreneurs had gotten off to a fast start.

For me, a lifelong resident of Manhattan, the new job meant embarking on a career of reverse commuting. I started with the train, but, needing to visit construction sites, I soon changed to the car. I must confess to feeling a measure of guilty pleasure cruising comfortably north as hordes of drivers braved incredible crowding on the way into the city. Of course, for construction people who work on a job site, the commute is part of life, their destination changing from year to year, or often day to day, and I have found them generally stoical about that circumstance.

Arriving at the office for my first day of work, I was welcomed with jovial sentiments, then promptly presented with the plans and specifications for the next project to be bid. I remember it well: the repairing of wooden fenders on the Cross Bay Parkway Viaduct in Queens. The work consisted of removing and replacing large creosoted timbers along with some of the wooden piles to which they were attached. Below the waterline the connections consisted of metal brackets, and a considerable amount of underwater welding was required. This was not like anything I had seen before, but an estimate is an estimate—labor, materials, and equipment—the bid was due in about a week, and I set to work. After a bit of quick research, I was able to speak somewhat knowingly on the telephone with the owners of piledriving companies—also with experts in marine carpentry, and most important, with a diver named Barney who specialized in underwater welding.

Barney came to our office, studied the plans carefully, assured me that he could handle the job with no difficulty, and told me how much of his time to allow in our estimate for each connection—let us say it was one hour—totaling seven connections per working day. To be on the safe side, thought I, better make it six. Barney also quoted me his hourly rate, a staggeringly high amount; but, after all, underwater welding is not your everyday construction activity.

I worked assiduously on the estimate and reviewed it carefully with my new employers. The cost, including a small contingency amount and a 15 percent markup, amounted to $105,000. Barney's work represented about $20,000 of the total.

To our surprise and delight, we were the low bidders. To our consternation we left a goodly sum "on the table," that is, the amount between our price and the second bidder. But, all in all, we started the job in great spirits.

That is until Barney called after visiting the site. "Damn," he said. "You didn't tell me about the tide." The tide? It seemed that the tide going in and out under the viaduct was so powerful that a diver could only work for about an hour, at high tide or low when the water was still. No six connections per day—only two. No $20,000 cost for the welding, but three times as much. With a $40,000 over-run, our $15,000 profit would be replaced by a loss of $25,000. The tide! Who could have known? Well, we all should have known, including Barney, who felt "awful, just awful, guys!" but he hadn't given us a guaranteed price. It was an object lesson in the financial hazards of construction, and it threatened to be fatal.

But, rather than default, we determined to plow ahead, trying desperately to find ways to maximize Barney's rate of production. Production wasn't helped when, on October 8, 1956, word spread that Don Larsen of the Yankees was pitching a perfect game against the Dodgers in the World Series. Our superintendent, Bill Mullaly, announced that the job was going to shut down an hour early and all the men would gather at a bar at Rockaway Beach to watch the final innings. Bill was buying the beer. Larsen's perfect game is history, and the crew enjoyed their beers. But that was the only pleasant episode to report. Despite our best efforts—and Barney's—a devastating loss seemed inevitable.

And then, on a miraculous day when the tide that threatened our ruin proved to be our salvation, we learned another object lesson in construction, and in life. It is possible to get lucky. A tugboat, misjudging the very tide that we had disregarded, was swept into our work area, smashing into the timbers, piles, and welded braces. The work we had accomplished was substantially destroyed. But the company was saved. An insurance claim provided a happy ending to what could have been a tale of woe.

A few weeks later I met Jacques Kreisler, Sr., for the first time when he visited our office, and I discussed with him our escape from disaster. You needn't fear a financial setback, he said, or even failure. He went on to tell me how he had come to this country as a young man, founded a jewelry business with a partner only to have to close their doors in 1932 during the depths of the Depression. The business was restarted after a year and eventually flourished. "But I never had to worry," said Mr. Kreisler, smiling. As a youth he had been apprenticed to a goldsmith, and as he put it, flexing his fingers, "I had a trade in my hands." Because of his training and his skill, he felt that he could always make a living. That sentiment has resonated in my own consciousness (along with the somewhat contradictory advice of the elderly man in Florida who told me to think of "partnership"). If all else failed, I had a trade, not in my hands exactly, but in my mind: the ability to estimate construction costs. Building construction is an essential element of human civilization, and every project begins with an estimate of cost. After that discussion, I was comforted by the thought that if worse came to worst, I could always get a job.

EVERY morning we received in the office a mimeographed newsletter— *Brown's Letters*—that listed the projects in our area for which bids were being solicited. The jobs in the small-heavy category were few and far between, while the number of schools being planned was growing exponentially. The facts spoke for themselves. Let's go for it, I suggested, and agreement was instantaneous. We'll build schools. Selecting a project in Pawling, a community somewhat north of our office, sort of exurbia, where we thought the competition might not be too fierce, we sent for the plans and prepared to bid. As usual, we inspected the site of the proposed building. I undertook the task—this time, thinking about the tide fiasco, ever so carefully. I noticed that within the bounds of the proposed building there were several large outcroppings of rock, so large, in fact, that I took some measurements and made some rough calculations. The bid documents stated that rock excavation would be extra to the contract, and it was up to each bidder to insert a proposed unit price for this work. This unit price was not to be taken into account in calculating the competitive price for each bidder. Since there was no limit or stated penalty for a high unit price, I suggested that we submit a figure—about double the cost—that would yield a handsome profit on the rock work. This would enable us to make the base bid truly competitive. Lo and behold, we were the low bidders, and we didn't leave a large amount "on the table." Best of all, our unit price for rock excavation, while on the high side, was considered acceptable.

We were already making plans to get started on the job when word came that, before an award was made, we had to be interviewed by members of the school board, some of whom had questioned our qualifications. Not a happy development. I was selected to go to the interview, since I was the only one of us who had any experience in building schools. It was a dark, forbidding night, and I felt increasingly anxious as I drove up Route 22, past Heidi's Motel. I was heading toward the first of many interviews I was to have through the years—with school boards and building committees for many different sorts of organizations.

In Pawling I had reason to be concerned, since I was representing a company, now in its second year, that had never built a school—or much of anything else for that matter. Thinking realistically, it was not likely that anyone would try to disqualify us, since public funds were involved, our price was the lowest, and, perhaps most important, as required by the bid documents we had submitted a bid bond, indicating that an established bonding company would post a guarantee of our performance under the contract. Still, I was nervous and had to answer some serious questions about the firm's lack of experience. I spoke of my own previous experience, and Borg's as well, and I like to think I won some friends by stressing our desire to do a top-notch job for Pawling in order to build up a résumé of satisfied clients. The day was won when the architect rose to declare that he had every confidence in our firm's ability and intentions. The architectural firm was Coffin & Coffin, descendants of an early American New England family, indeed the founders of Nantucket, as straitlaced and confidence building as people can be. "Everybody has to begin somewhere," declared the Mr. Coffin who was present, earning my silent sworn commitment to do right by this group, to build them the best damned school it was possible to build.

The job turned out very well, and our path as school builders was blazed. Over the next five years we built a dozen schools in Westchester, southern Connecticut, and Rockland County.

This experience with public schools helped qualify us for private bid lists, and we found ourselves building a school for Temple Israel of White Plains and the Jewish Community Center in Harrison. These in turn earned us invitations to bid for synagogues in New Rochelle and Riverdale, bids that proved to be successful. At this point, one of our in-house comics suggested that we could advertise ourselves as builders of "schools, shuls, and pools."

Before we could give this idea our full consideration, we broadened our ecclesiastical profile by building an ecumenical training center for the Presbyterian Church. Also, we discontinued the installation of swimming pools—the emotional crises encountered in digging up the backyards of private residences was too distracting. And as for schools, the market began to dry up as populations stabilized. Suddenly the "schools, shuls, and pools" byline was yesterday's joke. The changing business environment became a matter of serious concern. Fortunately, this change did not find us totally unprepared.

I have read a number of articles and even books telling building contractors that the best way to survive and prosper is to specialize. In some ways it seems logical: become an expert in one field, know it well, and get to know the people who are the dominant forces within it. Also, avoid the pitfalls awaiting those who blunder into unfamiliar realms where dangers lurk—technical, personal, and political. This approach has served a number of firms well. On the other hand, those who specialize in a product for which there is suddenly no demand may find that they have contrived their own demise. I recall that the radio comedians Bob and Ray used to feature soap opera episodes sponsored by an imaginary firm, the Rotman

Corporation, "makers of fine buggy whips for nine hundred years." Well, concentrating on suburban schools in a fully developed suburban area began to seem uncomfortably like making those buggy whips.

We managed to avoid the pitfalls of specialization, partly by happenstance, taking advantage of opportunities that came our way. During the half dozen years when we were concentrating on schools and religious structures, we also took on an interiors project for the New York Telephone Company in White Plains and built two small office buildings for the Lawrence family in Bronxville. Also, at the behest of friends, we ventured, ever so cautiously, into the big city, New York, performing alterations in a law office and a printing plant.

Most memorable in the nonschool category—from a historical point of view certainly—was the work we performed in 1957–58 for the U.S. Army Corps of Engineers on the Nike missile system. It is little remembered today that during some of the most tense years of the cold war the New York metropolitan area was defended by a series of surface-to-air missile batteries. A total of nineteen such batteries were built around the city, and several hundred others deployed in a nationwide system. They represented a last line of defense against the feared coming of long-distance Soviet bombers. Within a decade, as intercontinental ballistic missiles became the threat, these sites were abandoned; but when they were being built there was understandably a sense of urgency. Our firm had no experience in working for the military, and no dream of entering that remote and forbidding field. But when bids were publicly solicited for "sanitary facilities" at a site in the Kensico area of White Plains, a stone's throw from our office, plus two other sites just across the Hudson River, Orangeburg and Ramapo, we thought, why not give it a try? This was for sanitary facilities, mind you, not for the rocket launchers themselves. Not many contractors seemed to be interested in this unusual-sounding project, and our bid of $211,000 was the lowest of the few submitted.

Since the batteries in question were located in wooded areas on rocky hilltops, the sanitary facilities could not be simple septic fields, but rather consisted of large tanks, each containing a prefabricated miniature sewage-treatment plant. The tanks, as I recall, were more than ten feet in diameter and perhaps twenty feet in height. Our contract work consisted of purchasing the ingeniously designed sewage plants from the Dorr-Oliver Company in Stamford, Connecticut; excavating a pit in the rock large enough to receive the tank; and then hoisting the tank off the truck on which it was laboriously brought up the hill, getting it settled properly in place, and performing all the ancillary plumbing and electrical work required. The project progressed as well as could have been wished. Too perfectly, as one of our men superstitiously said, and how right he was. The night before the excavated holes were scheduled to be backfilled, a heavy rainstorm struck the area. In anticipation of such a contingency the tanks had relief valves located near the bottom allowing exterior water to enter an empty chamber and provide enough weight to prevent the tanks from floating. Unfortunately, on one of the tanks, where a protective coat of tarlike waterproofing had been sprayed—to prevent rusting underground—the heavy black goo had been applied carelessly, making the relief valves inoperative. As a result, the enormous tank was lifted like a toy duck in a child's bath and tipped sideways, hitting the edge of the excavated pit, resulting in a nasty dent and an unknown amount of interior damage. Water seemed to be our special nemesis.

The first order of business, with no time to be wasted, was to repair the damage—which we were able to do in a few days of round-the-clock activity. Then, using our crane, we had to resettle the tank in its proper spot, complete the necessary connections, backfill the hole, and turn over the project so that the missile-launching equipment could be brought in. The next matter to resolve—second in importance to the military security of New York City perhaps but critical to the continued health of our construction company—was payment for the extra work performed. We put all of our cost figures together for the operation, much of it overtime, and saw that the amount was surprisingly large, more than we could afford to lose.

On an appointed day we drove up to what seemed to us a very fancy office building in Stamford to meet with the top executives of

Dorr-Oliver. In subsequent years I've been in fancy corporate conference rooms, sometimes as a board member of charitable organizations, and often with bankers and lawyers in connection with real estate projects. But I believe that the meeting with Dorr-Oliver was the only occasion on which I've met with "corporate America," with the manufacturers of machinery, the tycoons of what used to be the core of American power and importance. I've wondered about that world and how it would have been to work in it, how, with its departments and titles and organizational formality, it differs from the world of construction.

On the day in question my thinking was more concentrated: how were we going to come out of this mess whole. An accepted business approach is to enter into a negotiation with a considerably higher figure than the one for which you're willing to settle. Then be prepared to be flexible. In this instance I decided to play it absolutely straight, give the real figures with meticulous documentary support and stand firm if necessary. To my surprise and delight, the men in the dark blue suits, after a brief conference among themselves, accepted our figures as presented. Of course, the amount that seemed so large to us—I forget the details but recall that it was several tens of thousands of dollars—must have seemed small when compared with the Dorr-Oliver operation. Additionally, these people clearly felt guilty about their careless workmanship and wanted the incident gone and forgotten, especially by the army, as quickly as possible. Finally, we were the small guys in the equation, obviously in distress. In any event, another crisis had passed. The nation had its defensive missiles deployed, and our company was still in business.

WITH the completion in 1961 of an addition to the Hawthorne Junior High School in Yonkers, our suburban school-building days at last came to an end. With fewer schools to build, and also the entry of new companies into the marketplace, competition had become more intense. I think back on those five years, starting with the Pawling school in 1956, as a halcyon time, almost as the "good old golden-rule days" of sentimental song. Seventeen structures built in placid country settings, with mostly agreeable people: architects, workers, inspectors, school boards, and—where we were adding to existing buildings—teachers and children. Not that every minute of every day was carefree.

In Ridgefield, Connecticut, for example, where we built a high school gymnasium that featured laminated wooden arches rising thirty-two feet and spanning one hundred and twenty feet, a gust of wind came along at an awkward moment during erection and tumbled the arches into a splintered pile on the ground. It was a construction accident, embarrassing and costly; but no one was injured, and the broken materials were speedily replaced. Yet when news of the mishap got around—when a photo of the broken timbers appeared in the local newspaper!—the townsfolk were in an uproar. Parents envisioned their children under that heap of debris, and demands were made to change the threatening, hazardous, recklessly unsafe design. With some effort the architect and design engineer were able to convince the community that the arches, as part of a completed structure, would be sound as sound could be. The finished building turned out to be reassuringly stable, and handsome as well; but the experience showed that the "owners" of a school could be challenging clients indeed.

Thinking back to those happy days, I tend to forget the pressure of competitive bidding. Almost every week we submitted a formal proposal for a publicly advertised project. The frenetic combination of taking off quantities and pricing the trades as best we could, while at the same time contacting dozens of subcontractors by phone and trying to obtain the most favorable bids—sometimes "making a deal" with a sub, other times trying to gauge what bottom figure the broadcast bid was meant to imply—then debating how to price low enough to get the job while high enough to make a profit; then making sure that the bid was submitted by the immutable deadline (usually by telephone contact with an individual standing by at the appointed spot), then waiting to hear the results, damn, out of the running most of the time, frightening news when we were the successful bidder—well, those were harrowing experiences.

Then there were the wild and woolly episodes that the years only make more hilarious in recall. My favorite is the time we decided to bid on the replacement of four small concrete bridges in Connecticut. This was a throwback to our small-heavy construction concept, selected for a try during a month when there were no schools to be bid. There were no last-minute phone-call hysterics with which to contend since the price was established totally in-house in collaboration with a concrete subcontractor. However, the bids were to be opened in the state capitol building in Hartford, and the question arose of how best to see that our proposal got to the right place at the right time. Being a bit compulsive about such things, I resolved to deliver the document personally, and since I didn't fully trust my maps and was uncertain about parking facilities near the capitol, I decided to take the train. Allowing ample time, I drove to Stamford, boarded the train according to a schedule, and settled back comfortably, congratulating myself on cautious planning. Until . . . the train slowed down and came to a complete halt. Well, these things happen, and I had allowed myself plenty of time. After a few minutes the conductor's voice could be heard: "Sorry, folks. The wind seems to have blown a tree down, and it's lying across the tracks ahead. We'll back into the station we just left; but we might not be able to resume our trip for an hour, or maybe more." Unbelieving, I was first off the train when it stopped at the station and hopped into what seemed to be the only taxi in sight. "The capitol building in Hartford," I said; "and step on it please." "You gotta be kidding," said the driver. "That's way out of my area. And besides," seeing me beginning to pull wads of money out of my pocket, "I'd have to change my license plates just to drive on the highway." "Well, let's get them changed, you name the price, and we'll add twenty dollars if you get me there before two o'clock." The plates were changed, and off we went.

But the adventure was just beginning. I sat up front with the driver, lit the cigarette that he said he needed because of the pressure, and we zipped along, not too much over the speed limit since getting stopped wouldn't have served our purpose. Bothered by the smoke, I opened the window and a glowing ash flew off the cigarette. Incredibly, without our noticing it, the ash, still aglow, landed on the back seat, which soon was darkening and belching smoke. "Jee-zuz!" screamed the driver, "we're on fire!" "Don't stop!" I pleaded, as I scrambled into the back and started throwing bits of smoldering upholstery out of the window. This sounds more preposterous every time I tell the story, but it actually happened. We arrived at the capitol building with time running short. I gave the driver practically all the bills I had and then started running up and down the marble corridors looking for the room where the bid was due. I made it for the opening with just a few minutes to spare. We weren't the low bidder, but I hardly cared. In fact I laughed for what seemed like a long time, laughed out loud as I recounted the incident to the incredulous people in our office, and smile even now as I think of the incident.

THERE are other reasons for me to think fondly of that golden age. In Kreisler Borg I had found my home at last. The fit was per-fect. I brought with me the knowledge and experience of my days with Thompson-Starrett and Joe Blitz—and yes, the Long Island housebuilders, the Venezuelan crews, and the never-to-be-forgotten Seabees. I will not assume a false modesty. But I quickly recognized that in Kreisler and in Borg there existed a commercial intensity that I lacked. Bob Borg was the negotiator, the "buyer" that every con-struction company needs. As evidence of the state of my limited bargaining skills, when our company name was changed from Kreis-ler Borg to Kreisler Borg Florman, my Thursday-night poker-game mates gave me a nameplate that read: "Kreisler Borg & Patsy."

In mentioning the change of name I'm getting ahead of myself chronologically; but I guess it's just as well. Within a year of my join-ing the firm in early 1956, I raised the idea of my becoming a part-ner, and the possibility quickly became a joint objective. The only question was the money: how much should I pay for a one-third share of ownership, and where was I going to get the cash? It wasn't easy to pin down an accurate book value for the stock, but with the help of friendly lawyers and accountants, and motivated by the desire to get the deal done, we settled on a figure. The only problem was that I didn't have enough money. My wife and I emptied out our savings account and sold my prized stamp collection. A shortfall was covered by a loan from my mother, and the deal was consummated in June of 1957.

Although the company was just over two years old at the time, we felt that the name Kreisler Borg should not be changed, that it was sacrosanct, sort of like Eastman Kodak. However, as through time we saw architects and lawyers changing their firm names to reflect changing personnel, we eventually decided to change ours, which we did in 1969, making it Kreisler Borg Florman, often KBF for convenience. This wasn't totally consistent, since we didn't delete Kreisler from the name, even though by that time Borg and I had bought out Kreisler's interest.

I'VE jumped ahead, but don't want to give short shrift to the firm's formative years. Soon after my arrival we established—willy-nilly and unplanned—a working relationship that was to serve us well for more than half a century. I was the estimator, Borg was the buyer, and we divided between us the oversight of the jobs, taking on only as many as we felt we could handle—personally. We rarely embarked on more than four new projects in a year, so that, allowing two years for each, we rarely had more than eight active at any given time, four for each of us. This enabled us to stay in personal touch with owners, architects, and subcontractors. Neither Borg nor I had "hardhat" personalities, and, recognizing this, we gathered around us a small force of talented field men. Tom Grasso acted as general superintendent, and after Tom's tragic illness and death, we promoted John Cricco, a capable and high-spirited young man of whom more later.

When I speak of only four new projects per year—eight in operation at any one time—it doesn't sound like an adequate foundation for an enterprise that flourished for so long in a uniquely challenging industry. Yet that's the way it was. From 1955 to 2010—fifty-five years—the number of our contracts totaled approximately two hundred and twenty. That's four per year. Some of these contracts, particularly with New York City agencies, consisted of supervising several projects—police stations, firehouses, armories, and so forth. And many of the contracts were for multibuilding projects. So we have surely built more than three hundred buildings, even many more, depending on how one counts. But the crucial fact is the way in which the owners of the business were able to personally remain in control of the work. This is a selling point that many firms are pleased to use: personal attention from the principals. And, while watching a job closely is no guarantee that things can't go radically wrong—as we have seen and will see again—this approach helped protect us against the diseases of overexpansion and loss of control, diseases that have led to the failure of many construction firms. Looked at another way, this approach cut us off from the option of growing to be a giant in the industry.

There is another reason for following the management path we did, perhaps the most important reason, although never specifically articulated. By limiting our prospects for growth, we gained freedom to lead lives of our choice outside the office. First of all, Borg and I were family men. I remember my wife showing me a newspaper article one day that told of entrepreneurs who had made millions before reaching the age of forty. "Yes," I replied, "but they're not expected to be home by 6:30."

This is not to imply that we didn't work hard. We were in the office early and worked a full day. When estimates were due we often labored far into the evening. On a few such occasions I slept over near the office—and once found it awkward to be coming out of the Roger Smith Hotel in White Plains at sunrise, only to run into a friend of my mother's who looked at me askance. Yes, we worked hard, but had lots of fun, including a full quota of vacations. We weren't the type of contractor who prompted consultant Matt Stevens to entitle his book, *Managing a Construction Firm on Just Twenty-four Hours a Day.*

We valued our free time but didn't devote all of it to family and self-indulgent activities. As the years went by, Bob Borg became active in the American Society of Civil Engineers, where he was founder and first chairman of the Committee on Social and Environment Concerns in Construction. He was also a member of the board of directors of the American Arbitration Association and deeply involved with other professional and construction-industry organizations. I took to writing, mainly about the relation between technology and the larger society, first in periodicals—becoming a contributing editor to *Harper's* and *Technology Review*—then in books, of which this is the seventh. That avocation earned me invitations to speak at universities and professional society gatherings. I served on boards of directors—for a hospital, a private school, and a science museum—and also a term on the Board of Overseers of Dartmouth's Thayer School of Engineering. In later years, after being elected to the National Academy of Engineering, I accepted appointment to numerous committees of the National Research Council, which functions under the auspices of the National Academies of Science and Engineering and the Institute of Medicine.

Were these activities business-related? Only tangentially. They were related to our profession: engineering. And in some circles I suppose they earned us a modicum of respect as good citizens. Yet I liked the separation of this life experience from working for profit, from making a living. Students are taught in business school, and even in engineering school, that career success requires a quotient of "people skills," and I will not quarrel with this concept. I have had many occasions to try to sell myself as an expert builder, and I've never shied away from applications, interviews, and presentations to potential "owners." Yet I feel fortunate that I was able to make my way without devoting a lot of time and energy to what today is called "networking."

* * *

IN 1959, at four years of age, KBF had outgrown its snug little office (emphasis on the word little) and taken up residence in half a converted house on Cromwell Place, a backwater in the White Plains of that day. When I say half a house, I mean it literally; the four-story structure was divided vertically, one half ours, the other half occupied by our architect friend, Matthew Warshauer. The layout called for lots of trotting up and down stairs, which was good aerobically but had drawbacks when it came to ease of communication. In early 1964 Al and Mario Passeri, masonry subcontractors with whom we had worked, built a two-story brick structure on Montgomery Street, in Scarsdale, and persuaded us, along with Warshauer, to leave White Plains and become their tenants. Eventually we purchased the building. I've never been completely comfortable with the address—Scarsdale being known as an affluent bedroom community. But the post office location determines such things, and Scarsdale it is, even though our building is located a mile south of the village, technically in the town of Eastchester. Most important, we overlook a lovely small park adjoining a pleasant suburban-commercial avenue and have been comfortable, a convenient commute for our people, who hail from many surrounding communities.

In later years our work required us to set up satellite offices: first in the Bronx, adjoining buildings we rehabilitated for the New York City Housing Authority; then in Rego Park, Queens, where we operated a "mentor" program for the School Construction Authority; next in Long Island City, to be close to the city's Department of Design and Construction. In 1999, after we built the Korean Trade and Distribution Center in Queens, we moved in as a tenant, only to find two years later that the owners desperately wanted us to get out and make way for the powerful film and television production facility Silvercup Studios. We agreed to make way by moving into available space in the original Silvercup Studios building for two years before leaving the theatrical world behind for an office back in Long Island City on Borden Avenue.

BUT this takes us into the future. The good old school days, 1956–1961, remain in the memory, special and serene. For the nation those were the Eisenhower years, the calm before the sixties. For our firm they were the suburban years, before we ventured into the big city; before the high-rise towers, aggressive developers, wily politicians, and bureaucratic agencies; before encounters with the powerful unions, a scandal-ridden building department, crooked cops (pre-Serpico); before the ferment of aroused communities, "affirmative action" and its shocking criminal aftermath; before we had even the slightest idea about the role played in our industry by the Mafia.

The Innocents Abroad. That's the title of a book by Mark Twain; but it expresses my feelings about the changes that lay before us.

SEVEN | *Dollars and Cents*

WE TEND TO THINK of buildings as objects of steel and concrete, brick and glass. Often we conceive of them in terms of grandeur and beauty, utility and social benefit. I recall my years in the industry in terms of drama and excitement, risk and danger. But none of us can ever forget that each building is intimately related to numbers. And when I say numbers I refer not only to dimensions, dates on a schedule, stresses and strains (actual as well as psychological) but also—indeed primarily—to money.

When contractors speak of "volume" they are usually referring to the dollar value of work on hand or accomplished. And when they use the word "capacity" they mean "bonding capacity," the amount of work a bonding company is willing to underwrite for them, an amount that often defines the outer limits of how much work a contractor can take on. "Profit," "loss," and "overhead" are other terms, well understood, that we express in percentages and numbers of dollars.

In addition to being important, statistics can be inherently fascinating, a fact to which any baseball fan can attest. For KBF, the 300-odd buildings that we've completed under some 220 contracts include 100 apartment projects incorporating more than 20,000 apartments plus 4,000 completely rehabbed. As I write these words, we are completing the tallest residential tower in the Western Hemisphere, the 76-story "New York by Gehry" in lower Manhattan.

I could list 30 schools; 20 hospital, clinic, and nursing home projects; 6 religious centers; dormitories for Columbia, NYU, and Brooklyn Law School; several suburban office buildings and shopping centers; a country club and a surf club; an innovative playground in New York City's Central Park; a yacht harbor at Battery Park City; and various other projects, including the never-to-be-forgotten facilities for the Nike batteries. Yes, yes. But what about the money?

A problem that confronts us at the start is inflation. Senator Everett Dirksen was quoted as saying, "a billion here, a billion there, and pretty soon you're talking about real money." Well, what *is* "real money" today? What do we consider a large amount? In discussing the equity value of Kreisler Borg when I purchased a share in 1957, I noted that the cost of living is about eight times as high today as it was then. Each of us has a favorite memory of what something cost in our childhood—a Coke, a movie, a ride on the subway: no matter our age, they were all so much cheaper when we were kids. We have learned to live with inflation, a phenomenon most often defined by changes in the Consumer Price Index. (A closely related number, COLA—Cost of Living Adjustment—was established by legislation in 1973, mainly to determine annual increases in Social Security benefits.) The cost of building construction usually moves in the same patterns as those of the general economy, but the industry has its own specific indicators.

The most widely accepted of these statistical records are the cost indexes established by *Engineering News-Record* starting in 1921. And the figure that I think of most often is the change from 1956, the year I joined KBF, to 2006, fifty years later. It's a convenient time span, this half a century, not only for discussing the history of our company but also because the onset of an international financial crisis in 2008 brought into question all future trends and patterns.

In 1956 the *ENR* Building Cost Index stood at 491. In 2006 the figure was 4,350, an increase by a factor of 8.86—886 percent. The

Consumer Price Index for the same period rose 741 percent. These are the facts. I will not attempt to convert everything that follows into "constant dollars." We all know that a million dollars isn't what it used to be.

IN its earliest years, that is, starting in 1955, our firm's annual volume of work completed was about $2 million. It rose steadily, even if not spectacularly, to $5 million at the end of our tenth year. Our first school, in Pawling, completed in 1957, cost $257,000. A larger school, built two years later in Greenburgh, topped $600,000, and we reached our first $1 million project with New Rochelle's Temple Israel, completed in 1962.

That same year we entered new territory, both technical and financial, with a $1–1.5 million building for Montefiore Hospital, and two years after that broke ground for the $1–1.5 million Peekskill Hospital. At about the same time, we ventured into the apartment field with a small project for the Yonkers Housing Authority, and then, for the same agency, our first high-rise, and almost our last—almost our last anything—the $2.7 million School Street Project. The project, bid in 1961 and completed in 1964 after incredible bureaucratic delays, its legal claims settled in 1966, was an experience deserving its own story, which will be told in the next chapter. We survived, thanks to the kindness of friends, and thanks to events that led us to the 1964 World's Fair, a fabulous never-never land where we were able to do work without bonding.

As we made our way out of the Yonkers debacle and into the late 1960s, we entered the world of Mitchell–Lama housing. Based on a 1955 New York State law, and implemented both by the state and New York City, the Mitchell–Lama program provided financing to construct apartments for middle-income families. The main incentive offered for investors was not the allowable 6 percent return on investment, which was rarely if ever realized, but rather the tax "losses" from building depreciation that, according to the then-existing tax code, could be deducted from ordinary income. Starting in 1968 this activity was supplemented by initiatives of the state's newly created Urban Development Corporation. Government sponsorship of housing, so soon to fall out of favor with a fickle public and changing administrations, flowered briefly at the very moment that we were ready to play our part in the movement.

We were introduced to these housing programs by happenstance and personal acquaintance, and, sensing the opening up of attractive frontiers, we followed through with zeal. Associating with non-profit groups who wanted to sponsor publicly financed housing and also with various private investors, we built a number of high-rise apartment projects, mostly running in cost from $2 million to $10 million. Sometimes we bid these jobs in competition; but often they could be negotiated, the guaranteed maximum costs required to fall within limits set by the various government agencies, and the final actual cost determined by thorough audit with authorized percentages for overhead and profit. Our average annual volume increased from $5 million to the $7 million range and, as we entered the 1970s, reached an average of $16 million annually, with three years topping $25 million. Of course, compared with contractors whose annual workload runs into the billions of dollars, we have always been very small potatoes. Still, we felt fortunate. While New York City underwent a severe financial crisis, coming close to bankruptcy in 1975, KBF was engaged in programs that weathered the storm.

In the 1980s, as the city struggled to recover from its financial ills, and as Ronald Reagan ruled in Washington, the Mitchell-Lama and UDC programs expired. Fortunately, we found a niche in a small federal program, HUD's 202, which provided funding to nonprofit groups for moderate-rent housing for the elderly. These projects, doled out with political acumen to nonprofit groups with a delightful variety of ethnic, community, and religious connections, usually contained about one hundred apartments. We were able to help such organizations apply for sponsorship and make their way through the maze of government red tape, and we developed along the way a number of very pleasant working relationships. At the same time we took on several New York City Housing Authority projects, upgrading large developments with the tenants in residency, an intimidating challenge that, happily, was handled with a minimum of stress. And, sensing that a decline in publicly funded housing would persist, we began to pursue privately financed work with several of New York's prominent developers. We also kept our estimating skills sharp by bidding in the marketplace and were able to find some interesting work with hospitals and nursing homes. The average annual volume for the 1980s exceeded $30 million.

It was satisfying to see growth and a modest degree of success. Yet time has a way of flying, and, as Kreisler Borg Florman celebrated its thirtieth anniversary in 1985, there was a new kind of number to consider: the ages of the principals. Entering our sixties, we started to think seriously about succession. We had in the firm several outstanding people—knowledgeable, personable, and energetic—but none with the entrepreneurial ambitions that seemed called for in a CEO. Fortuitously, we were introduced to Joseph Zelazny, a talented engineer-builder born in Poland who had made his career in New York City, rising through the Starrett Corp. and HRH to a top position. Joe had overseen construction of a number of important projects, including the Javits Convention Center, and was well acquainted with many people in our industry, including those in the private development sector. Having business sense to match his technical skills, he seemed well equipped to take on a leadership role. We invited Joe to join us in a partnership position, which he did in 1987.

We were at that time already at work as construction managers for private developers, building the Corinthian, a $100 million project for Bernard Spitzer, and Columbus Green Apartments for Steve Ross of the Related Companies. Joe moved vigorously into this field, negotiating additional projects with the Related Companies and gaining contracts with the developers Leonard Litwin, the Rose Organization, the Dursts, the Manocherian Organization, Toll Brothers, Forest City Ratner, and several others less well known but equally satisfying to deal with. We also pursued work with the city of New York through the Department of Design and Construction and the School Construction Authority and were retained to oversee numerous small city jobs under multitask contracts. The HUD 202 program, although curtailed, managed to survive, and we got our share of the few projects that were authorized. As a result, volume grew to an annual average of close to $100 million in the 1990s and $200 million in the first decade of the new millennium.

But so what? Or, as Groucho Marx would remark when asked "How's your wife"—"compared to what?"

IN 2008 *Engineering News-Record* marked its fiftieth anniversary of ranking American contractors based on size, that is, based on "construction revenue" in a given year. *ENR* celebrated the occasion with a feature giving detailed information, about "The Top 400 Contractors" (as of 2007). According to the editors, 2007 had been an "exceptional year," with the group having generated contracting revenue of $256.86 billion domestic and $47.50 billion abroad. Future prospects looked ominous, but the recent past "was close to the best of times."

The companies were ranked by total construction revenues in 2007, with breakdowns provided in percentages not only between domestic and international but also by types of market: general building (53.1); manufacturing (2.1); power (6.3); water supply, including dams and reservoirs (1.5); sewerage/solid waste (1.8); industrial process (6.6); petroleum (11.6); transportation, including airports, bridges, roads, railroads, and piers (11.2); hazardous waste (1.7); telecommunications (1.2); and other (2.9). These percentages indicate that just about half the construction by the top four hundred firms is in the realm of general building—the realm in which KBF lives—the other half in the category popularly known as "heavy." The two companies topping the overall list were Bechtel, headquartered in San Francisco, at $17.7 billion for the year, and Fluor Corp., of Irving, Texas, at $13.3 billion. Both of these firms showed more than half their work as international, and also more than half in industrial and petroleum, practically nothing in the general building category. The giant in our field, building construction, the number three firm in the overall industry, was the Turner Corp. of New York City, with $9.4 billion, all domestic, 84 percent in general building. Rounding out the top ten were KBR, of Houston; Kiewit Corp., of Omaha; Skanska USA Inc. and Bovis Lend Lease, both headquartered in New York City; PCL, of Denver; Perini Corp., of Framingham, Massachusetts; and Jacobs, of Pasadena, California. Of this group, following Turner, only Skanska and Bovis Lend Lease, at about $5.5 billion each, and Perini, at $4.6 billion, are mainly domestic and building construction.

Thinking of my home territory, I look for other firms I would call "New York builders of buildings" and find Structure Tone, number 17 on the list with an annual figure of $3.3 billion; HRH, number 169 at $420 million (three years later, the company was bankrupt, a lesson in caution amid the recitation of riches); Barr & Barr, number 177 at $394 million; Gotham Construction, number 241 at $298 million; Henegan Construction, number 288 at $250 million; E.W. Howell, number 364 at $183 million; Hunter Roberts, number 385 at $169 million; and DeMatteis, number 394 at $162 million. These names may mean little to the average citizen, but to those of us who comprise the New York City building industry they are as familiar as this morning's headlines.

Incidentally, we New Yorkers tend to think of our city as the center of the universe, which perhaps it is not. Still, in the world of building construction it does have a prominent place. According to McGraw-Hill Construction Research and Analytics, the New York City building construction market as a percent of the total U.S. market was, for the five years from 2005 to 2009: 17 percent, 27 percent, 31 percent, 36 percent and 41 percent. Of course, much of the work done in the city is performed by companies whose headquarters are elsewhere. And the unit costs in New York City are very high, so that the square footage of new buildings doesn't match the percentages quoted, which represent money expended. Nevertheless, what happens in New York City construction clearly counts in the scheme of things.

Our firm has never filed financial figures for publication; but it appears that in recent years, with a volume in excess of $200 million, we would have made our way into the lower ranks of the hallowed list of four hundred. Except—and this is a big except—the meaning of these figures is not what it first appears to be.

What, exactly, is the definition of "construction revenue"? I pick up an issue of *New York Construction,* a McGraw-Hill publication, as is *ENR,* and find as number 1 on a list of "top contractors" in our area Tishman Construction Corporation (with $2.8 billion revenue for 2008 in the Tri-State region) and, on top again in 2009, dubbed regional "Contractor of the Year." Of course, Tishman is known to be one of the biggest around, and yet that name doesn't even appear on the *ENR* "Top 400" list. How can this be? I check with the folks at *ENR,* and they tell me that I will find Tishman listed as number 13 nationally on the *ENR* list "Construction Management-for-Fee Firms." Oh my gosh, *a separate list for a separate category.* And as I look further I see that there are also lists for "Construction Management-at-Risk Firms," "Program Management Firms," "Design-Build Firms," "Firms in Combined Industry Revenue," and "Firms in Combined Design and CM/Professional Service." Obviously this list making is a more complicated business than it first appears.

Obtaining a copy of *ENR*'s guidelines for filling out their survey form, I see it clearly stated that *only at-risk work* is to be included in calculations for listing among the top 400. Our firm's volume of work, especially in recent years, includes several projects for which we have not provided a guaranteed maximum price. So, strictly speaking, if we were ever to submit our figures to *ENR,* such projects would have to be eliminated from our calculation of volume. However, although President Clinton was once ridiculed for saying that the truth sometimes depends on what the meaning of "is" is, I venture to argue that there is a question of whether the term "no risk" really means no risk.

I look at some of the no-risk construction-management contracts our firm has signed and see that we sometimes provide guarantees concerning certain particular aspects of the work. But more important than any such specific item is our general agreement to monitor the work "in order to avoid defects and deficiencies" and "ensure that the work is performed in strict accordance with the project schedule approved by the developer." Imagine what such language can mean should a serious problem arise.

Consider not in the abstract but an actual case: an eminent contractor who served "without risk" as construction manager on a large building. This contractor recommended strongly against the use of certain clamps for attaching curtain wall to the structure. The curtain wall manufacturer persisted, the architect approved, and the construction manager reluctantly deferred. When the clamps failed, the construction manager was brought into the ensuing lawsuit and was found liable for a sizeable portion of the repair expense. "No risk" did not mean no risk.

THE world seems to grow ever more complex, and construction contracts are not exempt from the trend. In our firm's early days contracts were almost always lump sum. Simple and clear-cut. Based on a complete package of drawings and specifications, and in competition with other contractors, we would submit a lump sum proposal. If the owner was a public agency, the bids would be due at a specified time at a specified place, opened in public, and the figures read out loud for all to hear. The firm submitting the lowest bid would—barring some exceptional circumstance—be awarded the contract. If the owner was a private entity, then the process could be informal, with such timing, secrecy, and negotiations as the parties chose to employ. Public or private, the final contract would say in effect: "The contractor will perform the work as defined by the contract documents for the agreed price," and and often within a specified time.

During the course of my career I have seen a gradual shift away from major reliance on the lump sum approach, particularly in the New York City marketplace, and particularly in the private sector. As the cost of land escalated, and the cost of borrowing money as well, a developer planning a project often found that waiting for plans and specifications to be completed cost more than savings that might be achieved by competitive bidding. A solution was for the developer to create his own internal construction organization—which most developers don't care to undertake—or to hire a contractor as "construction manager," performing as a contractor but not guaranteeing the final cost of construction. A side benefit of this arrangement was that, in the absence of having to guarantee the cost, a contractor was content to charge a lesser fee. And the developer had total flexibility to make changes without having to dispute prices with his contractor. So, for a while it became fashionable to hire construction firms who took no financial risk but served as professionals, charging a fee for their services.

This had advantages; but the absence of fixed limits to cost can be troublesome. So the pendulum swings. Developers became more cautious, asking for guarantees, often limited or qualified as dictated by each situation. Then suddenly it was the banks who began to require developers to obtain assurances that construction costs would not escalate. Out of the yin and yang of what is desired and what is achievable, there has evolved an almost infinite variety of contractual arrangements. We might quibble about exactly where risk fits into the picture, but it is clear what the *ENR* criteria are, and no gainsaying the differences that exist between their various lists.

ENOUGH about volume. What about profit? This is the single number that seems to provoke the greatest amount of interest. But how is profit to be defined? A number of dollars has little meaning unless it is related to—what? Return on capital invested? That is the usual figure by which the success of a business venture is defined. For construction companies that are publicly owned this figure is certainly what most interests their investors. But most construction companies are privately held, bringing many other factors into play. If the principals draw salaries, this reduces the business "profit." If the principals have "perks"—cars, entertainment allowances, insurances, and so forth—all within permissible IRS guidelines, of course—these reduce the business "profit." If, from time to time, the principals remove invested capital and retained earnings, in effect take bonuses, the equity will decrease and future profit, expressed in percentage return on equity, will increase. It can readily be seen that ultimate flexibility makes it difficult to set standards or evaluate "success."

I have read in various places that whereas the average business should aim for a return of 15 percent on equity, a construction company, since the business is so risky, should shoot for 30 percent or even 40 percent and that the most successful quartile in the industry achieve such results. At KBF this figure is not one to which we pay much attention. We have no investors other than the principals, and we leave in the business only as much equity as is required to operate and to satisfy the bonding companies, banks, or the occasional fussy client. Retrospectively I see that the figure has been slightly more than 20 percent, which is not a bad return on investment, although it is not, to be sure, an attractive reward for a very risky investment. Yet, to repeat, since our salaries, perks, and bonuses are included in the firm's overhead, percentage return on equity has never been for us a particularly meaningful figure.

A more interesting figure is profit expressed as a percentage of revenue, that is, a percentage of the value of work completed.

ENR reports that for the top 400 in 2007, a banner year for the industry, the average profit on domestic work was 4.6 percent—exactly double the 2.3 percent figure reported in 2004. *ENR* reports only the average, promising not to reveal individual figures. I'm willing to bet, however, that the 4.6 percent—also the 2.3 percent—is comprised of higher profits for firms in heavy construction (who generally invest in equipment and have large payrolls) and lower profits for roughly half the firms specializing in building construction (who mainly use subcontractors).

I find on the Internet a copy of Turner Construction Company's financial statement for 2004, which reports $69 million earned on $7 billion value of construction completed—a one percent profit if I have counted my decimals correctly.

The management consultant Matt Stevens of the Stevens Construction Institute reports that in the building construction industry (excluding heavy construction), "Average net profit before tax is approximately 3 percent for all contractors. Specialty contractors hover around 4 percent and general contractors are south of 2 percent." South of 2 percent.

EVERYTHING I learned early in my career, everything I saw at Thompson-Starrett and Joseph P. Blitz, and everything I had picked up through shared information and gossip led me to believe that in bidding for lump sum work—on schools for example—one tried to attain a gross profit of 10 percent but was usually forced by competition to settle for closer to 5 percent—gross. This is what we discovered in KBF's early years bidding on schools and other buildings—often against ten or more competitors. On the many housing projects that formed the bulk of KBF's work through the years—under the Mitchell-Lama and HUD 202 programs—gross markup was specified, usually 7 percent, composed of 2 percent overhead and 5 percent profit. I don't know who established those figures and how, but that is what the government dictated and that is what we worked with: a gross markup of 7 percent. When, later, we took on large contracts—in the tens of millions of dollars—for private developers, often with no price guarantees on our part, or with only limited guarantees, the marketplace dictated fees as low as 2 percent. And keep in mind that we are talking about gross income from which has to be deducted something called overhead—the salaries of the principals and office personnel (estimating, bookkeeping, purchasing, the writing of contracts, etc.), rent, telephone, insurances, legal and accounting fees, and so forth. So putting this all together—gross markup of 7 percent on standard government-financed housing projects, and occasional net fees as low as 2 percent on very large private projects with no price guarantees—well, a net profit "south of 2 percent" seems to be a reasonable assumption.

There are many general contractors who achieve much higher profit margins. I would like to be among them. They may do specialized work, have excellent relations with affluent clients, or have special contacts—political or social—or whatever. I am proud of our firm's reputation and standing in the scheme of things. But, aside from the unique work we performed at the 1964 World's Fair, we have had to function in a competitive environment and to cope with the low profit margins that are typical in our industry.

I will not provide a bookkeeping analysis of the net profits achieved by our firm or the salaries and benefits drawn by the shareholders. Yet it can be seen that in the ordinary course of affairs a company of our size is not likely to have been the source of great fortunes—as fortunes are defined these days. In fact, it sounds as if we have been constantly operating near the edge of a precipice.

Yet considering the ever-present dangers, numerous crises, and occasional reversals, our earnings, however limited, proved to be gratifyingly steady. I attribute this to meticulous estimating, capable "buying," and committed field supervision, and for this I pay tribute to all of the firm's talented people. But I must also credit—forgive the touch of conceit—my own fierce determination to protect the profit figure, however slim, in each and every project. I have not looked to harass the owner with claims for extras, but if changes came from the architect or any other source, I would be sure to alert the owner with a change-order proposal. This had to be done tactfully and with care not to spoil the congeniality that is so important for a project's success. But it had to be done. And we needed to apply the same protective alertness to the subcontractors. Every claim from that source had to be studied and dealt with. Sometimes the actions of one sub could be the cause of claims from another—a careless plumber, say, might damage masonry or drywall. Again, diplomacy was important, but being lackadaisical could be costly. In addition to averting shrinkage of our calculated profit, I paid particular attention to our cash flow. I saw to it that monthly requisitions were prepared and submitted at the earliest possible time and that approvals and payments were followed up conscientiously. As with claims, tact was essential, but persistence was essential as well. A timely flow of funds helps a project in many ways: it gratifies our subs, our bank, and our bonding company. It also provides crucial protection against the consequences of an owner's financial difficulties. Also, during the years when interest rates were very high, cash flow could have a significant effect on our firm's bottom line. Since profit margins were not large, attention to detail was important.

HAVE we at KBF been adequately compensated for our risk? If, in defining "compensation" one includes the quality of our work experience—the excitement and the satisfactions as well as the hazards—the answer I give is yes. Yet I say this as a survivor at the end of a long career. I do not urge everyone to "jump right in, the water's fine."

We could go on indefinitely talking about numbers. But I have a tale to tell.

EIGHT | *Deus ex Machina*

ALL WAS GOING WELL. The transition from schools to other types of buildings, particularly apartments, seemed to have been perfectly timed.

In late 1961 I was introduced to a developer who had three building sites in the Bronx and plans for three old-style six-story apartment houses with wooden floor beams and fire escapes—metal exterior fire escapes—ancient history really, the type of "semi-fireproof" design that nobody was using anymore. But, ancient history or not, this developer was determined to move ahead quickly, before his permits expired and the codes changed, and in his hurry he decided to take a chance with us, novices as we were. The project was a great success, and I still think fondly of those buildings whenever I see a fire-escape scene in an old movie.

At the same time we had an opportunity to bid on an honest-to-goodness high-rise apartment structure on East Seventeenth Street in Manhattan: a doctors' residence for Beth Israel Hospital, nineteen stories high with 142 apartments. The project, named the Stuyvesant, was financed by a city agency, and since we managed to get qualified and obtain a bid bond, we were able to submit a proposal. Our price of $1,899,000 was a winner, by a nice, slim margin.

Elated, we went for a third residential project, bidding to the Yonkers Housing Authority for the so-called School Street Apartments: 279 units in three buildings, two with thirteen stories and one with seven. Our bid of $2,728,000 was right on the money. Bingo. A trifecta! We looked forward to the holiday season, and the coming of 1962, with barely restrained glee.

NOT that we ever expected our work to be completely free of difficulties. Early in the new year, excavating at the Stuyvesant, we encountered an influx of water that prevented us from proceeding with the foundations. The building was located close to the East River, the soil proved more porous than had been anticipated, and the challenge was to control the water without incurring the expense of installing a coffer dam. One of the workmen—a prankster at heart—announced to one and all that "the angry river devils" were invading our work site. Fortunately, with the help of an experienced soils engineer, we were able to install a wellpoint system—an array of vertically placed perforated pipes attached to a pump—that kept the river at bay. Still, the rumor about the "river devils" took hold. In fact, early one morning our superintendent discovered that the bottom of the excavated area was covered with an assortment of dead fish. Evidence of the threatened invasion? No, the work of our prankster, who had purchased the invaders from a nearby fish market!

But our good mood was destined to be short-lived. On the Yonkers job we were abruptly stopped from proceeding with work on one of the three buildings. Absolutely stopped; forbidden to proceed. That particular building, we learned, was located on a short street scheduled to be eliminated, except that the street had not been demapped by the highway department. A mere formality, of course. But no. It seemed that a political war was being waged in the city of Yonkers, and out of spite the highway department was refusing to sign the necessary documents. Just a temporary nuisance, we were told: proceed with work on the other two buildings, and all will be well. And proceed we did.

Our schedule for constructing the three buildings had been prepared with exquisite care. We had given the superstructure concrete work to a young firm—M.D.A. (for Mario de Acutis, the owner)—

short on corporate experience and limited in capital but technically knowledgeable, energetic, and well equipped, so we thought, to take on this particular project. And, yes, Mario's price was attractive. His plan was based on using a crane on railroad tracks, cleverly laid out to circle between the three buildings in an operation that featured a concrete pour almost every day. With one building held up, however, the schedule became a shambles, and the carefully designed operation yielded to chaos.

The Yonkers Housing Authority officials urged us to continue with the work, assuring us that the missing permit would be issued at any moment and, equally important, assuring us that we would be compensated for the costs of the delay. We considered stopping work on the entire job but decided that proceeding as ordered would be the lesser of two evils. Unfortunately the additional costs mounted precipitously.

The permit was finally issued, but too late. Mario had run into financial difficulty, and in order to keep him working we had advanced him more than $200,000 for payroll. He ran out of money again, and this time we did not have the funds to keep him afloat. Our own on-site costs also rose, and other subcontractors began to request increases because of lack of continuity.

As for the monetary relief promised by the housing authority, it was not forthcoming. It seemed that officials of the Public Housing Administration in Washington, funders of the project, were reluctant to pay for political intrigue in Yonkers.

After many fruitless meetings, we received the fateful news: we would have to institute a lawsuit. A lawsuit! We were assured that this would be a friendly process, but given our growing desperation and the authority's embarrassment, the mood became—how best to describe it?—let us say tense. I suppose it didn't help that the initial legal papers were served on Emmett Burke, the famously feisty chairman of the authority, in his home one evening, just as he was sitting down to dinner.

Friendly or hostile, mood was now beside the point. Our firm appeared to be on the brink of financial ruin. And all because of a political feud in Yonkers. Who could have predicted such an occurrence? How might it have been averted? There were no answers.

We were still assured that the matter would be settled somewhere along the line. And we figured that we could somehow survive if we had additional funds to tide us over—but we didn't. Our bank was not inclined to support us as we embarked on legal proceedings against the government. And, as soon as our bonding company got wind of the problem, their traditional amiability turned to frosty suspicion.

In ancient Greek and Roman drama, when the leading characters in a play were confronted with disaster, the apparently insoluble crisis was often solved by the intervention of a god. The god—Zeus, perhaps, or Apollo or Athena—was brought on the stage by an elaborate piece of equipment, a sort of miniature crane, and lowered, as if from the heavens, to set things right. This literary device became known as deus ex machina. Translation: "god from a machine." Our firm had been saved five years earlier by an actual machine—the tugboat that crashed into the Cross Bay Parkway Viaduct fenders in Queens. Another miraculous intervention seemed too much to expect.

As it turned out, our salvation required not one god but four, two very decent subcontractors whose generosity made it possible for us to complete the Yonkers job and two hot-tempered titans whose fierce clash made it possible for us to do other work when our bonding capacity disappeared.

It all began with Joe DePaola. As I've mentioned previously, I met Joe in the early 1950s when I was working for Joe Blitz while Joe D., graduating from simple foundation work, was making his mark as inventor of the two-day cycle for superstructure concrete. By 1961, when our firm embarked on its first high-rise buildings—the Stuyvesant in Manhattan and the accursed Yonkers project—Dic Concrete, Joe D.'s firm, had become a dominant force in New York high-rise construction, a position it was to maintain until the company was dissolved in 1982. It was logical for us to have Dic do the superstructure work on the Stuyvesant, which we did; but on the Yonkers job we couldn't resist Mario de Acutis's most attractive price. After

M.D.A.'s collapse my first instinct was to call Joe and tell him of the fix we were in. I really don't know what I expected. First came a fatherly lecture, which I might well have anticipated. "I guess you young fellows have learned a lesson." By that he meant the risk one takes in hiring an underfinanced subcontractor for a critical trade. Yes, we surely had. "And I guess you want me to come up to Yonkers and finish that job." Yes, that would be great except that we didn't have any money. "Well, the job's got to get done," said Joe, who then added, "and you'll pay me when you collect from the government." I was stunned.

I was equally stunned when I went to Phil Rosen, our masonry subcontractor on the job, told him about our calamitous situation, and received similar reassurance: we'll finish the job, and you'll pay us when you can. Deus ex machina, and disaster averted.

But not quite. The help from Joe and Phil stemmed the bleeding, as it were, allowing us to finish the concrete and masonry in Yonkers without laying out additional funds. Yet the firm's survival still was not assured, since we needed income to keep our office in operation. The second part of our dramatic salvation remained to be played out. We had to get more work, and soon. Our bonding company was becoming increasingly skittish, although, as we provided additional personal guarantees, they agreed to provide a bond for one more job.

Restraining the impulse to cut our prices recklessly, we missed out on a few close bids. But then, in January 1963, we successfully landed another doctors' residence, this one for Memorial Sloan-Kettering Cancer Center. The 157-unit building was eleven stories tall, and our contract was for $2,283,000. Not only did this project help with income for 1963, but, equally important, it led miraculously to our work at the New York World's Fair in 1964 and 1965, wonderful, profitable work that required no bonds at all. This final piece of our deus ex machina escape was vital, since the Yonkers lawsuit was not finally resolved until 1966.

Two hot-tempered titans. The first of these was Norman K. Winston, sponsor of Memorial's doctors' residence, a building that was in fact called Norman Winston House. Mr. Winston had made his fortune investing in real estate and building thousands of middle-income homes in suburban areas after World War II. As a political activist and major Democratic Party fund-raiser, he became a close friend of Robert F. Wagner, New York City's mayor from 1953 to 1965, and of Robert Moses, whose multifaceted career led to his becoming president of the 1964–65 World's Fair. During the summer of 1962 Norman Winston was appointed by President Kennedy to be United States Commissioner to the Fair, with rank of ambassador, specifically charged with supervising development and construction of the Federal Pavilion.

When we first met Mr. Winston, early in 1963 on his visits to the Norman Winston House construction site, we found him to be a tough guy as advertised, but also benevolent in watching how these "kids," as he regarded us, worked hard to get his building done right and on schedule. The thought crossed my mind that maybe we could somehow get in on that World's Fair activity. But I soon saw that this was out of our league. With Congress having appropriated $17 million for the Federal Pavilion, the construction contract went to Del Webb, famed developer of Sun City, Arizona; owner of the New York Yankees; golfing buddy of Howard Hughes, Barry Goldwater, Bing Crosby, and Bob Hope; an all-around big shot pictured on the cover of *Time*. Out of our league indeed.

But then, sometime late in 1963, as if we had written it into the script of a play, the two titans clashed. I never found out whether Del Webb walked off the job or whether Norman Winston threw him off, and I didn't care. All I know is that Winston got hold of us one day in November and told us to get our asses out to Flushing Meadows and finish the goddam Federal Pavilion. Webb was off the job, and the fair was scheduled to open in April. In a flurry of papers we were given a contract by the U.S. Commission, technically an arm of the Department of Commerce. No bond was required or even discussed. Webb's subcontractors would complete their work under supervision of government inspectors. We were to perform miscellaneous finishing items and provide "general oversight"—whatever that meant. Our original fee was a measly $45,000; but this amount grew rapidly as the scope of our activities increased. By the time the fair closed in 1965 we had billed some $2 million, on which we earned approximately 20 percent in gross profit. It's not as if we engaged in any form of price gouging. We were in a different world from any we had known before, a world in which charging "10 and 10"—10 percent for overhead plus 10 percent for profit—was the norm, a world of "special" work, following the directions of theatrical designers, lighting virtuosos, and flamboyant decorators. The $400,000 added to our bottom line meant everything to us. To the people around us it was a drop in a tempestuous ocean.

The U.S. Pavilion, the frame and exterior of which were basically complete before we arrived, was a splendid structure. Designed by Charles Luckman Associates, it was a 150,000 square foot building, two stories in height, floating twenty feet above ground, supported by four columns and featuring a luminous facade of multicolored glass. The main feature for the visitor was a fifteen-minute ride called "the American journey" in which moving grandstands, each carrying fifty-nine passengers, passed by movie screens of varied shapes and sizes for a "you are there" experience of our nation's history from the time of Columbus to the beginning of the space age. The project was designed and installed by the Cinerama company; but there was much work needed to prepare the space to suit their needs—mechanical services plus carpentry, plaster, and paint. The building also contained spaces for standing displays and lectures and movies, as well as an information center sponsored by the American Library Association.

The "library of tomorrow" was equipped with a Univac computer. Encountering the Univac—in 1964, ten years before the first consumer computers were produced—was a most remarkable experience. The large machine contained more than five thousand vacuum tubes and consumed a huge amount of electricity. We were required to install a powerful air conditioning system in the glass-enclosed space it occupied. When the massive machine was pronounced ready for action, I was given the opportunity of playing with it a bit, and I was particularly taken with a program that taught basic mathematics—interactively. The work was at once a challenge, an education, and an entertainment.

Just about every day I went out to the fairgrounds, along with John Cricco, our leading project manager, who at about this time we made a vice president of the firm. We were given so many change orders and put in charge of so many workers that we were hard-pressed to keep up. As the fair's opening day approached, there developed a sort of underground competition between contractors who tried to steal workers from one another. I recall one payday when Cricco and I drove out to the job carrying $18,000 in cash to cover payroll and to maintain the loyalty of our crews.

There were chaotic moments, but somehow the work got done—at least to the point where the pavilion could safely receive crowds when the fair opened on April 22, 1964. On that memorable day, Norman Winston proudly hosted President Johnson, who toured the U.S. Pavilion and spoke to a gathering of invited guests. I was tasked with ushering a selected group of VIPs to a specially prepared men's room. For a few unforgettable moments I found myself standing in a line in front of the urinals, flanked on one side by Adlai Stevenson, then U.S. ambassador to the United Nations, and on the other by FDR Jr., a past congressman serving at that time as undersecretary of commerce. Stevenson, who had twice run unsuccessfully for president against Eisenhower, was a special hero of mine, and I was hoping he would say something memorable. Mostly, however, his conversation consisted of jovial complaints about how a politician has to put up with long waits between pit stops. As a building contractor I've spent many occasions—mostly groundbreakings and ribbon-cutting dedications—in the company of New York's governors, mayors, congressmen, and other assorted famous figures. But this particular moment, side by side with Adlai Stevenson, stands out in my memory as something very special.

The fair was our company's financial salvation, but I remember it mainly for the glamour, for the excitement, and also for the spirit of the time. It was the early 1960s, the era of Beatlemania. The Vietnam War hadn't yet become the affliction it was soon to be, and the fair, with a theme of "Peace through Understanding," was dedicated to "man's achievement on a shrinking globe in an expanding universe." It was a treat to see my young sons enjoying the fabulous exhibits, especially those few to which I could gain special entrée.

As the summer flew by and the fair's winter closing approached, we were pleasantly surprised to find ourselves called on to perform additional work. In anticipation of the fair's second opening in the spring of 1965, the U.S. Pavilion was adding a new project, the Hall of Presidents, and the contract was given to us without competition. This exhibit featured memorabilia of thirteen presidents: Washington, John Adams, Jefferson, Jackson, Polk, Lincoln, Cleveland, Theodore Roosevelt, Wilson, Franklin D. Roosevelt, Truman, Eisenhower, and Kennedy. I especially remember Jefferson's combination drawing board and desk and also the sword that Jackson waved during the battle of New Orleans. We didn't handle any of the precious materials, but we did provide the display cases, the special lighting, and other architectural features.

Also, through recommendation, we were retained to build the Winston Churchill Pavilion, converting a building that previously had been called simply the Pavilion and used for special events. This installation consisted of a reconstruction of Churchill's study at Chartwell, his country estate. Also featured were twenty-five of the great man's paintings, plus medals, films, recordings, a letter from FDR, and other fascinating materials. The project was sponsored by People-to-People International and paid for by Joyce Hall, president of Hallmark Cards.

In connection with these second-year projects, I attended a meeting chaired by Robert Moses. I reported on our progress, which I thought was excellent, but Mr. Moses looked angrily at me and said we had to do better. At the time I was irked; but in retrospect I savor the memory of being growled at by this famously surly powerbroker. As the fair neared its end, Robert Moses, in the final phase of his career, was truly a lion in winter.

All ended well. Still, I am amazed to find in my file the following letter:

> *April 23, 1965*
> *Dear Mr. Florman:*
> *We have watched the progress of your work on the Joyce Hall "Churchill" exhibit with appreciation and a considerable degree of amazement.*
>
> *Through the almost super human efforts of yourself and the able assistance of John Cricco, Project Manager, and Vincent Barilli, Job Superintendent, you were able to pursue construction rapidly and adjust quickly to the multitude of changes which are inherent in a "plan as you build" type of operation.*
>
> *It was exceedingly gratifying to me to see the "Churchill" exhibit virtually completed on Opening Day and available for the pleasure and enlightenment of our Fair visitors.*
>
> *Again, my thanks for a job well done.*
>
> *Cordially,*
> *Robert Moses, President*

Cordially! So different from the man as I encountered him. I take pleasure in the rereading.

AS pleased as we might have been with the World's Fair, we couldn't forget the lawsuit with the Yonkers Housing Authority. I don't recall that experience with any of the bitterness that accompanies my memories of several other disputes. After all, there were no villains, at least none we could identify. The Yonkers Highway Department meant us no harm. We were the innocent victims of their quarrel with other politicians. And the housing bureaucrats, both in Yonkers and Washington, were simply doing what they considered to be their job in defending against a claim. Clearly we were entitled to some compensation; the problem was simply how much, which is not to say that this wasn't a very important matter, at least to us.

In the past we had been involved in a few minor contract disputes with subcontractors, mostly resolved by arbitration rather than in court. But this was something big; there was no provision for arbitration, so our only course was litigation. We were advised to seek the counsel of Nevius, Jarvis & Pilz, a highly esteemed firm that traced its roots in construction law to the 1880s, and we felt honored—and encouraged—when they agreed to accept our case. They did so on a contingency basis, their fee to be 20 percent of our recovery. That's the way things were done in those days. More pleasant for the client, certainly, than the general practice today, which is—except for personal injury matters—paying the lawyers currently for their time spent, regardless of how long it takes to resolve a matter and how much, if anything, is recovered. As it happened, the grand old firm of Nevius, Jarvis & Pilz was approaching its time of dissolution, and we ended up as the client of the young man they had put in charge of our case: Harry P. Sacks. Harry did a fine job, but moving a matter through the courts can be frustratingly slow. We had bid the job in late 1961, started construction in early 1962, and achieved completion in 1964, taking more than two years to build a project that we had figured to build in less than eighteen months. I don't recall exactly when we instituted suit but surmise it must have been early in 1963. Resolution, as I've said, didn't come until 1966, three years later. We settled for a sum that, after legal fees, was barely enough to make us whole on the job. With alacrity, and great thanks, we paid Dic Concrete and Phil Rosen their bills in full.

WHEN Joe DePaola came to our rescue in 1963, he not only finished the concrete work in Yonkers but, equally important in the long run, he introduced us to Jim Lee. Jim was a friend of Joe's, and his firm, Clason & Lee, was one of the top bonding agencies in the New York area. An amiable Irishman who seemed to be a pal of everyone of any importance in the construction industry, Jim Lee could order up a bond with a snap of his fingers. And with Joe to recommend us, we were in clover.

In bonding, money is at the heart of the matter; but confidence is also a key element, and Jim Lee was a master of building confidence. His personality was winning, and, combined with savvy and a history of success, it made him an imposing force.

A performance-and-payment bond is an insurance policy that guarantees to an owner that his builder will fulfill the terms of the construction contract. Performance and payment. "Performance" means that the contractor will build the building, complete, in accordance with plans and specifications. "Payment" means that the contractor will pay all his bills, not leaving any unpaid obligations that would subject the building to liens or claims of any kind. A bond protects the owner against default, mainly against the possibility of the contractor's failing financially or, less likely but possible, simply walking away or disappearing. This does not make the bonding company the owner's partner. If there is a legitimate dispute between the contractor and the owner, the bonding company is not obliged to side with the owner, not by any means. But, in the end, if the contractor fails to perform, the bonding company will step in to complete the work and pay the bills.

Bonding companies charge a fee for providing this guarantee, traditionally on the order of 1 percent of the amount of the contract, although for certain types of work and under special circumstances the fee might be as high as 2 or 2.5 percent. The bond is obtained by the contractor for the benefit of the owner, and the fee is recognized to be a legitimate cost of the work. Naturally, bonding companies vie for client contractors who are well capitalized, well experienced, and who associate with owners and subcontractors of good repute. However, in a competitive and imperfect world, a situation often arises in which a contractor wants to secure bonds—achieve a bonding capacity—beyond the limits of what a bonding company considers a prudent risk. So bonding companies, guided by their underwriting experts and also by their desire to do business and make profits, study the figures and negotiate with contractors. A convenient rule of thumb is "ten to one." A contractor can achieve bonding of ten times his working capital. If your financial statement shows equity of $1 million, the bonding company will write bonds up to $10 million in value. The rule of thumb, of course, is just the beginning of the story. If the contractor has a good record, valued experience, and worthy clients—if the economy is booming, if planets are properly aligned, who can tell?—the ratio might be fifteen to one, twenty to one, twenty-five . . . or whatever the situation seems to warrant to the parties involved. Often, to reach the figure that the contractor requires, the bonding company will ask for personal guarantees. Or guarantees provided by third parties.

When our firm was in its earliest days, with very little experience, very little equity, and ambitious designs on the size of jobs we wanted to bid, we provided personal guarantees. Next, we agreed to have our wives sign on the guarantees. And finally, in an explosion of ambition and hubris, we went out to members of our families, receiving guarantees from them, subordinated to the bonding company, notes for specified amounts on which we paid interest.

We were daring, but not totally immune to apprehension, and as soon as we passed the crisis in Yonkers, we returned, with great thanks, the guarantees to our families. Then, we removed our wives from any responsibility, and eventually we were able to free ourselves of personal liability except for rare cases when we signed for limited amounts in connection with specific jobs.

As was to be expected, a few successful projects had made us darlings of our bonding company. But the moment they realized the extent of our problems in Yonkers, the company cut our bonding capacity to zero and prepared glumly to observe our demise.

Jim Lee knew that KBF would be OK because Joe DePaola told him so. And when Jim vouched for us with a new bonding company, they looked kindly upon our financial statement, not dwelling on the footnote that mentioned our lawsuit with the Yonkers Housing Authority.

Did Joe sign any papers on our behalf? I would guess it wasn't necessary. Those were different days, and a wink and a nod—and a handshake—carried a lot of weight. I never asked, and even today I can't be sure of what transpired.

When, in September of 2005, Joe DePaola, then aged ninety-five, came up from his Florida retirement to receive the Humanitarian Fellow Award from the Concrete Industry Board Foundation of New York, and I went over to shake his hand, Joe smiled, pulled me close, and whispered in my ear, "I helped you guys." He certainly did.

Joe did practically all of our high-rise concrete work from 1962 to 1982, when he closed up shop. His firm name was Dic Concrete until 1972, when he joined forces with Walter Goldstein as Dic-Underhill. We relied on his prices, and doubtless the few other concrete firms knew of our friendship. Yet Joe's prices always compared well with our own estimates, and in some cases seemed to help us be low in competitive situations. As the years progressed and Joe and colleagues sponsored several middle-income housing projects, they retained our firm as construction manager. And even after Dic-Underhill ceased operations in 1982, we jointly sponsored a building in Battery Park City.

But my most vivid memory of Joe DePaola will always relate to that call I made when we faced disaster in Yonkers. "I guess you young fellows have learned a lesson."

MANY is the lesson I have learned since the early 1960s—although I confess that I still take an occasional chance with an undercapitalized subcontractor, but not for a major undertaking. A more important lesson, learned from Joe D. and others along the way, is that the people one meets—and can relate to—are often more important than any technical skills and financial savvy that can be developed. And, of course, if a friendly Greek god can be dropped on the stage at the right moment, so much the better.

NINE | *A Happy Family*

WHEN I THINK about our company as it started to grow in the mid-1960s, what comes to mind is the picture of a happy family. Do I romanticize? Perhaps a bit. But serious reflection leads me back repeatedly to the same conclusion.

"Happy families," wrote Tolstoy in the famous opening sentence of *Anna Karenina,* "are all alike; every unhappy family is unhappy in its own way." This is a great beginning to a great novel, but many a reader has wondered to what extent the proposition is valid.

Scientist Jared Diamond, applying what he calls "the *Anna Karenina* principle" to the animal kingdom, asserts that there are a number of different characteristics that make most species impossible to domesticate, unable to live together peacefully in flocks like happy families. For example, there are animals with a nasty disposition (like the zebra and the African buffalo), there are those with a tendency to panic (like deer), some with an inclination to be independent loners (like cats), others with a drive to seek territorial priority (like male antelopes in breeding season). Families, Diamond suggests, in order to be "happy," must be free of *all* such characteristics. In this way they are "alike."

And this is how I think we were at KBF: free of all antisocial characteristics—good people who liked each other and liked working together.

Of course, undomesticated wild animals can be satisfied and

successful in their own ways, and so it is with contractors. In fact, one might argue that "unhappy" contractors—nasty, nervous, independent, and competitive—are likely to be more successful in business than the "happy" family folks described by Tolstoy and Jared Diamond. In fact, I have previously alluded to the aggressive streak that often reveals itself as an element of construction activity. Joe Blitz certainly believed in belligerence and made it pay. When I pointed out to him that his secretary and his bookkeeper, two people in an office of only five, were constantly feuding, he said that he was pleased to have it that way. And at every opportunity he would hassle his supervisory employees in the field. Joe DePaola, the most successful concrete contractor of our time—and an individual whom I idolized—argued, yelled, and harassed his crews, and once told me that he liked it when a man quit and then later returned to the company because he had "learned that it's a tough world out there." Certainly the large construction firms contain their share of aggressive, competitive types not inclined to cuddle up together around a family hearth. Even blood family firms have their share of battles.

Speaking of blood families, I was very well pleased to see my two sons following independent professional careers (although they did spend a few summer weeks employed as laborers). Two of the Borg children worked for the firm for a few years but eventually took off happily to distant realms. And when Joe Zelazny joined us as a principal in 1987, his two sons were already set on life paths far removed from construction. While this eliminated potentially useful long-range succession options, it also eliminated the tensions that often build when next-generation relatives are active in a closely held business.

In any event, happy family is how I remember us—at least from the mid-1960s to the mid-1980s. In the company's first few years, people were just getting acquainted, and there were the pressures of an uncertain beginning. After 1987, as a new CEO came on the scene, and as the firm grew in size and many of our people worked out of satellite offices, it wasn't possible to maintain the cozy familiarity that seems in memory to have been so special. However, the goodwill, the essential decency of practically all our people, and the friendly feelings persisted—even though we gathered as a group much less frequently.

I must confess to a couple of disappointments. And I'm sure that there was some nastiness, or even impropriety, I knew nothing about. But, in an imperfect world, in a rough-and-tumble industry, I earnestly believe that our clan evolved harmoniously into something very special.

Trying to discover the roots of this phenomenon, I can't claim credit for the owners of the firm. Yes, enlightened self-interest supported our instinct to treat people well and to share such prosperity as we might enjoy. But in this we were not unique: there are many well-meaning employers. I've concluded that the special family feeling in our firm came originally from three very special people: Virginia Crowley, John Cricco, and Peter Cettina.

Virginia came to us as a teenage secretary in the summer of 1961, meaning that she has spent—is it possible?—half a century with the firm. During this time, from her vantage point at the center of things, answering the phone and greeting visitors as they come up the stairs to our office, she has been the very heart of KBF. Everybody who has had any contact with the firm knows "Ginny," and knows her with great fondness. She is the ultimate diplomat, overseeing schedules for the principals and for many other busy people. She has taken on executive duties relating to insurance, employment benefits, office maintenance, and much else, becoming corporate secretary, while only grudgingly accepting help in the most ordinary secretarial chores. She has been adviser and confidante to dozens of employees, ambassador of goodwill to all the firm's clients, and friend (or expediter, critic, adversary as the situation may dictate) to subcontractors, suppliers, attorneys, and salesmen. Resenting the technological revolution that has taken away her beloved typewriter and made obsolete her shorthand skills, she has nevertheless mastered the computer. Becoming a mother figure for the company, she has at the same time been a mother to her own fine family.

John Cricco came to the firm a few months after I did in 1956, and he retired in early 1997 after a career of more than forty years. He had started in construction as a teenager, partly, he used to say, to keep in shape for the football he played at White Plains High School. After earning a degree in construction technology from Westchester Community College, he worked for a housebuilder, and then joined our swimming pool "subsidiary," Pools Unlimited, subsequently moving up our corporate ladder from assistant project manager to vice president in charge of construction operations, finally to become executive vice president. The timing was fortuitous of course, and John knew a lot about construction from a technical point of view. But as the hero sings in the opening number of *The Music Man*, "You gotta know the territory," and John's two greatest assets were his intuitive grasp of our territory—construction, Westchester County, and then New York City—and, perhaps best of all, his feeling for people: blue collar and white collar, workers and bosses, tough guys and police officers, brassy broads and genteel ladies, bureaucrats and executives—he liked people and they liked him. John became a solid citizen in Pleasantville, husband and father, and active member of the volunteer fire department, where, as could have been predicted, he was elected chief. Whenever we started a new job I could be sure that within a few days John would be on friendly terms with dozens of people in the neighborhood and be well on his way to establishing pleasant relationships with those individuals whose visits to the site would be important—union delegates, building inspectors, cops, and community bigwigs, even the bookies. Within the firm, John was a friend to every employee, and a mentor to many a young newcomer.

Pete Cettina was a "latecomer," hired in 1965 and retiring in 1995, as we needle him when he attends our annual holiday party, "after only thirty years." Pete had earned an engineering degree from Polytechnic Institute in Brooklyn and also a professional engineer's license. After several years working as a field engineer, first for another construction firm and then for KBF, we brought him into the office to work with me on estimating. In short order he proved himself, and I was happy to have him take over as chief estimator. Eventually he became a vice president and a leader in our company. Pete Cettina could have come out of central casting as the good brother in a film about an Italian immigrant family. Solidly established in a house in Queens, husband, father of six, active in his community, a volunteer in his local church—he was the kind of guy you could call on to lend you a needed tool, or, more likely, a helping hand, with any problem that might arise. Our main difficulty with Pete was his being, as the expression goes, honest to a fault. If he came to a meeting in which we were negotiating with an owner about the value of a change order, you couldn't count on Pete to shade the facts, even ever so slightly, in the interest of making a better deal.

Ginny, John, and Pete gave us a personality and a reputation that we cherished and that Borg and I could never have established on our own. Also, since Borg and I are Jewish, the addition of two solid Italian Americans—with families in the old country—and one good Irish woman brought us into perfect harmony with the New York City construction industry of the mid-twentieth-century. Actually, the only thing Irish about Ginny was her name, which she got from her husband. Her father came from a German family, and whenever she showed impatience with what she regarded as foolishness, John would start to call her "fraulein."

Indeed, many new waves of diversity—racial, national, and religious—have swept over the New York construction industry in recent years, and the civil tolerance that is now encouraged is certainly a good thing. But there was something pleasant in the jovial bantering about recognized differences that used to flow so freely. Jews and Italians were particularly active in construction, and they shared not only the zest and ambition characteristic of the field but also the burden of widespread social prejudice. Anti-Semitism is a centuries-old phenomenon, although blessedly reduced in America in our time. Largely forgotten, however, is the anti-Catholic sentiment that prevailed not so long ago, compounded, in the case of Italians, with a hostility toward immigrants. When Joe DePaola was my guest for lunch at the Yale Club (where the club of my alma mater, Dartmouth, is ensconced) he noticed that the Yale seal emblazoned on the menu contained Hebrew words as well as Latin. Bursting out with laughter he said, "you Jews get in everywhere." He knew full well that both of us, if our backgrounds were known, would be regarded by some of the people in that room as interlopers. He enjoyed making light of it, as did I. Today prejudice is diminished, but so is the freedom to make the jokes we used to make. Political correctness hasn't come without some sense of loss.

Leaving that aside, the important fact is that the wonderful threesome—Crowley, Cricco, and Cettina—were the center of our corporate family.

THINKING of family, I browse through old files and find a photo of a company picnic dated 1973, some twenty-odd employees plus spouses and lots of children. That really was a family affair, and we held several until the group seemed to grow too large—and the children suddenly too old. In the office, for a few years, a group would gather at lunchtime on the last Friday of each month to congratulate those whose birthday had recently taken place. But, as we grew in numbers and opened satellite offices, this custom became a casualty.

Thereafter we tried to compensate with our once-a-year holiday party. For that it had become a tradition for me to get gag gifts, in the early days a carefully selected item for each individual, giving way to "theme" items, usually decorated with the company name.

AS the years went by, I spent more and more of my time in our office, or in other people's offices, and less time visiting the jobs. So my recollections of the field and the people who were in the field actually running the jobs are less vivid than I wish they were. I know that we had many terrific superintendents, and I recognize that they contributed much to our successes and to our reputation. But I hardly know where to start in giving credit where it is due. If I were to make up a list, surely at the head would be Howard Louie, who has built a dozen jobs for us, including some of our biggest, starting in 1981. Howard is—possibly in part because of his Chinese heritage—one of the calmest people I have ever known. How he has managed to excel in the tempestuous atmosphere of an active construction site remains a mystery to me. A very pleasant mystery, I must admit.

At the other end of the emotional spectrum I have to put Norman Bernstein, who was with us from 1969 to 1982. "Stormin' Normin," as we called him, was a graduate engineer, very smart, informed on many subjects, and very well spoken—indoors. But when men or materials didn't show up on the job as promised, or when things didn't go as they ought, his ferocious temper would take over. Because of his schooling and obvious smarts, I thought that he might make a good estimator or in other ways use his skills to advantage in our office. But when I mentioned this to him, Norman replied with great seriousness that I wouldn't have made that suggestion if I knew him better. The real Norman, he said, was a volcano ever ready to explode, and it was only in the field, in the open air, where screaming and swearing were acceptable, that he could spend his working day.

Probably my secret favorite of all field people was Frank Stila, who, for nearly thirty years starting in 1961, was our number one punch-list man. It was Frank's job to come into a building that was nominally complete and to take care of any blemishes or complaints. He would usually work with a list prepared by the architect, but often had to address a complaint voiced by the owner, or sometimes by one of the tenants. Frankie was an artist, master of many trades, and he had magical ways of curing imperfections. But I loved him for the way he could deal with the people, particularly the senior citizens who moved into our "housing for the aged" projects. Such individuals are often nervous, understandably so. I was particularly charmed by the story about an elderly lady who complained bitterly that her kitchen counter wasn't level. One of our men checked it out every which way and reported to Frank that, although it was perfect, the woman was convinced that this wasn't so. Frank took over, agreed with the distressed lady that things didn't look quite right, took out a hammer and started tapping various spots around the counter. "Still not quite right," he said a few times, until finally, "there, that's it—perfectly level now." "Oh, yes, thank you," said the aggrieved tenant, and the crisis had passed. Yes, Frank was a favorite member of the family, and, speaking of family, Frank's son, Billy, grew up and worked for us, first as a laborer, then a foreman, and finally as a job superintendent.

I could go on at length talking about our field people as well as the good folk who joined the KBF family in the office: about Bob Hewett, who was hired to assist Borg in the buying activity—Hewett, a super pianist with a high IQ (a member of Mensa) and an ingratiatingly silly way of telling stories to children; about David Stein, the young accountant, who took over as treasurer and has managed for years to placate people, within the firm and without, who haven't been paid what they considered a proper amount of money in what they considered a timely manner. The chief money man does a lot to establish the reputation of a firm, the intangible "quality" that means so much, and David, in his quiet way, has done more than his share to help. And there were representatives of a younger generation—John Nowak, Stephen Griswold, Arman Boyajian— who so impressed the people we worked for that they were continually being offered attractive jobs by others. With our reluctant but understanding approval, they left us to take advantage of what looked like wonderful leadership opportunities.

There are other individuals who will appear in the pages to follow—especially women and members of minority groups. According to my dictionary an employee is "a person hired to work for another." But I think I've made it clear how, at our firm, the employees have played a major role not just by working for another, but by shaping the company and determining its destiny.

TEN | *Extended Family*

THE TERM "EXTENDED FAMILY" is used by anthropologists to describe social systems in which the "nuclear family" finds it difficult to achieve self-sufficiency. Clearly the general contractor, no matter how talented the people in his own organization, is not self-sufficient, but rather depends heavily on subcontractors.

The day is long past when the president of Thompson-Starrett could proudly promise John D. Rockefeller, Jr., that his company performed masonry, carpentry, and other key trades with its own forces, "without resorting to subcontractors." In our complex world of high tech and specialization it is impossible to overstate the importance of subcontractors in the construction process. The subs, as we call them, are experts in their own discipline, and their firms are staffed with trained craftsmen. Subs purchase the materials used, everything from bricks and concrete to plumbing fixtures and the most complex electronic equipment; and they own or rent the cranes and bulldozers—most of the heavy equipment one sees on a construction site.

I've mentioned Joe DePaola and Phil Rosen, whose firms performed two of the most critical trades: concrete and masonry. Other key players are the excavator and the mechanicals: electrical, plumbing, heating and ventilating, and, in some buildings, sprinklers. Then we have elevators, steel and miscellaneous iron, carpentry and drywall, windows and exterior curtain walls, flooring, and so forth, all the way up to painting and the final landscaping. There are usually more than twenty separate companies, each one of which is critically important to the timely completion of the building and the quality of the finished product.

The general contractor, or GC, is responsible for providing and financing the so-called general conditions: his supervisory personnel, a force of general laborers, a teamster, hoists, rubbish removal, watchmen, and the like, which usually amounts to about 10 percent of the total building cost. He is also responsible for processing monthly payments from the owner to the various subs. It is a simple yet fragile process that must run smoothly—or else. If a subcontractor runs out of money it can spell disaster for a construction job, and for the general contractor as well. So much is obvious: the work must be performed well, and financed soundly, and the GC and his subs must work together to accomplish this.

A more delicate part of the relationship is the establishment of an agreed price, the amount of the subcontract. If the GC has guaranteed a price for the building, he and the subs are sharing—in a sense competing for—the money provided by the owner. If the GC has budgeted, say, a million dollars for the electrical work, every dollar paid to the sub over that budgeted amount comes out of the GC's pocket, and every dollar reduction in the sub's price is additional profit to the GC. It seems clear that the thing for a GC to do is take competitive bids from the subs and let the low bid win—other factors being equal. Ah, but other factors are rarely equal. A low price from the sub may be instrumental in the GC getting the job in the first place. Performance by the sub—in timeliness and in quality—may determine overall success for the GC on the present job and into the future. And, most complex of all, every successful sub must have relationships with numerous GCs—GCs who are often competing against one another—while GCs must have relationships with numerous subs, also competing among themselves.

Happily, things often have a way of working themselves out. On a given job at a given time, certain subs may be "right," well suited.

Perhaps it is a type of work at which the sub excels, or a geographic location in which he is used to operating. Or perhaps he is well regarded by the architect or the owner. Or perhaps we feel it is "his turn" with us. Or—thinking less of intangibles and more of the dollar—suppose he "needs" the work, having numerous men who are free, while his competitors are busy with all their best people occupied. His price will naturally be the lowest, and he will be well poised to handle the job.

Construction estimating is a fascinating activity, and there are countless books, pamphlets, and charts that tell one how to calculate cost based on productivity: so many bricks placed by a man in a day, so many square feet of wooden forms for concrete, so many yards of concrete placed by a crew of such-and-such size, et cetera. But anyone with experience—or even common sense—will recognize that the pace of the worker depends on his or her level of experience and/or training and/or motivation. I have in my office a book about estimating, published by F.W. Dodge Corporation in the 1950s, which describes in great detail how to determine costs based on productivity in the various trades. However, on the inside of the front cover, there is a chart that tells one how the costs so painstakingly determined might be adjusted for a variety of factors, among them: state of the economy; amount of work on hand; availability of labor and level of training; and adequacy of supervision. Based on this chart, the estimator is advised to adjust his prices by a figure to be selected— somewhere between 25 percent and 100 percent! Little wonder that subcontractors differ in their approach to each job.

And while the general contractor may think he has the upper hand in dealing with subs, since he has the contracts to award and he controls the money once the job is under way, the truth is that subs are not without their leverage, often founded in wits and experience.

It is fruitless to examine too closely what is often a serendipitous, only partly analytical element in a contractor's life. Our firm has been fortunate through the years to have established good relationships with numerous subcontractors, many of whom have contributed much to such success as we have enjoyed. We have even established warm friendships (which is different from doing business with people who have been lifelong friends. I'll examine that ticklish business in the next chapter).

I've already spoken of Joe DePaola and Phil Rosen and the debts owed to them. They were the only ones who saved our corporate lives, so to speak; but there were many who helped us get work, accomplish it well, and were a pleasure to deal with personally as well as financially. There were some we helped, taking a chance with the young, or sometimes old-timers down on their luck, usually to mutual advantage. There were a surprisingly large number who were fun to be with, who brought jolly spirits into our office or out on the jobs. I won't try to list, out of several thousand subcontractor firms, the good guys, many of whom are no longer with us, or the few with whom the experience ended badly.

Except, speaking of those who are no longer with us, I'll never forget Guido Civetta, the excavator, knowing that he had a terminal illness, coming to our office to "settle up" any differences we might have had, and more specifically to pay any debts that we might consider outstanding. And in the same mood of melancholy reflection, I recall attending the funeral of Fred Kornfeld, the plumbing contractor, and grieving for the loss of a man for whom I had great personal affection.

TO represent those few with whom we had problems, indeed did battle, let me select Sal Morelli, our masonry subcontractor on the $13.5 million building we constructed in 1986 for the Hebrew Home for the Aged in Riverdale. Or was he our subcontractor? We negotiated a mutually satisfactory price for the work and prepared a contract that was deemed agreeable by both parties. Morelli submitted insurance certificates, a trade payment breakdown for the agreed price, and other required documents. We submitted his name to the architect as our mason and received approval. Sal sent us samples of the brick he intended to use, which we forwarded to the architect, who approved them. Finally, Sal sent men to the job site and constructed a sample panel with a window installed, all in good order as required. But then the owner's inspector entered upon the scene. This individual, who had spent his long career in the construction industry, was, without question, the most difficult inspector I have ever encountered. He was a spiteful man who, in the opinion of the subs on the job—and I had to agree—lacked balance and all sense of fairness. I forget what particular remarks he made at a job meeting one day, but whatever they were they prompted Sal Morelli to stand up, say "I'm not going to put up with this sort of crap!" and stalk out of the room. I assumed that this display of temper would blow over. But within a few days our field people informed me that Sal was refusing to start work. And no effort of mine could persuade him to start. We were counting on him, I pleaded. Yes, sure, there was a difficult inspector, but we've all seen difficult inspectors before and we can live with that. And Sal, you've got a contract, you've submitted all your papers, your men have built a panel in the field.

"But I haven't signed the contract," said Sal, "and I won't." He hadn't signed the contract? Well, it was not unusual for the actual signing of a subcontract to come after the work had commenced. Once agreement had been reached we considered the signing to be a mere formality. At least that's the way we had felt in the past. Neither pleas nor threats were of any avail. Sal was gone. It was a busy time for the construction industry, local masons had a lot of work, and it cost us a large sum to find a substitute contractor on short notice.

We had always handled our very few unresolvable problems with subs through arbitration; but in this case, since there was no signed contract, our only recourse was to embark on a lawsuit. Today I would do anything possible to stay out of court. But this all took place before I grew older and wiser. After our lawyers told us they considered a contract to exist, I impetuously said, "OK, let's sue the bastard."

At least that lawsuit—unlike most litigation—moved ahead briskly before a single judge. Unfortunately, the judge ruled against us.

However, our lawyers had become increasingly convinced that we were in the right, and with them doing the work practically pro bono, we appealed. Ah well. Righteous indignation failed to carry the day. Appeal denied.

Engineering News-Record considered the case so interesting—and such an object lesson for general contractors—that they wrote about it. This was not exactly the sort of publicity we sought. But, with the passage of time, the matter seemed less distressing than it had once been. Also, our further experiences with that impossible inspector had proved so appalling that I secretly conceded Sal had done a very smart thing—even if not the most admirable—by walking away. Finally, I couldn't help but be amused by the *ENR* article's headline: "Deal was never cemented."

TANGLED relationships in the world of contractors and subs can occasionally lead to incidents so farcical that they defy classification. The bidding for Crown Gardens, a middle-income housing project in Brooklyn, is one such event. The year was 1971, the cost was over $9 million, we had several other jobs under construction, and, despite our good relationship with the bonding company, they had raised questions about our workload. With the bid hour approaching, it looked as if we would have no bond. Walter Goldstein, Joe DePaola's associate, called me to see how our estimate was coming along. I told him that it looked as if we weren't going to be able to submit a bid. As the story was told to me, Walter, when talking with another bidder, HRH, told them that KBF wasn't putting in a bid. This prompted HRH—who thought that we were the keenest competitor for the job—to add $200,000 to their bid price. In a fantastic turnaround, we got word at the very last moment that the bond was approved. A special messenger rushed to the bid site and delivered it to our representative. Submitted with barely minutes to spare, our bid was the lowest. But if HRH had not raised their price, the job would have been theirs. According to our spies, the HRH people were furious, thinking that they had been misled, perhaps intentionally.

When we heard of what happened, we had every reason to think that our confidence had been betrayed; and of course Walter felt doubly embarrassed. As he confessed later, he was truly convinced that we would not be submitting a bid, and it was simply his urge to gossip that undid him.

The tale points out the complex relationships that exist in the construction marketplace. All of us, contractors and subcontractors alike, occupy booths in a lively bazaar, a place where human foibles and deceptions can be found mingled with intellect, daring, charm, and trust.

IN addition to the subs, our extended family has always included our professional advisors: the lawyers and the accountants.

Lawyers are a vital part of every business enterprise, not least in construction. I don't consider our firm to be particularly legalistic in our approach to life. But as I think back through the years: forming a business, corporate affairs, taxation, contract forms, profit-sharing plans, wills and estates, litigation, real estate, equal employment laws, government regulations, joint ventures, potential mergers—ad infinitum—we have consulted with many different individuals, a multitude of firms. I do have one unique legal tale to tell, which I have designated to be my penultimate chapter. But, aside from that, I fear that reviewing legal history, or trying to list all the attorneys on whom we've relied would take me too far afield. I will mention Joe Levine and his successor, Donald Hamburg, who gave valuable guidance in personal matters as well as corporate, and Allen Ross and Fred Cohen, who ably handled most of our construction law.

With accountants, it's a concise story with a very small cast of characters. From the start, Howard Garlick was our stalwart friend and counselor. When Howard took his firm into a larger firm, as has been the way with accountants trying to keep up with the changing world, he took with him Fabio Berkowicz and Mark Levinson. And when Howard finally retired, Fabio and Mark carried on. We stayed with them, hardly noticing as they made several moves from firm to firm in an ever-changing, increasingly fluid profession. The profession may have changed, but our friends and advisers have been a steady and comforting source of good sense.

Also, in a pleasant surprise, Howard brought us some construction work. In the early 1960s, explaining aspects of the KBF financial statements to an official of a bonding company, he struck up a friendship, and this brought us an invitation to complete three projects on which other contractors had defaulted. Alterations to a state hospital in western Pennsylvania had me flying to Pittsburgh every two weeks and driving sixty miles to the coal-mining city of Connellsville. Another contract had us replacing generators in a pumping station on Ward's Island in New York's East River, and a third required taking a ferry to Riker's Island, where we repaired masonry and plumbing in the penitentiary—fascinatingly spooky.

I don't think that Howard was pleased when, in 1959, I wrote an article for *Engineering News-Record* entitled "Can You Anticipate Your Profits on a Current Job?" and started it with the observation that "a contractor's accountant is unable to tell him whether or not he is making money." But Howard had a sweet nature, mildness personified, in spite of having been a star tackle on the Franklin and Marshall College football team and having served four years in the Pacific during World War II as a captain in the Marine Corps. There is a moral in there somewhere about what constitutes a real tough guy.

ELEVEN | *Friends*

WHEN WE BECOME FRIENDLY WITH PEOPLE met in the course of doing business the concept of negotiating and dealing with money matters is there from the outset and seems a natural part of the relationship. Starting to do business with people who have previously been good friends—sometimes lifelong friends—that is a very different experience.

My first encounter with this disquieting phenomenon was in 1964 when KBF started work on the Federal Pavilion at the World's Fair. One morning my phone rang, and I picked it up to hear a roar: "Where's our money?" It was Jim Berman, my dear friend, my close friend since grade school—since we were kids and played stoopball on West Eighty-ninth Street. My shocked silence was followed by stammering until Jim broke in: "Just kidding, just kidding." Jim was a partner in the Raisler Corporation, one of the largest heating and ventilating contractors in the New York area. His father had been a partner before him, and after graduating from MIT, Jim had joined the firm. They installed the heating and cooling equipment for many of the largest office buildings in the city, as well as mechanical systems for sewage treatment plants and other enormous projects. Jim and I often traded stories about the construction industry; but since Raisler would never have any interest in working on jobs as small as KBF's, there had never been the slightest possibility of our two companies working together. The phone call came about because Raisler was the mechanical contractor on the Federal Pavilion, and when the general contractor, Del Webb, disappeared from the scene and our firm was brought in to finish the building, payments for the subs were funneled through our office. Luckily, I had no responsibility in connection with the timing and amounts of Raisler's payments, and Jim's question about money was just a prelude to a friendly chat. We shared a few laughs, but I was strangely shaken. What if we ever found ourselves in a contractor-subcontractor relationship? Fortunately the situation never arose.

A few years later, I was approached by another high school classmate, a graduate engineer who had worked for several heating and ventilating contractors before joining with an experienced steamfitter foreman to establish his own company. The new firm had done a few jobs satisfactorily, their prices were competitive, and I was persuaded to give them three of the relatively small apartment projects we were building at the time. The jobs were completed without any serious problems that I knew of, but apparently my friend-subcontractor lost money on each of them. He and his partner were experiencing problems on other projects as well, and after a few years they went out of business. A mutual friend chastised me for contributing to this good guy's problems. Being a villainous general contractor, I must have taken advantage of this poor, well-intentioned schoolmate. This accusation was irksome because I didn't feel the least bit guilty. But I did feel extremely sorry. And I still do.

Another instance—one that ended on a happier note—speaks to the same problem. A mechanical subcontractor had performed some work for us through the years, never with any problems that I can recall. But enter the villainous inspector on the 1986 nursing home. Not only had our masonry contractor, Sal, stalked off that job, but almost every major subcontractor had problems with this individual, including the mechanical sub to whom I now refer—let me call him Tom. What made this particular imbroglio unique was the fact that Tom and his wife had recently become social friends, changing perceptibly the business relationship. Tom was, and is, the most pleasant, good-natured individual one can imagine, and although the project ended on a sour financial note for all, not a harsh word passed between us. However, Tom's son, who worked with him, was a more conventional member of the construction community in that he had a fierce temper. His tantrums did not sit well with my people, nor, frankly, with me. Sensing that all was not serene, Tom's wife suggested that our friendship was more precious than any gains to be had in business, and it was tacitly agreed that our firms would not be working together in the future. I said that the story ended on a happier note, and it did, compared with what might have been. However, it seems a little bittersweet in the retelling.

THE most lamentable experience I've had working with a friend stems ironically from one of the most resplendent buildings in our company's portfolio—the Corinthian. To quote from Wikipedia:

The Corinthian is a 55-story apartment building that was New York City's largest apartment building when it opened in 1988. It was designed by Der Scutt, design architect, and Michael Schimenti. Its fluted towers with bay windows are unusual compared to the traditional boxy shape of buildings in the city, and it bears a resemblance to Marina City and Lake Point Tower in Chicago. The building incorporates a portion of the former East Side Airlines Terminal designed by John B. Peterkin and opened in 1953.

At 1,100,000 square feet it is the largest project of Bernard Spitzer, father of former New York Governor Eliot Spitzer. It occupies a full block between First and Second Avenues and between East 37th and 38th Streets, and overlooks the Manhattan entrance to the Queens-Midtown Tunnel. It has 846 apartments, 125,000 square feet of commercial space on the first through third floors, a 48,000-square-foot garage and roof deck.

The name of the construction manager is not mentioned; but we've become inured to such omissions in reference material. Well, almost inured.

I met Bernie Spitzer on a tennis court in the 1960s and we became friends. Along with three other men, we played on an indoor court in Queens most Monday nights during the winter season. It was peripheral that Bernie and I shared an interest in construction, he being an engineer and a successful developer. Working with a minimal staff, Bernie would construct one apartment building at a time, handling the purchase of land, arrangement of financing, and acting as his own general contractor. He retained architects but participated actively in the design process. He hired management firms but closely oversaw rental and management activities. I have not encountered anyone in the industry more smart and knowledgeable. Starting from humble beginnings, he had become very successful.

In 1976, on Bernie's recommendation, I was invited to join the Board of Trustees of the Hospital for Joint Diseases Orthopaedic Institute (HJD). The hospital was erecting a new building on Seventeenth Street and Second Avenue, and Bernie, as an active member of the building committee, felt that another construction professional would be helpful. I accepted the nomination, and we worked together until the new building was successfully completed. Shortly after the dedication ceremony, Bernie resigned to pursue other activities. I eventually became chairman of the building committee and served in that capacity on the hospital board until HJD merged with NYU Medical Center in 2006. During the years that we worked together on that hospital building committee, Bernie and I would often walk partway home together after the biweekly meetings. Among many topics, we would talk about construction, its pleasures and problems. We chatted as friends, and I never dreamed that we would ever be doing business together.

However, in late 1984 Bernie invited me to his office and, much to my surprise, asked me if I would be interested in being construction manager for two new buildings that he was about to erect. But why? I knew well that Bernie always handled the construction operation himself. True, but this was two big buildings going up at the same time, he explained, and besides he had partner investors who would be more comfortable with a professional contracting firm on board. One of the two buildings was the gigantic Corinthian described above. The other I'll call Building B, since it was never built and I'm not sure that the various parties would want the matter talked about. Bernie emphasized the fact that he had never functioned this way before, but that he thought we could work well together. He warned me that he was a tough guy to do business with. He didn't say how tough.

After more discussions, I concluded why not? and quoted a figure for our fee that I thought was fair and in keeping with industry standards. I wasn't surprised when Bernie said it was too high, asserting that we could practically do the two buildings for the cost of doing one. After all, Building B was on the East Side of Manhattan, not far from the Corinthian, and the Spitzer office would be the focal point for both projects. There seemed to be some logic to this, and, without much fuss, I lowered the figure. We reached agreement, the fee being divided more or less proportionately, according to cost, between the two structures.

We started preliminary work on Building B, which was to have structural supports running through an existing building, in March of 1985, and on the Corinthian in October, seven months later. So far so good. But early in 1986 we were told to stop our preliminary work on Building B, and in May we were informed that the Building B project was cancelled. We were reimbursed for our out-of-pocket expenses—mostly measuring, planning, and layout—but learned that we were not to receive our fee. I argued in vain that we had reduced our overall fee because of doing the two buildings at once, that we had put a large portion of the joint fee into Building B, and that the fee for the Corinthian could not possibly stand on its own. Bernie contended that we would make "more than enough" money on the Corinthian to make us whole.

What happened was we did poorly on the Corinthian—financially that is, not with the construction itself, which went very well. The building is an object of pride for all concerned. On top of the inadequate fee, we felt that we were not properly compensated for extra work performed. We thought surely that with a successful conclusion to the Corinthian there would be some accommodation, at least on the fee for Building B. There was not.

I felt responsible for getting our company into this mess; but we had to move on. The decision was to take our lumps on the Corinthian claimed extras but to institute a lawsuit based on the contract for Building B. Unfortunately, although the contract had been negotiated and agreed on, it had not been signed. A bit of déjà vu— when would we learn? However, the situation was quite different from what we had encountered with Sal the mason. Not only had we performed work on both sites, but there was ample evidence that the two buildings had been negotiated as a single undertaking.

Convinced that right was on our side, we told our lawyer to charge ahead. There were few preliminaries, since it was mostly a question of two people and the agreements between them. A jury trial was scheduled. In a final effort to bring this sorry business to an end, I reduced our claim to what I considered a token. Bernie countered with an offer of a lower figure yet. We met in his office, where we had met so many times before. In what I considered a move on behalf of civility in a harsh world, I suggested we split the difference. Bernie said no. In disbelief, I walked out.

A few days later, accompanied by our attorneys, we entered a courtroom. An elderly judge met with each of us individually, it being his objective to negotiate a settlement before proceeding with the selection of a jury. I recall saying—I think these are close to being the exact words—"Your honor, I appreciate your efforts; but I must tell you that this matter has a long personal history behind it. Just the other day I offered a most reasonable settlement, much more than reasonable, and will not now accept a penny less." A little while later my attorney came to me with the news that my settlement figure was now accepted, and that after I signed a release, a check would be forthcoming. I nodded my head and walked away looking straight ahead.

But the story doesn't end there. A few months later, one of my firm's people, a man who had been on the Corinthian job, told me that Bernie was contemplating construction of a new building and hoped we would consider being his project manager. When I sent back the message that I no longer wanted to work with him, he seemed, so I was told, genuinely puzzled. I came to realize that he felt the way a football player might if a friend, playing on an opposing team, objected to being pushed and knocked down. We might well have been long-time friends, but when it came to business we seemed to live in different worlds.

Bernie and I met again a few years later, at the funeral of one of the members of our old Monday-night tennis group. The tincture of time had done its work, and the grim setting helped give a sense of perspective. We shook hands and chatted for a few moments, mainly about our departed friend. Our paths crossed several times in the ensuing years, usually at the theater. The meetings were cordial but brief.

I will not generalize or try to tell others what to do, much less how to feel. But the lesson for me is plain. In embarking on business dealings with a friend, one puts the friendship at risk.

TWELVE | *They Say It's Who You Know*

ACCORDING TO CONVENTIONAL WISDOM, in order to get ahead in the business world it's important to know the right people. "It's not what you know, it's who you know." In the world of construction, the right people are primarily those who control the awarding of construction contracts, and secondarily the people who oversee performance of the work and approve payments.

This seems obvious; but things are rarely what they seem. Building construction usually involves some level of competition based on price, and where such competition prevails—fair competition, real competition—knowing the right people doesn't necessarily carry the day.

Competitive bidding is the process that is said to provide protection for the public, and for sensible private consumers as well. However, this apparent truism has its weaknesses. Consider the contractor who told me he bids low with every intention of making his profit through aggressively pressing claims for extras, manufactured as might be required. Needless to say, he works mainly for public agencies where being disagreeable is not grounds for disqualification. He delights in greeting an inspector on a new job with the pronouncement: "Nice to meet you. I'll stay in this half of the shanty, you stay in that, and I'll see you in court." Such an overtly belligerent approach may be rare, but many a contractor bids low with the intention—or a prayer—of eking out profit somehow, some way through change orders. Even if outrageous claims are not pursued, one can, more subtly, hope for extras related to the owner changing his mind or adjustments resulting from errors in the plans. Or perhaps a contractor is friendly with a representative of the owner, maybe an employee of the contracting agency, a friendliness that gives him assurance of favorable treatment once the job is under way—thus joining the knowing-the-right-people approach with the being-the-low-bidder requirement. There is even the possibility, in this imperfect world, that a contractor, having bid too low, might try to cut a few corners.

Owners can help protect the efficacy of the bid process by limiting the list of bidders, through prequalification, to firms of good reputation. However, for public agencies and not-for-profit organizations freedom of action is often circumscribed. It's not always simple to prove that a contractor is not "qualified." Open competition is what the public wants, usually the more open the better—that is, until a job runs over budget or bogs down in dispute, in which case outrage is expressed about a particular contractor having been included on the bid list.

Naturally, private owners who are truly private—not beholden to the citizenry or shareholders or partners of any sort—are free to select their contractor by any standard they choose. And it is totally proper for contractors to seek the esteem of such individuals and of the world in general. That is good business, good sense, and often begins with good fellowship.

AFTER considering all the pluses, minuses, and maybes, nobody will deny that having friends in high places can be an important asset for a construction contractor. *Friends in High Places* happens to be the title of a book: a critical study of the Bechtel Corporation, the largest American construction company. With forty-four thousand employees working in all parts of the world, the firm builds, designs, and often obtains financing for power plants, oil refineries, water systems, and airports, as well as every conceivable sort of building. A former

Bechtel associate, John McCone, was head of the Atomic Energy Commission from 1958 to 1961 at a time when the firm was building the world's second commercial nuclear power reactor. (Mr. McCone subsequently served as director of the CIA.) George P. Shultz, secretary of state under Ronald Reagan, was a past president of Bechtel. Caspar Weinberger, Reagan's secretary of defense, served as the firm's general counsel. Other Bechtel executives were associated with the George W. Bush administration.

In 2005 Bechtel was awarded a no-bid contract by the Federal Emergency Management Agency (FEMA) to install temporary housing for the Hurricane Katrina disaster relief effort. *The Wall Street Journal* reported that this led congressional Democrats "to renew the charges of cronyism they first leveled when the firm won lucrative work in Iraq." On Boston's "big dig," according to *The Boston Globe,* Bechtel "hired a team of deeply connected lobbyists and lawyers to help it influence local and state officials." No need to cite additional instances. Clearly Bechtel is a construction company that has benefitted from its association with people who rank high in important circles. I do not reproach, merely state a fact. Admirers of the firm cite its proud history of outstanding construction achievements. Stephen Bechtel, Jr., chairman emeritus, has been much honored for his service to the engineering profession and numerous worthy causes. And Bechtel, like other successful firms, is staffed by some very talented professionals.

Many companies, large and small, benefit, or attempt to benefit, from political contacts. That is the American way. It is permitted for elected representatives to assist those of their constituents who seek fair treatment from the government. And citizens are free to support politicians—with financial contributions and other forms of volunteerism—all within prescribed legal limits.

At KBF we've never tried to establish contacts in Washington, or in Albany, for advantageous connections. I say this not with pride. Maybe it would have been smart to be more active politically. People achieve influence in government offices not merely by cronyism, but often by dint of hard work, and within the bounds of propriety.

I was tempted once, in the spring of 1980, when, at a seminar on engineering education, I served on a panel with Michael Dukakis. He and I had interesting conversations followed by friendly correspondence. The man had been governor of Massachusetts, for goodness's sake, and was at the time preparing to attend the 1980 Democratic National Convention in New York City. One reads of how people meet politicians in this circumstance or that and become supporters and then friends, with incalculable consequences. When, in 1988, Dukakis obtained the nomination for the presidency, I had a brief pipe dream about how I might have become involved. Even after he was soundly defeated I wondered.

Similar fantasies struck when, in the fall of 1983, I met Walter Annenberg at a two-day conference on scientific literacy and had a fascinating chat, one on one, in the hotel where we were staying. This was not a politician, and he certainly didn't need financial support; but he was a powerhouse, a media magnate, a man who "counted" in high circles, and I fancied that he thought I was a bright fellow with good ideas. But what would it take to get meaningfully close to a person like that? And to what end? It didn't seem to be my sort of thing. That recognition, plus the press of more immediate concerns, plus good old-fashioned laziness prevented me from following through.

In New York City I couldn't have had closer access to political power than during the eight years (1966–73) when John Lindsay was mayor. My then brother-in-law, Dick Lewisohn, was a long-time friend of Lindsay and served in his administration in various positions, most significantly as purchase commissioner and then finance administrator. A "Rockefeller Republican"—a gentlemanly breed that appears to have vanished from the earth—Dick was more than willing to put in a good word here or there, help a kid get a place in a city-run summer program, arrange for invitations to some exclusive social event, and so forth. But he was not about to hand out no-bid city contracts, even if he could; and I was not about to ask him for underhanded favors, even if I had known how to go about it.

So I met John Lindsay mostly at ground breakings and ribbon-

GOOD GUYS, WISEGUYS, AND PUTTING UP BUILDINGS

cutting ceremonies, just as I met all the mayors: Wagner, Beame, Koch, Dinkins, up to Giuliani, who spoke at the dedication of a building at Bellevue Hospital that my firm had converted to new offices for the city's Administration for Children's Services. Giuliani was not my favorite mayor, but he did give our firm one of the nicest acknowledgments I can recall, complimenting us for our outstanding effort in completing the project exactly on schedule, which, he said, in his experience was exceedingly rare. As for Mayor Bloomberg, since we weren't building publicly financed housing during his tenure, I never had occasion to meet him on a podium. Although my wife and I did run into him on a Sunday afternoon in front of his residence. We wished him well, and he was exceedingly gracious. It is no great trick to meet politicians in New York City.

THE most impressive politician I've encountered in connection with a building project was Senator Al D'Amato. One morning we were dedicating a moderate-income apartment building for the elderly in Brooklyn, when, shortly before the ceremony was scheduled to start, a nondescript car drove up and its two occupants—Senator D'Amato and a driver—got out. The senator mingled with the crowd, shaking hands, smiling, chatting, clearly connecting. When the ceremony started and it came his turn to speak, he seemed to know everybody involved in the planning of the building, indeed, everybody in the community. He gave friendly credit to many, including us, the builders. As he spoke it began to dawn on me that he personally must have been involved in obtaining the financing that was a key to the success of the project. After his departure, a number of the local people spoke, with sincere affection, of his many visits to their neighborhood. D'Amato was not a man with whose political positions I often agreed; but he was obviously a person who could get things done. Could he be helpful in getting us work like the housing project that had just been dedicated? Were we foolish not to pursue the possibility?

As I've noted, it is easy to meet politicians in New York City, and this is particularly the case if one contributes even modest sums to campaign funds. John Kennedy, Lyndon Johnson, Richard Nixon, Bill Clinton, Al Gore, Charles Schumer, Nelson Rockefeller—those are just a few of the many whose hands I've shaken and to whom I've been able to mumble a few words, sometimes about construction-related matters. In addition to attending ribbon-cutting ceremonies and campaign gatherings, politicians meet with small groups in the homes of supporters and often address luncheons and dinners—gatherings of housing-industry people, for example—or galas sponsored by numerous charity organizations. Some of these affairs I attend of my own personal choosing; but many are at the behest of clients. If a private developer asks us to support a political candidate, we may well buy a seat, or even a table, at that candidate's fund-raiser. It may seem costly at the time, but it's never been the type of contribution that brings with it influence, much less meaningful clout. (Needless to say, we stay within the legal limits, personal and corporate.)

IT is well known that real estate developers in New York City give large contributions to politicians, usually to both political parties and sometimes to opposing candidates. This gives rise annually to a number of jaundiced newspaper articles. In the fall of 1986, KBF was one of three successful bidders to be named developer of apartment houses in Battery Park City, a state-sponsored public benefit corporation. According to the *Daily News,* although the bids accepted were indeed the most competitive, the announcement came after the gubernatorial election "amid suggestions that the decision was delayed for months to avoid the appearance of impropriety on the part of Governor Cuomo's reelection campaign." The article went on to say that two of the successful bidders, Milstein Properties and PaineWebber, "were heavy contributors to Cuomo's reelection campaign." And then: "The third winner, Kreisler Borg Florman Construction Co., was not a contributor." A friend who called the next day said that while it was nice to see our name in the paper, we'd never make it to the big time if we weren't going to play the political game. He was kidding of course, and yet . . .

I don't want to imply that in pursuing work we've relied solely on being the low bidder. No, certainly not. It's true we've always assumed that, even with good contacts and excellent references, our prices had to be reasonably competitive. Yet we've sought to nurture our reputation and, in the old Dale Carnegie way, to win friends and influence people.

In our early days in Westchester, we learned that if we satisfied a school board, a government agency, a private developer, or particularly architects, we had friendly advocates, sources for recommendations. "These young fellows are reliable, competent and energetic, and they really aim to please." That's what we liked to hear. Jack Kreisler made it a practice to obtain letters of recommendation from satisfied customers. Bob Borg oversaw the production of brochures and sent out press releases. And I, through my speeches and articles—and eventually books—about the role of technology in society garnered friendly notice, and even a few awards, from universities and professional organizations. All of this seemed to help, not in ways we could measure, but, we fancied, in receiving friendly receptions from prospective developers, board members, and architects.

As we entered the New York City construction arena, our realm of social-business contacts broadened. It just seemed to happen. We joined various contractors' associations and organizations that sponsored the cause of publicly financed housing. Then, in addition to public housing, there was the world of "good causes": the Salvation Army, the Congress for Racial Equality (CORE), Catholic charities, Israeli bonds, and so forth.

Somewhere along the line we became season subscribers with the New York football Giants, the Knicks, and the Rangers, finding that tickets could be used as an incidental gesture of goodwill. At Christmastime, it was standard practice to distribute bottles of wine or whiskey, first to the subcontractor foremen, then to assorted office personnel. Across the industry there was sort of a standard pattern, almost comic when you think about it: we gave to the people "above"—owners, architects, and civil servants—and received from the people "below"—subcontractors and suppliers. To certain individuals, particularly architects and chairs of not-for-profit boards, I would sometimes send a carefully selected book. Within the company I was teased: "They'd rather have the wine and whiskey." Perhaps; but in some cases I thought not.

Full disclosure: there were a few people to whom we would send a "tasteful" gift, always purchased at a store where the item could be exchanged. One year I sent a box of cigars to a city administrator who I knew loved a particular brand, and he returned it with a note of thanks but regrets. I shared this story with a fellow contractor who smiled and told me I would have been better served had I slipped a couple of thousand dollars into the man's pocket.

Aside from Christmas, occasionally someone in our broad circle of acquaintance would ask for a favor, a load of gravel for a driveway, for instance, or a shower door of a special size that they couldn't locate—more a matter of convenience than of money value—and we would oblige or ask a subcontractor to do so. But this had to be minor stuff. I won't play Goody Two-shoes; we liked to ingratiate ourselves with "the right people." But contractors have gotten into trouble—big trouble—performing gratis work for clients or for employees of clients. There are enough risks in the rocky road without adding to them recklessly.

Of course, rectitude can be carried to ridiculous extremes. Like the time there was a death in the family of a city inspector on one of our jobs and our field people asked us to send a basket of fruit to the home with a note of condolence. Incredibly, the following day an "inspector general" came to our office carrying the basket and delivering a stern warning about inappropriate behavior. We never found out how this ludicrous turn of events came to pass.

* * *

WE weren't about to buy our way into the good graces of anyone—motivated, I must admit, as much by fear as by principle. When an employee of a television company said that for a "finder's fee" of $35,000 (the figure sticks in my mind these many years later) he could see to it that we would receive a handsome contract for building a new studio, I recoiled.

Of course, a finder's fee, defined as compensation given to an intermediary in a business transaction, is perfectly proper and legal—when it is perfectly proper and legal. To us this means open and above board, known and approved by all appropriate parties. We did pay such a fee, on two occasions. In 1985 Sam Kohl, president of Herbert Construction Co., came to us with the suggestion that we might take on a contract that had been offered to his firm but that was, he felt, somewhat more in our line than his. The project was a large new building in Westchester County, whereas Herbert's extensive experience was mostly on interiors in Manhattan, notably with a number of the city's most prominent department stores. We had met Sam in 1966 when our two firms had been joint-venture contractors on an extensive conversion of the old Vanderbilt Hotel into apartments and offices. One of the sponsors of the Vanderbilt project was a neighbor of Bob Borg's, and another one of the sponsors was a friend of Sam's; so a marriage had been made that turned out to be a happy one. Our two firms hadn't had occasion to work together again for almost twenty years; but when the opportunity arose we were pleased to renew the association. In the case of the new building, rather than a joint venture, Sam suggested to the owner that KBF take on the contract but that he would "keep an eye" on us. For making the introduction, and for his participation, Sam's firm would receive an agreed portion of our fee. The chairman of the institution's building committee approved the arrangement.

The other finder's fee we paid to Reuben Glick, a respected New York builder, when he introduced us in 1990 to Linda Hoffman, president of the New York Foundation for Senior Citizens. Reuben, recipient of an achievement award from the National Housing

Conference, had been selected by Ms. Hoffman to be the builder for one of her organization's projects; but, having decided to retire and close down his long-established business, he recommended us as his successor. To compensate him for the estimating and other preconstruction work that he had performed, and with the agreement of all concerned that he was entitled to such compensation, he was paid a portion of our fee. KBF's relationship with Linda Hoffman and her organization—"dedicated to helping New York's seniors enjoy healthier, safer, more productive and dignified lives in their own homes and communities"—flourished. Linda was a tough taskmaster, but always in behalf of her worthy objectives, and over the next sixteen years we built six housing projects together, all financed under the HUD Section 202 Housing for the Elderly Program. It was a happy day when Reuben Glick introduced us to her.

It so happens that over a similar period of time and under the same HUD program, we also constructed six projects for Community Housing Management Corp., a Westchester firm that assists community groups in creating and operating housing for the elderly. Reminiscing about how we were introduced to Linda Hoffman, I tried to recall how the long and close relationship with Gene Conroy, president of Community Housing, got its start. Drawing a blank, I called Gene, who also was hazy about the past. "Gee," he finally said. "I think you were recommended by an architect, but I don't really remember who." So much for knowing the right people.

POSSIBLY the most important "contact" in my career was totally unexpected, almost accidental. When our firm was a newcomer to the New York City market in the early 1960s I realized that this was a vast, mysterious territory in which we had to find our way. I had heard about the Mitchell-Lama middle-income housing program and thought, that's for us; but how, and to whom, were we to present our qualifications?

One evening in 1964 my wife and I were having dinner with my mother and her dear friends, Henry and Ethel Engel. Responding to

GOOD GUYS, WISEGUYS, AND PUTTING UP BUILDINGS

questions about "what are you doing at the office these days?" I told Henry a bit about my interest in housing construction. I was just making conversation, trying to be polite. But Henry listened intently. "Housing," he said. "Government subsidized housing? Wait a minute. I've got a cousin who I think has something to do with that."

As it turned out, Henry's cousin was Walter Fried, one of the three commissioners of New York City's Housing and Development Administration (HDA), the very agency that managed the city's Mitchell-Lama program. Walter had graduated from law school in the 1930s, the midst of the Depression, and had entered government service. He had risen through the Housing and Home Finance Agency, precursor to today's HUD, to become a regional administrator, and in 1960 had taken on his then current position with the city. The very next day Henry called his cousin to tell him about a young friend of the family who was a whiz-bang builder of apartment houses and to arrange for me to visit with Walter Fried in his office.

Walter was a quiet, avuncular, kindly bureaucrat who didn't talk politics and asked no favors. I don't believe that I saw him more than a half dozen times between that meeting in 1964 and his retirement more than twenty years later. But the single phone call that he made during my first visit to his office at HDA was enough to put me in his debt forever, a debt that I never repaid in any way, except to say thank you. I believed then and now that he would not have been pleased to receive any tangible expression of my gratitude. He was a good guy who took pleasure in putting in a helpful word for a cousin's good friend.

The call made by Walter Fried that day was to Henry Foner, president of the Joint Board of Fur, Leather and Machine Workers Union. Known as a "social activist," a fighter for causes from civil rights to wildlife conservation, and a leader in labor unions' opposition to the war in Vietnam, Foner was interested in housing for working people. He had just recently pledged union support for a middle-income project in Coney Island, and, since no contractor had been selected, the timing of my visit was exquisitely opportune. I gathered from hearing Fried's end of the conversation that my commitment to government-subsidized housing (as opposed to private luxury condos), and my presumed social conscience, were credentials just as important as my technical ability. Right then and there, over the phone, it seemed that my firm would be very much in the running to build that project in Coney Island. Naturally, any selection was subject to Foner's approval of me after meeting face-to-face, and, as I learned from others, a very careful check of my firm's performance on previous projects. The agreement also had to be approved by Foner's colleagues and Fried's fellow commissioners. So it wasn't just a simple phone call. Yet that's how it seemed to me then and that's how I think of it still.

The project that the union was to sponsor, with government funding, was to be named Sam Burt Houses, in honor of the late union president who had died in 1961 and to whom Henry Foner was the successor. KBF, as the contractor, would be required to meet the HDA cost parameters and provide a satisfactory payment and performance bond.

Our career as builders of Mitchell-Lama housing was launched, and as relative pioneers in the program we soon found ourselves accepted as "experts"—by subcontractors, architects, and, most important, by potential sponsors. Knowing the right people. I guess it counts, along with fortuitous timing and, not to discount our own abilities, appropriate experience.

SHORTLY after my epochal meeting with Walter Fried and subsequent agreement with Henry Foner, another encounter took place at the HDA office that was to prove auspicious. Bob Borg, dropping by, simply to get the lay of the land and become acquainted with some of the agency people, found himself sitting in a reception room waiting for admission. Another individual entered, announced the purpose of his visit, and was told to take a seat. Starting to chat, just to pass the time, the two men discovered a shared interest in the HDA programs and began a conversation that was to evolve into a lifelong friendship. The congenial stranger was Robert W. Seavey, an attorney, and he was visiting HDA on behalf of a client. The client, interestingly, was Councilman J. Raymond Jones, newly elected leader of the New York County Democratic organization, who was currently doing battle with another political powerhouse, Representative Adam Clayton Powell, over control of two proposed housing projects in Harlem.

Although Bob Seavey is white, he was in the early 1960s living in Harlem. He had joined the Carver Democratic Club and become an active participant in uptown politics. KBF never got involved in the titanic battle between Jones and Powell, where other contractors had already been engaged. But by happy chance Seavey was at the same time providing advice to the New York City Mission Society, a venerable organization founded in 1812 and active in Harlem since the 1920s. At the time of the Borg and Seavey meeting, the society leaders were discussing, with the HDA, the construction of a community center on Lenox Avenue and 142nd Street. This facility, to be called Minisink Town House (after the society's upstate camp), would contain a library, an auditorium, a gymnasium, and offices; and a master plan called for the building to be flanked by a Mitchell-Lama housing project. The apartment building was to be named Bethune Tower in honor of Mary McLeod Bethune, the famous African American educator who had died in 1955. Bob Borg's chance meeting with Bob Seavey, coupled with the positive glow surrounding our commencement of Sam Burt Houses, resulted in our firm's being selected to build the community center, paid for by the Mission Society, and Bethune Tower, financed by a Mitchell-Lama loan. On the apartment house, we used part of our fee to join Seavey in equity ownership.

Bob Seavey, with his wife, Phyllis, also a lawyer, successfully combined the practice of law with business enterprise. Bob maintained his interest in politics and occasionally was appointed by Democratic administrations to various positions of responsibility. But his main activities centered on real estate development and management. In the years that followed, although KBF's path as a general contractor led us off in a different direction, we did work together with Bob on three additional middle-income housing projects. Aside from business, the friendship lasted, and we never have forgotten that fortuitous meeting in the HDA reception room.

THERE are also lessons to be learned from the jobs that one does not get, jobs that went to another because of friends in high places. Failure is often more memorable than success.

No sensible contractor, knowing that time is money, will chase after jobs in totally strange territory. But sometimes a job that seems within reach is found on investigation to be unattainable. Like the institution for whom we had worked successfully but whose CEO told me that the next job was committed to another firm. Why, for goodness's sake? That other firm did not seem anywhere near as qualified as KBF. Not only didn't they have the experience to match ours, but they came from far away, unacquainted with the local subcontractors, building department, or labor unions. Yes, we were told confidentially, but the firm's owner had a brother (or was it a cousin?) who was high up in the government agency that set the reimbursement rates that were crucial to the institution's well-being. No more needed to be said.

More bitter to swallow is the job one has in hand that is suddenly snatched away. In 1961 our firm had built an infirmary building in Yonkers for the Jewish Guild for the Blind—a successful job, a happy job—so when, in 1969, the guild planned a new building in Manhattan, we thought surely we would be the contractor. And we were, agreeing on a price and the wording of the contract. With endorsement by the architect and owner, we filled out the necessary forms, arranged for appropriate insurance, and obtained a permit from the Department of Buildings. We assigned a superintendent to the job and prepared to get started.

Then, suddenly one morning we received a call from the guild's executive director, who, somewhat abashed, said sorry, but it had been decided that HRH would be the contractor. What? Well, sorry, but it is just one of those things.

The president of HRH in those days was Richard Ravitch, whom I had met socially and found to be a likable fellow. Trying to maintain my calm, I called him on the phone and was pleasantly surprised when he readily agreed to see me in his office. When we met I said something like, "Dick, this is our job, you can't just take it away." To which he responded, "Sam, the owner wants us to take over. You and I are in a competitive business; we win some and we lose some." I left, shaking my head and mentally thinking of going to war. I wasn't without weapons. In particular, since the building permit had been issued to KBF, how could HRH even show up at the job site?

Indeed, within a few days we received a call saying that Bernard Mendik wanted to meet with us to talk about our giving up the building permit and turning the project over to HRH. Mr. Mendik, a real estate tycoon, was then, or shortly was to become, president of the guild, also chairman of the Grand Central Partnership, trustee of the Citizens Budget Committee, and vice chairman of the Fifth Avenue Association. Oh, and lest I forget, he was the longest serving chairman in the history of the Real Estate Board of New York.

Dick Ravitch, active in Democratic politics, had, at the time of the Guild for the Blind construction, already been appointed to the United States Commission on Urban Problems and elected president of the Citizens Housing and Planning Council. He was destined to sell HRH in 1977 and go on to an amazing career: chairman of the Metropolitan Transportation Authority, chairman of the Bowery Savings Bank of New York, candidate for mayor of New York City, and chief labor negotiator for the Major League Baseball owners. In 2009 he was appointed to the position of lieutenant governor of New York State.

I can't claim that in 1969 I could foresee the future; but Mendik and Ravitch were clearly forces to be reckoned with. And more important—although I had my contentious side and was tempted to fight for my rights—our firm's interest would not be well served by doing battle with a worthy institution providing services for the blind. So we relented and cooperated in transferring the building permit and other critical documents. We were compensated for the time spent by our estimator and our superintendent—a pittance—shook hands and wished the guild well. When, in 1971, the building was dedicated and I learned about some of the notable philanthropists who had provided the funding, it occurred to me that one of them could well have been instrumental in the decision to change contractors. The "who you know" factor might sometimes be part of a social web more complex than an outsider can appreciate.

ALTHOUGH I can't say that I've ever enjoyed losing out in the quest for a job, there are some projects that were fun to chase even though there was no realistic chance of success. High on this list is the residential compound established in Riverdale, New York, in the early 1970s by the Permanent Mission of the USSR to the United Nations. Bob Borg had traveled to the Soviet Union twice with committees of the American Society of Civil Engineers, and he had established enough professional contacts to gain our firm an interview. But our firm certainly lacked the connections required to contend seriously for the contract. Yet it was great sport to be ushered into a lavishly decorated conference room in the heart of the Soviet consulate and to sip specially selected Russian brandy while presenting our credentials. The cold war was still very much a factor in everyday life, giving the experience a special fascination.

The part of the interview I recall most clearly followed Borg's checking some estimate figures with his newly purchased handheld pocket calculator. This remarkable gadget, invented at Texas Instruments in 1966, had only recently become available to the general public, and the Russians showed great interest in it. "Gentlemen," said Bob, taking advantage of the moment, "if we are your contractor, you will each be presented with one of these remarkable devices to help you in checking our work." "Ah, Mr. Borg," replied the head of the interviewing team, "if you are our contractor, you will deliver to us a truckload of those little machines!" This remark was followed by great hilarity, and we left the premises well pleased with our presentation. Of course, the contract was given to another company—selected by the higher-ups in Moscow. I wonder if a truckload of pocket calculators was part of the deal.

ONE more "we didn't get the job but enjoyed the chase" story: Billy Rose's Island. This takes us back to 1957, a year after I joined Kreisler Borg, at a time when the company was still engaged in building swimming pools. Billy Rose was a famous theatrical showman whose most celebrated production was "Billy Rose's Aquacade," a feature of the 1939 New York City World's Fair. That extravaganza starred Eleanor Holm, an Olympic star whom he married after divorcing his first wife, the comedienne Fanny Brice. Rose divorced Holm in 1954 and married the actress Joyce Matthews two years later, only to divorce, remarry, and divorce her. He was, in short, a colorful character. Some wealthy individual for whom we had built a super-pool gave Rose our names and arranged for us to visit him on his small private island just off the coast of Connecticut near Darien. We were told that Mr. Rose wanted to totally redo the landscaping on his island and that we, as pool builders and general contractors and aggressive young entrepreneurs, would be just right for the job. Rose was full of wildly extravagant ideas that he set forth in rapid-fire showman's delivery. As best I could understand his master plan, he wanted to bring in topsoil to cover the many sandy areas on the island and plant gardens rich with colorful flowers. I didn't foresee problems in obtaining the flowering plants he wanted; but when I started to calculate the quantities of topsoil that would be required, tried to imagine bringing the soil to the island by barge, and then put a dollar value to it all, I came up with an incredibly high figure. "No big deal," said Rose expansively. Then after a pause: "But maybe we'll think about plan B."

He thereupon outlined an alternative scheme that featured using the sandy areas as part of a giant stage set, putting the hulls of old boats here and there, with nets and other fishing gear. Then came a thought that seemed to delight him: how about chests and shovels to hint of buried pirate treasure! Waving his arms and pointing to various spots that he conceived as dramatic centers of attention, he became increasingly animated. The impresario was planning his next theatrical production. "I'll get some of my theater designers working on it," he concluded, already ushering us toward the boat that was waiting to take us back to shore.

Our follow-up calls to Billy Rose were not returned, and I never found out what sort of landscaping work was done, if any. From a business point of view I suppose we had wasted an afternoon. Yet if the positive side of "who you know" includes fascinating encounters with legendary people, our visit to Billy Rose on his island was a huge success.

THIRTEEN | *Architects and Technocrats*

ARCHITECTS: A UNIQUE BREED. They are artists yet also technologists; creative free spirits yet agents of their clients, private and public. Most people think of them mainly as designers; but, like it or not, they are entrusted with oversight responsibility, both technical and economic. Like ordinary mortals, they compete for commissions, pay rent, and have payrolls to meet. Most contemporary American architects, including the great ones, take pride in their ties to the Bauhaus school and pay homage to that famed institution's articles of faith. In the first proclamation of the Weimar Bauhaus, dating from 1919, the architect Walter Gropius proclaimed: "The artist is an exalted craftsman . . . Let us create a *new guild of craftsmen,* without the class distinctions which raise an arrogant barrier between craftsman and artist." Bravo, say the builders of this world. Yet a barrier does exist, not necessarily arrogant, but undeniably real. I am proud to be an engineer and a builder, but I regard architects—the great ones anyhow—with respect verging on awe.

Thinking of architectural titans, Frank Lloyd Wright stands in the top rank. In 1991, the American Institute of Architects singled him out as "the greatest American architect of all time," a statement that sounds fairly definitive. I never worked on a Wright building, but I almost feel as if I did. In my final days at Thompson-Starrett, in the fall of 1953, Wright was completing plans for the Guggenheim Museum, to be located at Fifth Avenue and Eighty-ninth Street, and there was a lot of talk about the unusual design that was contemplated. One day, without prior notice, a set of the building's structural drawings came into the office, and I remember being dazzled by what I saw. Tons and tons of reinforcing steel seemed to swirl within the curved concrete walls of that remarkable structure. I was less enchanted when it looked as if the firm might be bidding on the job and I might have to work on a reinforcing steel quantity take-off. When the decision came down from on high that we were abandoning plans to prepare a cost estimate, I was relieved—but also disappointed.

Construction on the building didn't begin until 1956, and although I played no role in the work, I found myself stopping by the site every so often to see the progress. And since its completion in 1959, the year of Wright's death, I have viewed the building with the reverence it deserves and imagine that I can see those reinforcing bars swirling within the concrete walls.

I feel another connection to Wright, almost as tenuous as my dreaming about the Guggenheim, and that is the time I spent in the 1960s with a Wright apprentice, Edgar Tafel. Mr. Tafel has been considered the "unofficial guardian of the Frank Lloyd Wright School." At least that is what he was called in 2001 when he was awarded an honorary doctorate by SUNY Geneseo. And that is how Tafel thought of himself. He spoke often about his days with Wright at the famous Taliesin studio in Arizona. When Tafel left Taliesin to strike out on his own, a rift had developed between the student and his mentor. Despite this falling out, the self-anointed disciple wrote books about the master and produced a prize-winning film, *The Frank Lloyd Wright Way*. I got to know Tafel when he was chosen by the New York City Mission Society to be the architect for the Minisink Town House and the adjoining apartment project, Bethune Tower. I also met him socially when he designed a house in New Jersey for relatives. He was an excellent architect, a pleasure to work with, and a delight to listen to. Yet I had a strange feeling that he never seemed to be totally absorbed in the work at hand: the community center, the apartment house, or the suburban residence. I fancied that he couldn't stop thinking about those celebrated Wright projects on which he had worked in years past: Fallingwater, Wingspread, and the Johnson Wax headquarters.

ONE very famous architect with whom I did spend some time was Marcel Breuer. Recognized as a founder of the modern movement and celebrated for his furniture designs as well as his buildings, Mr. Breuer was born in Hungary and educated at the Bauhaus, where he also taught. He immigrated to the United States in 1937, and, after teaching at Harvard, moved in 1946 to New York City, where he practiced and resided until his death in 1981. I never worked on a Breuer building, and I met the gentleman under unusual circumstances; but that encounter was for me most memorable.

My firm had entered into an arbitration. It may seem as if we were constantly involved in such battles, but perhaps ten or twelve confrontations, some quite minor, over a period of fifty-five years doesn't sound excessive. In any event, the year was 1962: we had moved against a subcontractor who had abandoned a job, and one of the three appointed arbitrators was, much to our amazement, Marcel Breuer. Mr. Breuer was already well-known and much honored. Why in the world would such an individual serve as an arbitrator in an ordinary construction matter? Perhaps he was curious, perhaps he felt an obligation to serve, or perhaps he had time on his hands and was attracted by the fees to be earned. Putting this in context, we must recall that the arbitration took place a year before he received the commission to design the building that was to gain him much acclaim, the Whitney Museum of Art in New York City.

Mr. Breuer was dapper in dress and courtly in manner. Totally disregarding usual courtroom decorum, he started to chat with us, the parties to the proceedings. He sought our opinions on shows currently playing on Broadway and discussed them with verve, along with dissertations on art, music, and other cultural events. It was all very pleasant, although the first morning session started late and didn't progress as expeditiously as we had hoped. Then at lunchtime the three arbitrators disappeared and didn't return for more than two hours. During an afternoon break, attorneys for the two parties cornered the chief arbitrator and asked if the lunch intermission had to be so long. Our attorney reported back that apparently Mr. Breuer had selected an elegant restaurant for the arbitrators' dining and had insisted on ordering a bottle of fine wine that was to be savored at their leisure. The chief arbitrator was apologetic but confessed that he had enjoyed a most civilized repast. Well, civilized it might have been, during the proceedings as well as for the arbitrators at lunch, but instead of being completed in three days as we had hoped, the arbitration took seven or eight hearings over a four-month period.

But what an experience! I had come to an arbitration and found myself participating in a seminar with Marcel Breuer. How cultured the man was. And what a luminous personality. I couldn't believe that this was really happening. The legal fees ran to a lot more than I had anticipated. But I came to think of the expense as tuition. And to top it all off: the decision came down in our favor.

A world-famous architect our company could properly list in our brochure is Philip Johnson. He was architect for an apartment house we built—or rather *co*architect, and therein lies a tale. As reported in *New York* magazine, when the new millennium dawned, and the Manhattan market in luxury apartments boomed, it became popular for developers to hire a famous architect who would "sprinkle some pixie dust" on their buildings. I don't know precisely how much Mr. Johnson contributed to our project. But he did attend several meetings, old and frail, yet still an individual very much worthy of respect.

There is a top-tier architect who I think of in a much more personal context, and that is James Polshek. Although he started his career in the office of I. M. Pei, served as dean of Columbia University's School of Architecture for fifteen years, has received much praise and many honors, and although he can speak before audiences, including prospective clients, with charm and erudition, Jim Polshek is, in my experience, more of a practical builder's architect than some of the legendary names I've mentioned. KBF's first experience with the Polshek firm was on a government-financed housing project we built in the Bronx in the early 1970s. At that time we had no say in his selection. However, our experience with the Bronx job was delightful, so when in 1990 we were cosponsors of an apartment building at Battery Park City, we happily endorsed the choice of the Polshek Partnership as architect. I say "endorsed" since Jim was what one might call the designated choice. Well beloved by the Battery Park City officials, he had achieved something of an "in" status. Yet we found him—and his staff—uniquely able to blend artistic creativity with technical knowledge and good sense, to work cooperatively with a builder, and to take budget restraints into consideration.

In 1999, when I served as chairman of the building committee of the New York Hall of Science, I had the unique opportunity of participating in the selection of an architect for the hall's new addition. Quite an exhilarating change of status: a member of the selection committee instead of being an anxious candidate vying for consideration. The Polshek firm was one of twenty names coming out of a computerized lottery process that had winnowed down a larger group of prequalified architects. A final decision was to be made by a committee comprised of representatives from the New York City Department of Design and Construction (DDC) and the Department of Cultural Affairs (DCA), as well as people from the hall's board and administration. The city representatives had a majority of the votes, not unreasonable considering that the city pays for and builds the Hall's buildings—as they do for thirty-three of New York City's cultural organizations. Polshek was an obvious choice, favored by several of us from the hall. However, some of the city representatives argued that he had become too much the "architect du jour," having recently completed the dazzling new planetarium for the Museum of Natural History and been named as architect for the Clinton Presidential Library. They felt that it was time to give some other deserving firm an opportunity. Although we could see both sides of the argument, the appeal of a proven creative force was most attractive to us. The museum, originally built as part of the 1964 World's Fair, designed by Wallace Harrison, a famous architect in his day, featured an outdoor display of early space-age rockets and an eighty-foot-high undulating concrete wall containing 5,400 panels of cobalt blue glass. An addition, we felt, should be worthy of the original, and the pro-Polshek argument finally prevailed. In the end we felt vindicated by the sparkling building that arose—and by the *Architectural Review* article proclaiming that the Polshek addition "brings vitality and new life to the Hall." (Postscript: in 2010, several years after Jim Polshek retired, the firm's name was changed to Ennead Architects.)

Fortunately, most of the architects with whom I've worked have been sensible and down-to-earth, as they would have to be to gain repeat commissions in New York City designing apartment houses, schools, hospitals, and the like. Paradoxically, however, the most craftsmanlike architect of all I have encountered; the one most interested in materials; the most curious, probing into the details of structural supports, masonry, waterproofing, glazing, and mechanical systems, was the man renowned for designing more than fifty synagogues: Percival Goodman.

At a 1947 conference of the Union of American Hebrew Congregations, Goodman had argued that instead of continuing to copy models of older churches and synagogues—the classical domes and such—builders of new religious structures should think in terms of modern architecture. As annunciated by the architecture critic Paul Goldberger, it was Mr. Goodman's belief that "the vocabulary of modern architecture could be transformed into something rich enough to express religious feeling." This concept was well received and gave rise to numerous commissions for new buildings. Not only was Goodman successful in unifying modern architecture with spirituality, but he was a lifelong student of utopias, who wrote, with his brother, the philosopher Paul Goodman, *Communitas,* a blueprint for ideal communities. Yet this artist-philosopher-idealist was passionately concerned about every construction detail. He pressed me relentlessly for precise technical information, insisting on discussion of minutiae with the subcontractors and even, occasionally, with tradesmen. During the 1960–62 period KBF built, to Percival Goodman's designs, and with his assiduous participation, Temple Israel in New Rochelle and Conservative Synagogue Adath Israel in the Riverdale section of the Bronx.

IN 2008 KBF became construction manager for a most amazing building designed by perhaps the most celebrated "starchitect" of the moment, Frank Gehry. Beekman Tower—upon completion renamed "New York by Gehry at 8 Spruce Street"—is a seventy-six-story apartment house in lower Manhattan, glimmering over the entrance ramps of the Brooklyn Bridge. The building, sheathed in stainless steel panels, incorporates a four-story school and a floor for New York Downtown Hospital, concessions to the local community by Bruce Ratner of the development firm Forest City Ratner. The concessions were needed to gain consent to build a taller building than zoning would ordinarily permit, and the choice of Frank Gehry as architect certainly helped as well.

In mid-2008, just when the foundations were completed—an enormous concrete-lined hole in the ground—the nation, indeed the world, was struck by the most terrible economic crisis since the Great Depression. For a while it was uncertain whether work on the superstructure would proceed, but after a few months of uncertainty, financial arrangements were in place and off we went. Then, in March 2009, as we reached the thirty-eighth floor, the project was put on hold, and word began to circulate that the building would stop there, "50% less Frank Gehry?" as one real estate blog put it. Our estimates showed that at the stage we had reached, with major commitments made, worthwhile construction savings would be difficult to realize. Also, social and political reverberations argued against such a radical change. Finally, at the end of May the order came for full speed ahead, some savings having been realized by renegotiation with subcontractors and citywide concessions by the unions.

In the meantime, conditions in the construction industry grew increasingly bleak. In this dispiriting atmosphere it was difficult to celebrate the unique spire, clad in a skin of angularly placed stainless steel panels, rising in a helical pattern that a *New York Times* architecture critic called "intoxicating," but celebrate it we did. A topping-out party was held at the site on November 19, 2009. And, by coincidence, that very evening we attended the annual awards dinner of the New York Society of Architects, where KBF was given the Distinguished Achievement Award "for the significant contributions your company has made to the architectural profession by maintaining the highest standards in construction without compromising our design." There was little question that in building an apartment house designed by Frank Gehry—in the midst of a recession, without compromising his design—we were specially qualified for that award.

Another celebration had been scheduled at the site more than a year earlier, May 30, 2008, to be exact, but that celebration had been cancelled under unusual, indeed tragic, circumstances. That was the day that New York suffered its second serious crane collapse in three months, killing two workers and seriously injuring a third. The accident occurred about 8:00 A.M. at Ninety-first Street and First Avenue, and since the concrete contractor affected was the same firm that was working at the Beekman, many hardhats rushed uptown in concern for their fellows. Bruce Ratner wisely cancelled the festivities, scheduled for noon. The occasion had been planned "to celebrate the design and construction of the Beekman Residential Tower and home of Lower Manhattan's New Public School." In addition to Mr. Ratner, featured speakers were to have been the New York State Assembly speaker, the New York City schools chancellor, and "Pritzker Prize–winning architect Frank O. Gehry." I arrived at the site at about 10:00 A.M., totally oblivious to what had occurred on the Upper East Side. Our superintendent filled me in on the latest tragic news, but, as long as I was there, he took me to see the nearby space that had been rented and decorated for the occasion. Centrally featured was an impressive display of Mr. Gehry's many conceptual models for the building. And as I entered the hall, who did I see in the middle of that display but Mr. Gehry. I had never met the gentleman—this project being completely under the supervision of our CEO, Joe Zelazny, and his professional staff—so I introduced myself. Mr. Gehry greeted me cordially, and we chatted for a few minutes, but I could tell that he was anxious to get back to the several men whom he had been addressing. Reporters and architectural critics had come to cover the event for various publications. I gradually drifted away from the group, my thoughts returning to the disaster unfolding at the uptown construction site. It may not be fair, but my abiding memory of Frank Gehry is of a lecturer proudly addressing a small audience of people he clearly considered important, declaiming about his work, oblivious to the outside world.

Probably this view of the man is colored by my ambivalent feelings about his work. I appreciate Gehry's talent, and I know that I shouldn't be trapped in an antiquated attachment to traditional building forms. Indeed, I admire the Frank Lloyd Wright circular museum and other modern artistic statements. But with Gehry I feel that all restraint has been cast aside, and it makes me uncomfortable. The famous Guggenheim Museum in Bilbao, for example, with its "crinkled" shapes that could never be designed, much less built, without computers—is that where architecture is headed?

Yet I came to admire the Beekman building, sheathed as it is in stainless steel panels. The apartment-tower anatomy precludes the use of wild, curving, flying forms, and, thus disciplined, the Gehry genius impresses without irritating. Increasingly I find myself pleased by the thought that my firm is constructing one of the greatest of buildings in the greatest of cities.

SPECTACULAR buildings are few and far between, and I'm forced to recognize that most of the building I've done has been in the company of architects working under pragmatic constraints. I've spoken about the creative giants of the age because they fascinate me, as they do most people. As Mario Cuomo has said about politics, we campaign in poetry but must govern in prose. So it is in construction.

This is not to say that some economy-minded, roll-up-the-sleeves architects are not creative geniuses in their own way. Take Peter Claman, long a partner in Schuman Lichtenstein Efron (in recent years reconstituted as SLCE Architects). Pete has always been "a quick man with a pencil," as *The New York Times* portrayed him two decades ago, with a reputation for "maximum effective use of interior space." Come to think of it, apartment layout requires conceptual artistry, combined with an appreciation of how people live and what people want, as well as what can be built economically. Pete's special talents have long been in demand by knowledgeable developers. When I say "long" I know whereof I speak, since our first work with his firm goes back to 1959. There are at least a dozen projects on which we've worked together, mostly apartment houses but also hospital work and a community center—Pete enjoys his reputation as a genius in apartment layout but doesn't like to be typecast.

Recalling longtime relationships, Richard Dattner came into our firm's life back in 1966 when we built the Adventure Playground in New York City's Central Park—a remarkable project: novel, historic, iconic. Instead of the standard array of swings and slides, Dattner's design featured a stone fortress, a climbing pyramid, and a water-play area. We long thought of Richard as a playground specialist—his book, *Design for Play,* was published in 1969—and as an urban planner. But he expanded his practice into many areas, and when in 1990 we started to work for Linda Hoffman and her New York Foundation for Senior Citizens, we found that Richard was her architect. This led to our working together on six apartment projects.

A third architect who seemed to travel in our world, retained by organizations, public and private, for whom we worked—on housing and nursing homes—was Peter Samton of Gruzen Samton. That was a late-blooming relationship compared with Claman and Dattner; we didn't meet Peter until the 1970s. But we did some half dozen projects together, including one for the New York City Housing Authority that had multiple stages and lasted for several years.

When I say "our world," in doing repeat jobs with these three firms, and a few others, I came to realize that we traveled in circles, public and private, that intersected. I also learned that architects and contractors, different as we might be—artists compared with "workers"—shared many problems. The owner was always a third party in a complex relationship, and the Department of Buildings sometimes a difficult fourth. Architects, along with contractors, have to balance the demands of good workmanship, time, cost, and safety. An architect has mundane obligations, such as processing approval of shop drawings in a timely manner, that could be a critical factor in job progress. And errors, by the architect or his engineers, or even—conceivably!—by the contractor, have to be overcome.

I'll always remember how Peter Samton, on that unhappy nursing home project with the "villainous inspector," was commissioned by the owner to resolve a dispute. The subcontractors were up in arms, and I was furious, ready to carry the argument to the Supreme Court. But Peter persuaded us to accept a compromise. Looking weary, resigned to forces beyond anybody's control, he said, in effect, "These are the people we have to live with. This is the community in which we have to make our way." I can't say that these words completely extinguished my combative instincts; but they had a lasting effect.

There are a hundred other architects with whom I've worked, most long gone; the firms don't often outlive the founders. Many of these architects were fine people, several superbly talented, some a bit eccentric, a few—but only a very few—unpleasant or seemingly incompetent.

AND I could write volumes about the engineers, structural and mechanical, who were retained by the architects and often had a tremendous influence, not only on the quality of the finished building but also on the efficiency of the construction process. We all know that mechanical and electrical systems have become increasingly complex and ever more central in the evolution of the modern building. But I am moved to mention an old-fashioned structural engineer, relatively unheralded, who, during the time of my career, made an important contribution to our industry. Robert Rosenwasser was uniquely able to design a reinforced concrete slab, according to code of course but using a minimal weight of steel bars per square foot. Invisible to most people, this skill reduced building costs by an appreciable amount. Were other engineers less talented? Or were they just a bit—not lazier perhaps—but less persevering? Through the years a lot has been written about engineering ethics. In my humble opinion, the philosophers have not given enough credit to simple diligence.

Finally, on a lighter note, I must mention another professional who worked as a design engineer on several of our projects. Joe Goldreich showed up in my life, unexpectedly, several decades after we had traveled together to the Philippines as newly commissioned ensigns in the Seabees. Aside from the pleasure of an unanticipated reunion, it was intriguing to consider the different roads we had traveled. Both of us had started at the same place and with identical educations in civil engineering. Joe had followed the career of a designer, and I had become a builder. Each of us half envied the other and speculated about how it would have been to trade life history.

FROM architects, through the design engineers, I come naturally to another group of professionals, those I think of as the "technocrats." I refer to the civil servants, usually trained in engineering or accounting, who are employed by the various government agencies with whom we have worked on so many projects. The term may sound menacing if one thinks of Big Brother, government control ceded to technicians. But if we accept the Merriam-Webster definition of "technocrat": "a technical expert; *especially*: one exercising managerial authority," that's simply a feature of a modern society. As citizens we want smart, trained, efficient people overseeing government programs. As contractors, we also want them to be reasonable, define that word as you will.

At the beginning of the previous chapter I observed that the supposedly "important" people for a contractor to know are primarily those who control the awarding of construction contracts, and secondarily the people who oversee performance of the work and approve payments. Upon reflection, "secondarily" may not be the right word. It's great to know the people on top, but the workers in the trenches, particularly in a public agency, can be crucially important. Inspectors in the field, as I had learned from my earliest days, can occasionally be troublesome. But the office people have, in the long run, more critical control. In many government-financed housing jobs—for KBF most notably in the Mitchell-Lama program—while the contracts may not have been bid competitively, the price had to compare favorably with the agency's estimate and also be approved as falling within established government guidelines. Further, at project's end the final cost was subject to stringent audits. Finally, the agency's people had to OK the selection of subcontractors, the details of materials to be used, and all contractual and financial matters—monthly payments, extensions of time, change orders, and so forth. In short, these individuals had powers equal to, or sometimes exceeding, those of their superiors. The simple exercise of a red-tape delay, for example, is one of the greatest hazards a contractor has to confront. And if one happens to encounter an obstructionist, a contractor has to think twice, and think again, before trying to go over his head.

On our first Mitchell-Lama projects, built under the supervision of the Housing Development Administration (HDA), I must say we were fortunate. One could not conceive of a finer group of professional civil servants. They were smart, energetic, and decent. They were mostly young—as was the Mitchell-Lama program—which might have partly accounted for the good feelings that I recall. Al DeMeo was the top man, knowledgeable verging on persnickety, but fair, and in the end always reasonable. Charlie Pumilia, Pete Brady, Vince Ferrara—those are the names that come first to mind. Good guys, although never pushovers. I give credit to KBF people, particularly John Cricco and Pete Cettina, for showing our firm's better side, intent on getting things done, contractors not angels, but straight shooters. The relationship could serve as a model for the ideal society. If it sounds too good to be true, or if it seems as if I'm buttering up New York construction overseers in general, I hasten to add that my other experiences never came close to that "era of good feelings." (I borrow the phrase used to describe the period in United States political history, 1817–25, during which partisan bitterness is said to have abated.)

When KBF constructed buildings with New York State Mitchell-Lama financing instead of New York City, we dealt with a completely different crew and encountered very different treatment. I remember one particular incident in which our electrical subcontractor was ordered to replace hundreds of plastic outlets that varied in minute detail from the specifications and that the design engineer had ruled were satisfactory and represented no appreciable saving in cost. I made an appeal to a Mr. Milton Duke—how come I remember that name when so many others elude me? After I, and the pleading electrician, were turned down with what I felt was surly satisfaction, I asked the man why he was so unreasonable and so unpleasant. The answer took me by surprise. "If you'd been through as many investigations as this office has," said Mr. Duke, "you wouldn't listen to any soft talk about being reasonable." At least that was a rationale that one could ponder.

When the New York State Urban Development Corporation came along in the 1970s, under Ed Logue, the "urban renewal whirlwind" (to quote his *New York Times* obituary), obstructionist instincts were tempered by the enthusiasm to get things done, and the results were fairly satisfactory. I commented on this to one of the new administrators, and he said, "Give us seven years. A new enterprise like this has seven years before it starts to go stale, or even sour." An interesting thought.

Certainly when we did work for the New York City Housing Authority, a venerable institution founded in 1934, I found bureaucratic spitefulness firmly ensconced. One of the nastiest old-timers explained that "a career spent dealing with greedy, crooked, lying contractors" was enough to spoil one's disposition.

*   *   *

IT'S been many years now since I've dealt directly with office engineers in the public sphere, and I like to think back to the good old HDA—since 1972 known as the Department of Housing Preservation and Development (HPD)—and dream that all the agencies have evolved along those lines, leading to a more perfect world.

I have met contractors—in fact, people in all walks of life—who carry perpetual grudges against civil servants, claiming that they are officious or lazy or corrupt, an affliction that honest, hardworking, private citizens should not be forced to tolerate. I suppose that disputes about the benefit of public enterprise versus private are not going to moderate. In fact, they seem to gather more force as the years go by. To gain perspective I like to quote from an editorial that I came across doing research, in the July 5, 1906, issue of *Engineering News-Record*. "The old argument that municipal ownership was to be abhorred because it was a step toward socialism can no longer be used . . . The public has learned that there are other inefficiently managed industries besides those owned and operated by the government;" and further, "that there are grafters in private business as well as in public business." Written more than a century ago, but timeless.

It is my opinion that quality people, in the public sphere as well as in the private, are a fundamental element of a successful society.

FOURTEEN | *Developers*

ARCHITECTS, ENGINEERS, TECHNOCRATS . . . so much brilliance, so much creativity, so much artistry. Yet the most splendid plans in the world would never be realized in steel and concrete without one vital element: financial backing. There is public funding, to be sure. We take for granted government spending to meet community needs and to support many community aspirations in education and the arts. In addition, our society is blessed with private institutions and generous individuals, philanthropic, religious, and civic-minded, who sponsor museums, concert halls, and churches that enrich our lives. But what is the source of all those office buildings and apartment houses, the towers that define our magnificent urban centers? Entrepreneurs of course, investors looking for profit and willing to take risk. The growth of New York City springs mainly from the energy, courage, and optimism of a special group of individuals. We call them developers.

IN the November 1998 *Bulletin of the Century Association* there appeared an announcement: "Frederick P. Rose will speak at lunch on Monday, November 30, at 12:15 p.m. on *How Does Anything Ever Get Built in New York?* Reservations are required." I told Joe Zelazny—our firm's CEO—to mark the date in his calendar. "I'll reserve for two," I said. "We have to go hear what Fred has to say." The day arrived, we had a pleasant lunch, and as one might have expected, there was nothing new or revolutionary in Fred's remarks. He spoke humorously of the difficulties inherent in conceiving, financing, designing, and building a project in Manhattan, coping with the pressures of bureaucrats, politicians, bankers, and most of all communities. His solutions were upbeat. Be patient with the red tape; go the extra mile in observing regulations; and, of prime importance, be a good neighbor—protect adjoining property, respect as much as possible the desire for cleanliness and quiet, and, if special situations warrant, pay for a roof repair for the church next door or provide a few new windows for the local community center. Spotting Joe and me seated in the audience, Fred singled us out for praise as good-citizen builders who worked hard for the well-being of our marvelous city.

There were a few friendly questions that Fred fielded deftly, and as the event ended he came over to our table. "If you fellows have a few minutes," he said, "let's go over to the job." At the time our company was six months into the construction of a building for Rose Associates, a forty-eight-story apartment house on East Twenty-ninth Street, and we certainly had a few minutes, and more, for a visit to the site. We joined Fred in a taxi, and shortly we were climbing up the stairs of the partly completed structure. Fred scorned use of the hoist and seemed to relish the exertion. We finally stopped on a floor where some men were working, and we were joined by our superintendent. Fred asked some penetrating questions, particularly about the mechanical systems, and then requested an update on the progress schedule. He seemed very much at home in the surrounding chaos.

A really good guy, we agreed, after he departed. Our comments were based not only on the visit—in which he behaved more like a builder enjoying his trade than like a developer building for profit—but also on our previous experience with him and on his fine reputation. What a shock to learn of his death, just nine and a half months later, at age seventy-five. I don't know anything about the state of his health at the time when he cheerfully scampered up the steps of our building—his building. But my memory of him will always be brightened by the recollection of that brief site visit.

When I say fine reputation I am understating the case. Many of New York's wealthy developers are philanthropic, but Fred and his wife, Sandra, in the words of the chairman of the New York Public Library board of trustees, "enriched the cultural and educational life of the city with their dedicated involvement in a wide variety of causes and organizations." The Roses made multimillion dollar gifts, not only to the library but also to Lincoln Center and several of its constituent organizations, as well as to the American Museum of Natural History. Fred served on the boards of, and generously supported, Yale, the Metropolitan Museum of Art, the New York Philharmonic, and numerous other institutions. In addition to his philanthropy, Fred believed in service, devoting time as president of the Scarsdale Board of Education and participating in the activities of many worthy causes. He was trustworthy and honorable in his business dealings. "He was the closest thing to a saint," said his friend and oft-time partner in development enterprise, Charles Benenson.

All right, let's slow down a bit. We know that one can't be a real estate developer and landlord in New York City, or anywhere else, and qualify for sainthood. Also, since Fred didn't have to fight his way up from impoverished beginnings as did many other developers, a gentlemanly demeanor was perhaps to be expected. Still, casting aside superlatives, he was a good man who accomplished good things.

After Fred Rose's death in 1999, his son Adam carried on, with the help of able professionals. One never knows what lies in store as the "next generation" takes over, but in the ensuing years our firm built three more apartment houses for Rose Associates, among them the Helena on West Fifty-seventh Street (with the Durst Organization as codeveloper), 580 units, winner of a gold rating from the U.S. Green Building Council. There was one changed condition that we had to live with: Adam Rose didn't want our company signs displayed all over the job sites. Maybe we had overdone it in the past. Anyhow, his father had permitted it—or overlooked it—but Adam did not. With sad resignation, we agreed to this restriction.

★ ★ ★

THINKING of generational change, I was surprised to learn in late 2009 that the Elghanayan brothers, after four decades as partners, were breaking up their $3 billion real estate empire, partly because of problems relating to succession. The properties had been divided into three packets of roughly equal value, and the choices decided by the flip of a coin. Henry was going on his own; his two brothers, Tom and Fred, were off in a different direction together. I was particularly interested because in a small way our firm was involved in the Elghanayans' earliest success. The father, Nourallah, had been a prominent manufacturer in Iran under the shah, and, looking ahead, had moved the family to Queens in the 1950s. In 1970 the brothers, with a $100,000 family nest egg, started to purchase and renovate small buildings in and around Greenwich Village. In 1976, venturing into the big time, so to speak, they purchased a factory and loft building on East Forty-sixth Street, planning to convert it into a 340-unit apartment house with commercial space and a garage. This is where my firm entered the picture. By 1976 KBF had earned a respectable reputation as apartment house builders, and we also had done some conversion work, notably the Vanderbilt Hotel. We met Fred Elghanayan, the engineer brother who ran Rockrose, the family's construction operation, and were retained to be the construction manager on this complex enterprise budgeted at $8 million. I recall the project as a great challenge and a great success. I also recall it as being the only one on which we were fired. Well, maybe "fired" is not quite the right word, but then again maybe it is. About halfway through the job Fred called us in to say that he had decided he could finish the building on his own. He had learned a lot from us but now felt he'd like to carry on alone. He had the right to terminate our participation, which he was choosing to exercise, paying our fees and expenses up to that point. Did he really want to test himself by taking over the helm? Was he displeased with our performance? Was he simply trying to save the few dollars represented by our fees? We were somewhat shaken since nothing like this had happened to us before—or, let me add, ever after. Nevertheless, with a shrug, we decided to forget about the mystifying event and concentrate on the other work we had on hand.

But then there occurred the most intriguing part of the whole experience. Fred called to say that his father wanted to meet us, and would we join them for lunch? We accepted the invitation, and Bob Borg and I met Fred and his father at an elegant restaurant. As the conversation evolved it became clear to me that the older man, perhaps drawing on his experiences in the Middle East, wanted to be sure that the termination of our engagement did not lead to hard feelings. Maybe he had heard about violent crime in the New York construction industry and wanted to be sure that we carried no grudges. By the end of the meal I believe that the older man was satisfied that there was no bitterness about which to be concerned, and no doubt in person we didn't seem particularly intimidating. Indeed, in the years that followed, occasional contacts with Fred Elghanayan were congenial. I didn't follow the fortunes of Rockrose, although it was common knowledge that the Elghanayans were "successful." In fact, a $3 billion real estate empire! I like to think that maybe they learned a few things from us about how to build.

MUSING about families from Iran, the passing of years, and the succession of generations, the Manocherian family comes naturally to mind. I don't have any specific information about the value of their empire, but certainly they are, as *The New York Times* has put it, "one of the city's major builders and investment owners of residential property." In 2001 we built an apartment house for the Manocherians: the Caroline, a majestic building running the length of the block between Twenty-second and Twenty-third streets on the east side of Sixth Avenue. In addition to 440 luxury units, the building featured an enormous facility for the New York Health and Racquet Club, another Manocherian enterprise. I thought that the project was a great success, and when Joe Zelazny was invited to dine at Fred Manocherian's home and was asked to discuss government aid to housing with the guest of honor, Senator Chuck Schumer, I felt certain that KBF had a devoted client. I could hardly believe it when the next Manocherian construction job went to another contractor. The explanation? Fred explained to Joe that the choice was made by members of the next generation. The way of the world.

When I find that we have lost out because of decisions made by sons and nephews of people to whom we had been close, I instinctively think of a scene in Arthur Miller's play *Death of a Salesman*. Willy Loman, the aging traveling salesman, pleads for his job with the son of the man who hired him. Exasperated and fearful, Willy shouts: "Promises were made across this desk!" It is a powerful and moving moment in the theater. Of course, in real life no promises have been made to me about future contracts, and it is only to be expected that each generation will want to make its own mark. It is also to be expected that a displaced elder will be disappointed.

THE most dynamic and most successful developer with whom I've worked is, without question, Stephen Ross. With a fortune estimated by *Forbes* to have been $4.5 billion in 2008, doubtless reduced by the recession but still substantial, he personally—without a founding generation to give him a start—has become a giant, dubbed "King of Columbus Circle" in reference to his landmark Time Warner Center. Every biographical note about Ross makes mention of his wealthy and influential uncle, Max Fisher of Detroit; but aside from lending Steve money for college tuition, Mr. Fisher is not known to have been a critical factor in Ross's amazing success story. In fact, Steve says he borrowed $10,000 from his mother to help him get started in business. Everyone agrees that Steve Ross is smart and came to the development field well prepared with degrees in accounting and law, as well as experience with investment banking firms. But who could have predicted his meteoric career? In 1972, at age thirty-two, he ventured forth on his own, founding the Related Companies. His first efforts were in the field of government-aided housing, and that's where I come into his story—or, perhaps more notably, he into mine.

By the late 1970s our firm had built about twenty middle-income projects. Also, having teamed up with three established neighborhood organizations—Ballet Hispanico, the Church of Saint Gregory, and Claremont Stables—we had managed to be named sponsors for two sites in the West Side Urban Renewal area. When the city's planning commission got bogged down in political turmoil, the ballet company moved, the church revised their plans, and the owner of Claremont Stables decided against new construction (opting eventually to close the hundred-year-old landmark). Somehow our status was never challenged, and since there were no carrying costs involved with our sponsorship, we just let things ride.

In 1980 Steve Ross hired a young man by the name of Peter Joseph, a public housing expert who had worked at HUD and become deputy commissioner of the city's HPD (successor to HDA) before moving into the private sector. As executive vice president supervising Related's residential development in New York, Peter looked around the territory and saw KBF, a firm he knew from the good old days, controlling two fine sites. It was a perfect match: a real estate wizard, super savvy in the financing of government-aided construction, and reputable builders who didn't have the foggiest idea of what to do with the projects under their control. I don't recall who first contacted whom and when, but I have notes of a meeting in January of 1984 attended by Peter Joseph and David Wine of Related with Bob Borg and me. Peter was a pleasant, soft-spoken individual, as was David (later a Related vice chairman and eventually an independent developer). Things must have gone smoothly because after only two months, in March, there was a memo of intent and, six months after that, September 11, 1984, a letter agreement.

The concept was simple: KBF and Related were to be, more or less, fifty-fifty owners, KBF to provide the sponsorship and perform the construction for a fixed fee, Related to arrange for financing and eventually manage the buildings. We all swung into action, obtained the required approvals, and within a year plans were complete for a ninety-six-unit apartment building on the west side of Columbus Avenue between Eighty-seventh and Eighty-eighth streets. Construction commenced in late 1985, and the building, called Columbus Green, was completed in 1987. The project rented well and earned some modest profits. A number of years later the Related people received what they considered a favorable offer from a potential purchaser; a sale was consummated, and we received our share of the proceeds. The other site, on the west side of Amsterdam Avenue between Eighty-ninth and Ninetieth Streets, did not proceed until 1996, and in this case we sold our interest to Related up front, performing the construction of the 265-unit, Sagamore, in 1997–98.

It all sounds so simple, and in retrospect we were pleased to have dipped our toes, however gingerly, into the development ocean. But the picture is not complete without introducing the chief protagonist: Stephen M. Ross. The earliest meetings, held mostly with Steve's soft-spoken aides, had led serenely to initial agreement. But when we were ready to move ahead, and there were details to be negotiated, Steve took over. I recall him being rough, tough, and sardonic, especially sardonic as he came to realize how little Borg and Florman knew about the field in which he was such a genius. Rough and tough was nothing new in the construction industry, and I never claimed to be a good negotiator; but in most situations I felt well-informed, as smart as anyone in the room. Until now. Suddenly I was floundering in an ocean of exotic terminology: "credit enhancement fees," "principal reserve fees," "sinking funds," "mortgage administration fees," and more. Bonds were issued by HDC and backed by Fannie Mae. How exactly did that work? Once Steve sized us up—and it didn't take him long—he was relentlessly aggressive and eventually intimidating. My notes of a few of the meetings we held are peppered with his quotes: "Buy me out!" when he knew we couldn't; "No more money . . . I'm suing . . . That's it!" I'll never know if he resented us for controlling sponsorships he thought we didn't deserve, or if that was just his way. Or possibly he was under pressures that later abated as his success became assured.

Anyhow, with the turmoil long behind us, we look back at our Steve Ross experience with a rueful smile. While we might have been pushed around a bit, we never felt cheated. And, in fact, we never had a real falling out. After we finished site 32, the Sagamore, in 1998, our construction team had made such a favorable impression that the Related folks hired us to build the Lyric, an apartment house on Broadway running from Ninety-fourth to Ninety-fifth Streets.

Following the felicitous completion of that project in late 2000, Related gave us another contract, the Tate, a 313-unit apartment house in the Chelsea area of Manhattan. That building seemed to go smoothly enough; but after its completion in 2002, no further jobs were forthcoming. I don't know of any particular reason. Steve himself was occupied with very big stuff, building the $1.7 billion AOL Time Warner Building at Columbus Circle and planning even more epochal development of the West Side rail yards. His rising deputy stars, President Jeff Blau and Executive Vice President Bruce Beal, Jr.—touted in commercial journals as young "leaders reshaping New York"—had confidence in other people, other firms, the new-generation syndrome.

I've met Steve Ross only once in recent years, at a charitable event, and he was cordial, as I would have expected him to be. Steve was present to receive the What New York Needs Award from the Doe Fund, an organization whose mission is to help homeless individuals obtain housing and employment. The man is philanthropic. "There is no feeling like the one you get from giving back," said Stephen M. Ross on the occasion of his most notable gift, $100 million to his alma mater, the University of Michigan, where the graduate school he attended is now known as the Ross School of Business.

One more anecdote about Ross that I can't resist telling. Back in 1987, when Steve was just fifteen years into his independent career, still making his way up a perilous ladder of success, and when our firm was just completing Columbus Green, the first job that we built with him, the New York football Giants went to the Super Bowl. As longtime season-ticket holders we had the option to buy two tickets to this glamorous event. We weren't about to go to

Pasadena where the game was played, but, aware that Steve was active all over the country, and knowing that he was a great fan of pro football, we offered him our tickets, which he accepted with thanks. The Giants won the game, which was a happy outcome, and we felt like big shots having given our tickets to our business associate.

Twenty-one years later, in February 2008, Steve Ross bought 50 percent of the Miami Dolphin franchise, along with Dolphin Stadium and surrounding land, for $550 million. Then, in January of 2009, for $1 billion more, Ross closed on the purchase of an additional 45 percent. At the same time, when our firm was confronted with a $60,000 charge for a contract to keep the rights to our six seats in the new Giants stadium—simply the rights to keep buying the tickets at an elevated price—I said, no thanks, that's pretty steep, and we're not made of money.

THE topic of professional sports teams brings me naturally to another prominent dynamo of a developer. Bruce Ratner is the founder of Forest City Ratner; builder of the $1 billion Metro Tech Center, a high-tech office, academic, and retail complex in Brooklyn; and, more recently, partner-builder with *The New York Times* of the paper's new building in Manhattan. In 2004 Mr. Ratner purchased the lowly New Jersey Nets, and the following year he announced his intention to build a stadium for them in Brooklyn, centerpiece of plans for a huge surrounding development known as Atlantic Yards. A hostile community group arose, leading to a legal donnybrook that captured headlines for several years.

Along the way, Ratner arranged to build Beekman Tower in lower Manhattan, seventy-six stories high, containing a school, a hospital floor, and 902 apartments. I've mentioned the spectacular building previously in speaking of its architect, Frank Gehry. The construction management contract came to KBF, and it was by far our biggest project ever. The topping-out party took place in November 2009, coincidentally just at a time when the state's highest court was expected to rule on whether or not the Atlantic Yards project would be allowed to proceed—a do-or-die moment for the developer. By Bruce Ratner's behavior at the gala event one wouldn't have guessed he had a worry in the world. On an outdoor podium filled with politicians and union officials, the man radiated enthusiasm and good cheer.

As it happened, four days later the court ruled six to one in Mr. Ratner's favor. At KBF we were pleased since we hoped to play some small role in the planned construction. However, this great victory was followed by financial problems that threatened to sink the entire enterprise. Undaunted, Bruce Ratner sold 80 percent of the Nets and 45 percent of the arena to the Russian billionaire Mikhail Prokhorov and moved ahead in a blizzard of upbeat publicity. Even from my place on the periphery of these events, I couldn't help getting caught up in the excitement. Ebullience can be contagious.

WHILE I confess to finding the showbiz side of real estate exciting, I appreciate the serenity that surrounds some very successful developers who shun the spotlight. At the other end of the flamboyance spectrum from Steve Ross and Bruce Ratner one finds individuals like Leonard Litwin, who has been quietly successful in apartment construction and management for more than fifty years. On his buildings and on his Web site, in his advertising and publicity releases you will find the banner of Glenwood Management; no mention at all of the publicity-shy Mr. Litwin. Without a touch of personal glory seeking, Lenny Litwin has built and managed himself into the billion-dollar category. He has traditionally done his own construction—in recent years with the able assistance of his daughter, Carole Pittelman, who my people tell me is an absolutely top-notch construction administrator. In 2002, while fully engaged in constructing a large building in the Lincoln Center neighborhood, Litwin's proposed 287-unit project on Liberty Street came to fruition, and, under pressure to start but feeling stretched, he retained our firm to be his construction manager. The job went very well, but Lenny and Carole still wanted to be their own builders. They took a fancy to a couple of our talented people, and on several projects in the following years, under mutually agreeable terms, we worked these men into their operation.

I could continue discussing developers indefinitely, although I've covered most of the biggest and best known for whom we've worked. And so, one might ask, if I find the topic so engrossing, how about my own career as a developer? Many acquaintances, seeing our company's sign on some very large buildings, assume that I must be a titan of industry. Upon being told that I'm just a hired hand—a highly trained professional, to be sure, but still in the employ of the true owner of those monster enterprises—invariably I'm asked why I myself don't take on the role of developer. And naturally I have asked myself the same question. Looking back, I see that by investing some of our fees in several Mitchell–Lama projects, we benefitted from substantial tax-shelter benefits and retained an interest in buildings that may in the future have value. Also, although our dealings on two properties with Steve Ross were a bit rocky, the role of sponsor-developer proved to be financially rewarding. Of course, we discovered that there was a lot we would have to learn before embarking on a career in development. And then came the Cove Club.

I've already noted that in 1986 KBF bid on and won sponsorship of a project at Battery Park City. In 1989, when the job was ready to start, we decided to invest 20 percent of the equity, and we invited our friends from Dic Concrete (Joe DePaola and his lieutenant, Frank Phelan) and Underhill (Walter Goldstein and his lieutenant, Bernie Jereski)—by then long retired—to join us. They took 40 percent and brought in the developer Steven Goodstein and family for the final 40 percent. Paul Milstein, who had become, according to *Forbes,* the wealthiest developer in New York, briefly considered buying us out; but, since we wouldn't consider his ridiculously low offer, he told us to get lost. It made me nostalgic to hear the same gruff insults that were his specialty when I knew him fifty years earlier as an asphalt-tile contractor. While these negotiations were under way, my wife would jokingly ask in the morning: "Who are you going to see today, Goodstein, Goldstein, or Milstein?"

Our development group formed a partnership, obtained the required financing, and approved the lovely plan that was drawn up by Polshek Partnership. With all approvals obtained, we started construction in 1992 and completed the building on schedule in early 1993. We all assumed that the beautiful site on the Hudson, with a grand view of the Statue of Liberty, would be appealing to potential buyers, particularly people from nearby Wall Street. Everybody knew that the stock market had crashed in October 1987 and had been steadily recovering. But we never dreamed that just when our building, named the Cove Club, opened in 1993, the real estate market would have gone into a terrible slump. As Andrew Goodstein, Steve Goodstein's son, was quoted in *All Business,* a Dun & Bradstreet publication, "The market couldn't have been worse . . . We needed to do something aggressive." The aggressive action was a grand opening with an auction, followed by a second auction in Hong Kong. According to that same D&B article, "Goodstein's approach to marketing the Cove Club in a difficult market resulted in his winning the title of Sales/Leasing Man of the Year from the National Association of Home Builders." Well, I'm pleased that Andrew won his award; but he neglected to report that the prices obtained in the auctions were far below what was needed to keep the Cove Club from going into the red. Financially, the enterprise was not a happy one. KBF earned a small fee for overseeing the construction, and the Goodsteins earned the usual management and leasing fees; but that provided little satisfaction for any of us as investors.

Looking back, perhaps the benefits of the lesson learned were worth the cost. I found out from personal experience something that every fool knows in theory, that real estate development is a risky business. However, I'll always recall with satisfaction the harmony that prevailed among the partners. No second-guessing, no assessing blame. And Andrew Goodstein won his award.

*   *   *

AN interesting aspect of doing business with developers, at least in a place like New York City, is the celebrity status that is accorded to the most successful of them—and to the spectacular failures as well.

Sometimes I hear of them in unexpected places. In a Connecticut daily newspaper, in November 2009, I read: "Not your garden variety tree-hugger, real estate mogul Peter Malkin, the well-connected owner of the Empire State Building, is on a crusade to protect another landmark from deforestation." It seems that Mr. Malkin, chairman of the Merritt Parkway Conservancy, was concerned about the extent of tree removal being planned by the Department of Transportation. He can also be found in Manhattan, creating business-improvement districts to rid the streets of graffiti and other blemishes. Peter Malkin is indeed a well-connected real estate mogul—one of the biggest in New York City—but he is more a buyer-trader-manager than a builder, so why would an incidental article about him catch my eye? Well, just as I met the great architect, Marcel Breuer, when he served as an arbitrator, so was arbitration the stage on which I met Peter Malkin. Only in this case, in the summer of 1995, I was the arbitrator; in fact, I was the arbitrator selected by Malkin to represent him in a dispute with the Long Island Railroad.

In most arbitrations, three impartial arbitrators are selected from lists provided by the American Arbitration Association. There is, however, a type of commercial arbitration in which each party appoints an arbitrator, and the two party-appointed arbitrators jointly select a third to act as chair of a tripartite tribunal. The parties having opted for this latter form, on the recommendation of someone unknown to me, I was selected by Malkin and his lawyers. The party-appointed arbitrators usually are paid for their services, and it is assumed that they will be predisposed toward the party who appointed them. However, they are obligated to act in good faith and with integrity. Intrigued by the complex matter to be decided, and perhaps more by the cast of characters involved, I accepted the appointment. My "opponent" arbitrator was Brian Strum of the New York University Real Estate Institute, and the chair was Lance Liebman, Dean of Columbia University Law School. This was a high-powered group, and we were dealing with a matter of some importance, so my fascination with the procedure was tempered by concern about being up to the task.

Peter Malkin, in addition to being the primary owner of the Empire State Building, is a principal in Mid-City Associates, an entity that owns 1 Penn Plaza, a building across Thirty-third Street from Penn Station. The dispute stemmed from varying interpretation of agreements dating from 1927 and 1968 that dealt with allowable access through Penn Station to the street. Mid-City planned to construct stores in and adjoining the station that would have altered the location of corridors available to pedestrians, and the railroad asserted that their authority gave them the right to prevent these alterations, or, since public safety was not a factor, to demand payment of fees.

It was absorbing, and admittedly perplexing, to study old drawings and faded agreements and come up with logical and coherent conclusions. We arbitrators investigated the site, studied the available materials, and listened to presentations by attorneys for both parties. Then we met in several private sessions, and each prepared a written statement. Since the dean saw things pretty much the way I did, the Malkin side "prevailed."

Peter Malkin naturally was well satisfied with the result. His attorneys insisted that I submit my bill promptly, and it was paid within days. I was gratified that things had turned out well; but I must admit that it felt strange to be taking money when I hadn't built anything.

THERE seems to be an infinite variety of fascinating career paths followed by bright and ambitious construction-related professionals. A few memorable individuals have such multifaceted interests and talents that they defy typecasting. Not developers exactly or exclusively, they exhibit the same creative vigor as members of that enterprising breed. One such New Yorker, a man with whom I plan to conclude this chapter, is Sandy Frucher.

Meyer S. Frucher, known to all as Sandy, served for nine years (1988–96) as executive vice president of Olympia and York, a giant

Canadian real estate firm, overseeing their development projects in the United States. He followed this with a decade as chairman and CEO of the Philadelphia Stock Exchange, serving in that capacity until July 2008, when he arranged for the exchange's acquisition by the Nasdaq OMX Group. His curriculum vitae in public life, overlapping his private endeavors, includes five years as chief labor negotiator for the state of New York, five years as president and CEO of the Battery Park City Authority, a decade as trustee and then chair of the New York City School Construction Authority, and a short stint as head of the New York City Off-Track Betting Corporation.

Somewhere along the way, Sandy had contacts with Mario Cuomo, and gradually he was referred to in the media as an "important adviser" and "close confidant" of the man who became a three-term governor of the state (1983–94). At KBF, as we worked at Battery Park City and did a number of jobs for the School Construction Authority, Sandy Frucher became, in effect, an important client. And in this complex society, where we all find ourselves playing multiple roles, I found myself board chair of the Ethical Culture Fieldston School, where Sandy was a parent.

This all came together on the morning of December 19, 1991, when I hosted Sandy for breakfast, scheduled to make a pitch for the school fund-raising campaign. What I hadn't anticipated was that at the very moment we were drinking our breakfast coffee, Mario Cuomo was scheduled to fly to New Hampshire to enter the presidential primary race—unless he changed his mind about running. This "Hamlet of the Hudson" was notorious for his indecisiveness, and that moment of "the plane waiting on the tarmac" was destined to go down in the history of presidential politics. I hadn't thought I was taking Sandy for a "power breakfast"; but we happened to be in a place where such breakfasts were taking place, and I found that our table became the destination of numerous visitors, many of them looking vaguely familiar, most of them looking like citizens who counted in the worlds of commerce and politics, and all of them asking Sandy "will he or won't he?" Instead of being concerned about fund-raising and general contracting, I suddenly felt I was at the center of the world, privy to decisions affecting the presidency of the United States.

To each of the table hoppers Sandy gave a shrug, a smile, and a firm "I don't know." And to this day I have no idea what Sandy knew or didn't know. In the end, of course, Cuomo decided against taking the plane, Sandy assured me that he would make the contribution I sought, and we had one last cup of coffee. Sandy returned to his world of real estate development, city public service, and—underlying all—politics. I returned to my small corner of the universe, marveling at the energy and ambition of so many of my fellow citizens.

FIFTEEN | *La Cosa Nostra*

I STARTED THIS BOOK with an anecdote about intimidation, about a dispute on a construction job ending with a threat to kill. I followed this with two brief quotations from a report of the New York State Organized Crime Task Force, a study that describes with specificity the dominant role played by the Mafia in our industry—my industry. In a letter to Governor Cuomo, accompanying the interim report submitted in May 1988, Ronald Goldstock, director of the task force, wrote: "The picture that emerges is one of long-standing, pervasive corruption and racketeering touching virtually every phase of the construction process and dominated by the operation of criminal syndicates . . . The implications of Cosa Nostra's domination of the construction industry are profound." Considering the accusatory nature of this report and the details contained within it, response from the city's contractors has been notably muted.

The Manhattan district attorney, Robert Morgenthau, explaining the reluctance of contractors to speak out about the Mafia, has said, "Their fear of physical harm is too great." Governor Mario Cuomo suggested a different source: "The fear of upset, the fear of delay, the fear of impediment to construction, and then the ease with which the builders can put those added costs in the price of the job." In other words, contractors go along to get along. Or, even further, using words from Goldstock's letter to Cuomo, contractors regard the Mafia as a force "providing stability ar d predictability . . . an organization which can provide valuable services." In a state of exasperation, *Engineering News-Record* editorially condemns those who "have a feeling that, if you operate in New York City and you learn how to play the game, you are somehow stronger and better than anyone anywhere else."

I hardly know how to react. For more than fifty years I have worked in this industry purportedly dominated by the Mafia. But for most of that time I was totally unaware of what was happening, and for all of that time I have been practically unaffected by the tumultuous events recorded in the newspapers. It's as if a tornado came roaring through my village and left my house intact. Or a widespread plague has spared my tiny corner of the world. Probably "tiny" is the operative word. Friendly subcontractors may have served as buffers, and our relations with the unions have always been cordial. But I do believe that size has been the key factor in our favor. Large enough to construct monumental buildings, we have still been inconspicuous enough to fly under the radar.

It has been a remarkable drama, the rise of Cosa Nostra in the New York construction industry, and I wish that I had some dazzling insights to share. Yet every small piece contributes to an understanding of the whole, so let me relate my own limited personal experience.

LIKE other children growing up in the 1930s, I saw a number of gangster movies. They made their mark, and I think of them often when I consider the role of the Mafia in today's society. In those movies the gangster was a villain; but in rebelling against a corrupt, hypocritical society—those were Depression days—he became a champion for a disenchanted public. And, of course, violence has always had its vicarious attraction.

This popular appeal carried over, for me, into adult life, making me an avid fan of the *Godfather* movies (1972, 1974, and 1990) and an absolute junkie for the *Sopranos* TV series (1999–2007). Although I had no foolish illusions about the true nature of criminality in America, my righteous feelings of disapproval were tempered by subtle affirmatives that are not easily defined. But this was the world of movies and fantasy. In the real world I had no personal experiences to make me feel that the mob had anything to do with me personally, or with my chosen profession, engineering, or even—for most of my life—with my business, construction.

Like the rest of the country I was interested in the Senate hearings of the Kefauver Committee on Organized Crime in 1951, although I think that *Life* magazine overstated the case when they wrote that, partly because of the newly evolving technology of television, "never before had the attention of the nation been riveted so completely on a single matter." The hearings did popularize the legend of a highly organized crime family called the Mafia, imported from Sicily. But details of malfeasance were scant. Concerns related mainly to gambling and drugs, and evidence was lacking. After the initial excitement died down, nothing much happened.

Six years were to pass before the next big stir, the Apalachin meeting of November 14, 1957. In a small town in upstate New York about one hundred Mafia leaders gathered, presumably to settle controversies that had arisen between the several "families." The notorious killer Albert Anastasia had recently been gunned down in a New York City barbershop, and earlier in the year Frank Costello, a known Mafia leader who had testified at the Kefauver hearings, survived an assassination attempt in the lobby of his apartment residence. This internal war had to be addressed, and there were many other business matters to discuss.

The Apalachin police, suspicions aroused by the arrival of numerous expensive cars in their remote hamlet, investigated. Then, calling reinforcements, they conducted a raid. This sent the participants scrambling away into the woods. Fifty-eight men were apprehended, but since they all claimed to be simply visiting a sick friend or talking ordinary business, they had to be released. Eventually they were called in for questioning, and twenty were indicted, tried, and convicted for conspiring to obstruct justice by lying to law enforcement officers. But the convictions were overturned by a United States court of appeals, and the Justice Department decided not to take the matter to the Supreme Court. By this time it was 1960, and knowledge about "organized crime" was widespread; but there had always been crime, and in the absence of specific newsworthy events, public interest waned. I knew no more nor less than any ordinary citizen. If and when I thought about crime, I thought about longshoremen—after all, as far back as 1954 I had seen Marlon Brando in the movie *On the Waterfront*. Also the manufacturers of clothing—everybody seemed to know that Carlo Gambino and his gang controlled trucking in the garment district.

A few years passed, and then suddenly, in September 1963, the Mafia was front-page news again. Joseph Valachi, a low-ranking member of the Genovese crime family, serving a life sentence for narcotics offenses and a murder in prison, was persuaded to tell his story, the story of the Mafia, complete with all the events to which he was privy, plus names, terminology, and dramatic description of the secret rituals. He testified before the Senate Permanent Investigations Subcommittee, chaired by John L. McClellan of Arkansas. "In millions of homes," reported *The New York Times,* "TV watchers shuddered at his lurid, gory picture of Cosa Nostra." "And yet," continued the reporter, "where will this public airing of material long familiar to police and law enforcement officials lead?"

The hearings did not result in any indictments; but they did contribute to pressures for Congress, over the next few years, to pass laws strengthening federal racketeering statutes. And Robert Kennedy, attorney general at the time, used the moment, in his words, "to encourage, arouse and sustain the vigilance of the public."

Yet in my role as a general contractor just beginning to do highrise work in New York City I saw and heard nothing out of the ordinary. In a final summing up of the hearings ("Robert Kennedy Defines the Menace," *New York Times Magazine*, October 13, 1963), there was specific mention of gambling, narcotics, prostitution, bootlegging, numbers operations, and loan-sharking. "Extortion" and "corrupt labor relations" were mentioned, but not in connection with any particular business. The only mention of construction was as one of a number of legitimate industries in which racketeers were beginning to take a financial interest.

I like to think that I'm not totally naive. The world of New York City construction has always seen its full share of illegal behavior; the 1960s and 1970s were no exception, and I wasn't wearing blinders during that period. It's just that, until the 1980s, I failed to recognize the prominent role played by the Mafia. Before the 1980s people were cheating—each other, institutions, and the government—falsifying, colluding, threatening, doing whatever bad things immoral, greedy, or desperate people have always done. Employees of the New York City Department of Buildings have been involved in graft and corruption for two hundred years. When KBF started working in the city, the police were taking payoffs, picking up monthly payments at construction jobs, using the threat of summonses for noise or dirt in the street. The testimony of Frank Serpico in late 1971 put a stop to police corruption, at least as far as we were concerned. Even the threat of a summons no longer fazed us since we could complain to the judges about harassment and invariably be spared a fine. Actually, after Serpico, behavior of the police changed dramatically, and gradually the ethos as well. A hopeful sign, incidentally, that codes of honorable behavior can be cultivated and that morality is not a lost cause.

At the Department of Buildings, however, improvement is still a work in progress. But this had little direct effect on our firm. Coping with municipal inspectors has always been, in the main, a problem for our various subcontractors, and as long as we were assured that neither quality of the work nor safety on the site was compromised, we let the subs handle things in their own way.

As for the Mafia, encountering no personal difficulties, I thought of its existence as merely a part of the human comedy. In fact, since Italian Americans played a prominent role in the industry, and since I took a liking to most of those I met, the thought of some stray Cosa Nostra presence wasn't without a certain appeal. The names were mellifluous, starting with the five families: Genovese (with Luciano and Gigante), Gambino (with Castellano and Gotti), Bonanno (with Galante and Massino), Colombo (with Profaci and Persico), Luchese (with Corallo and Amuso). Occasionally word would spread that one of the "made men," or a relative, was working on one of our jobs, or possibly just visiting, and there would be a ripple of excitement. In a few instances we were told that one of our subcontractors was connected to, or even owned by, one of the mob. To the extent that this might have been so—and in later years I was to see a few familiar names on lists of such firms—their prices were competitive and we could discern no irregularities in their performance. Attending social functions of Italian American societies—in lower Manhattan's Little Italy or certain defined areas in the outer boroughs—invariably the discussion would get around to how safe this particular neighborhood was, because the "community" wouldn't have it any other way.

Occasionally an Italian American group would express resentment at any association of their culture with criminal behavior. The director of the Italian Historical Society in America said that the Valachi hearings had "embarrassed 21 million productive, responsible Americans of Italian descent." This was something of a political hot potato, and New York senators Jacob Javits and Kenneth Keating took to the Senate floor to disavow any such implication. The fuss would die down, and life went on.

There appeared to be a heavy representation of Italian Americans among the various union officials, but that seemed natural since there were, from early days, many Italians among the ranks of New York construction workers. As a general contractor, my firm didn't deal directly with most of the unions—electricians, plumbers, carpenters, and the like. But those with which we did have contracts, that is, those who represented the few workers we had on our payrolls, seemed like pretty good guys, and by and large we got along with them very well.

There seems to be a lot of confusion about the rules that govern the ways in which unionized workers perform their jobs. Officials—and the public as well—complain about "featherbedding," seemingly

GOOD GUYS, WISEGUYS, AND PUTTING UP BUILDINGS

extraneous employees whose presence on the payroll drives up costs, and this is somehow associated with criminal behavior. The fact is that legally binding agreements are negotiated between the unions and contractors' organizations, and all contractors who are "union contractors"—which KBF has always been—have no choice in the matter. If we have a gang of laborers consisting of more than a certain number, we must hire a foreman; different types of equipment require operating engineers, and if there are more than a specified number of operating engineers on site then a "master mechanic" must be added to the payroll; elevator operators run the temporary elevators that carry workers up and down, while men from a different union handle hoists that carry materials, often making for a duplication that seems improper but is spelled out in formal agreements. Most notorious, a teamster must be hired for any project of a size specified in the current contract, the job of the teamster being to check all trucks delivering materials to make sure that the driver is a union member. Yes, these and other rules can seem outrageous. However, if we look back at the history of our industry we can see much inhumane exploitation of construction workers. So if the unions have managed to exert their powers in ill-advised ways it is perhaps understandable, a swinging of the pendulum that today, under fierce economic pressure, is already beginning to show signs of moderation.

In any event, the so-called featherbedding we pay for on our jobs is strictly legal and according to contract. All our competitors are subject to the same conditions, so we simply abide by the rules, pay the price, and figure the cost into our estimates. Naturally, if union leaders betray their members by giving up certain of their rights in exchange for bribes, that is another matter entirely. We have heard of that happening among a few subcontractors in the various specialty trades; but as general contractors, thank goodness, we have never been approached and would run fast in the opposite direction if we were.

There is one area in which we used to engage in a touch of friendly negotiation. With the teamsters, some of our jobs were marginal in cost and dimensions, just on the verge of the size that required a full-time union man. John Cricco, our friend of the people, would take on the role of the little guy, pleading poverty and promising to hire lots of teamsters once we made it to the big time. If he couldn't prevail on the basis of size he would play for time—"we're not really started yet, just pushing a little dirt around" or at the end of the job, "we're really finished, just doing a little patch-up; your man won't have anything to do." He did gain us a few weeks' grace here and there, particularly when he made a trip to union headquarters to plead his case. "Shows respect," he was told. A couple of the teamsters became friends of KBF field forces, following us from job to job, even showing up at our Christmas parties. They seemed to be good guys.

THAT'S the way it was all through the 1960s and 1970s. I had no idea of the ways in which the Mafia was gaining control of the unions and thus gaining the means to control the industry. And, of course, I was totally unaware of the fact that the FBI, using additional powers granted to them and moved by a new urgency emanating from Washington, Albany, and City Hall, had embarked on a campaign of taping Mafia conversations. I learned about this several years later, reading articles and books that rivaled in interest and excitement my favorite spy and detective novels. Incredibly, government agents were able to bug offices, cars, homes, and hangouts, recording many hours of talk between the bosses of the five families and their subordinates. It had always been frustratingly difficult to prove a connection between the top men and the crimes committed by their underlings. But now the evidence, from the bosses' own mouths, was piling up. Also, with the passage in 1970 of the federal law RICO (Racketeer Influenced and Corrupt Organizations Act), the means was finally at hand to prosecute the bosses even though they didn't involve themselves in the actual performance of murder and extortion. If it could be proved that an individual was "a member of an enterprise" that committed particular crimes, then that person could be found guilty of racketeering. Incidentally, harking back to my mention of the earliest crime movies, it has been speculated that the acronym for this law is a sly reference to the gangster hero-villain, Rico, played by Edward G. Robinson in *Little Caesar* (1930), often referred to as the grandfather of the modern crime film. When asked about this, the original drafter of the bill refused to either confirm or deny.

With these two developments gathering force—the Mafia's gaining power and using it, while FBI efforts were intensified and succeeding—an explosion was only a matter of time. In the late 1970s I began to hear rumors of troubles brewing in the construction industry, but the 1980s was the decade of denouement, and my true introduction to what was happening occurred in 1982.

I was attending a meeting with Joe DePaola and Walter Goldstein and a couple of their top aides, when Joe offhandedly informed me that they were closing down Dic-Underhill and completely retiring from the concrete business. I was shocked. Joe was in his early seventies, robust and fully committed to his work, while Walter, somewhat younger, seemed well satisfied to be engaged in a business that had been so fabulously successful. They made an odd couple: Joe, leader of Dic Concrete, boisterous field man and genius of the concrete trade, and Walter, founder of Underhill Construction, civil engineer graduate of Penn State, savvy in business, lover of fine wine and French cuisine. As explained to me by one of their people, the two had first worked together in 1961 and then more formally in 1966 as joint venturers performing the concrete work for Co-op City. In 1972 they founded Dic-Underhill and seemed to be living happily ever after. Here in 1982 they were suddenly giving it all up.

Why? I asked the question. Joe replied first: "I'm not as young as I used to be." Then, almost as an aside: "And I don't like the idea of going to jail." Walter's answer was more colorful: "I don't want to end up in the trunk of a car in the parking lot at LaGuardia Airport." I didn't ask any more questions.

Answers to questions I was tempted to ask were divulged three years later in the famous Mafia Commission trial. *Time* magazine called it the "case of cases." In February 1985 eleven Mafia figures, including the heads of the "five families," were indicted by U.S. Attorney Rudolph Giuliani under the RICO Act and placed under arrest. The charges included extortion, labor racketeering, and murder for hire. Trial before jury took place from September to November of 1986, and sentencing on January 13, 1987. During the course of that trial, Paul Castellano, one of the defendants, was murdered in Midtown Manhattan, another defendant died of cancer, and a third was granted a separate trial. The remaining eight were found guilty on all 151 counts, and each sentenced to serve one hundred years behind bars.

The Mafia was now the center of national attention, and right in the heart of it all was the New York City construction industry. A main feature of the trial was evidence attained from a bug placed in Paul Castellano's home. Recorded telephone conversations proved that the Mafia Commission had established a system to allocate all concrete contracts of $2 million or more to a preselected member of a "concrete club." The members of the club—seven in number, including Dic-Underhill—were to pay to the mob fees of 2 percent of each contract amount. Defense attorneys claimed that this arrangement benefitted the contractors, who, since the winning bidder was determined in advance, could raise their prices to exorbitant amounts before adding the 2 percent "fee" and that the process should be called bid rigging instead of extortion. But telephone conversations showed that the Mafia instigated the arrangement and used threats to enforce it. "I don't think I had much of a choice," testified James Costigan, president of the XLO Concrete Corporation. He related that Ralph Scopo, the Colombo soldier and president of the concrete workers' union, warned him that if he defied the system he would suffer unparalleled union miseries. And additional testimony revealed that Scopo would back up his threats of business destruction with threats of personal violence.

The concrete contractors, by turning state's evidence, were granted immunity from criminal prosecution. However, as evidence mounted in the criminal trial, the state of New York filed a civil antitrust suit claiming that this arrangement had been in place from 1978 to 1985 and that the contractors' overcharges had been on the order of 15 percent. The court subsequently granted summary judgement to the state on the charge of price-fixing, although not on the amount of damages. Eventually most of the contractors reached a financial settlement out of court.

The 1986 criminal trial was dramatic and breathtakingly revealing, but it didn't explain to me why DePaola and Goldstein, if they had been forced into the arrangement in 1978, would have abruptly closed their doors in 1982. Additional enlightenment came in the summer of 1987 when, in a second trial on racketeering, Joe DePaola and his top assistant, Frank Phelan, were called to testify. They told of meeting in 1980 and 1981 with Mafia boss Paul Castellano, who initially said that he wanted to buy Dic Concrete. "Mr. DePaola," wrote a *New York Times* reporter, "a feisty 77-year-old who is now retired," quoted Mr. Castellano as saying, "You are going to be my horse, Joe." To which Joe said he replied, "You better get yourself another horse, Mr. Castellano, because Joe DePaola is not going to be anybody's horse." The 2 percent arrangement was discussed, and DePaola also testified that, although he didn't sell Dic Concrete, he did sell his ready-mix supply company, Certified Concrete, to Biff Halloran, a defendant accused of controlling supply of concrete for the Mafia-run club.

At the end of this trial, Halloran was convicted of racketeering, along with Nicholas Auletta, owner of S&A Concrete, and two of his sidekicks, Anthony "Fat Tony" Salerno and Louis DiNapoli. As in the commission trial, the contractors who provided corroborative testimony were assured of immunity from criminal prosecution.

By the time this second trial was concluded I no longer wondered why Joe DePaola and Walter Goldstein had decided to close their business in 1982. I suppose they could have stayed at it for another three years, but caution, and perhaps some measure of moral discomfort, finally made the decision for them.

ANOTHER aspect of this trial that I found particularly interesting was the testimony of one Stanley Sternchos, owner of Technical Concrete. After Dic-Underhill ceased operations, we had gone out into the marketplace looking for a new concrete sub and found that Stanley submitted competitive bids. After checking his references, we gave him a job. His company performed well, and we were relieved to have found ourselves a new, seemingly reliable firm. During the period from 1982 to 1985 Technical did all of our high-rise jobs, five in number. I don't know whether or not we were assigned to Technical by the commission and the club, but their prices seemed right, and their work was good. In 1985 Stanley suddenly reported that he was having some problems, so we had to scramble out in the marketplace for someone new. And, sure enough, here in 1987 Stanley Sternchos was on the witness stand telling about his entry into the upper echelon of concrete subcontractors. He testified that in 1981 he had asked Ralph Scopo, the union leader and Colombo family member who had been convicted in the commission trial, to help him get a superstructure job. The amount of the contract was $3.5 million (higher than any concrete job on our books at that time), and Scopo, according to Stanley's testimony, had to check it out with Paul Castellano. Permission was granted, Sternchos paid the 2 percent— plus $10,000 for Scopo himself.

As I look back at the KBF records, after the departure of Technical in the mid-1980s we gave concrete contracts to a number of different companies: Riverview, Biltmore, Metro, Premium, Pinnacle, Sorbara. I trust that they were all independent, competitive, and competent and assume that the 2 percent Mafia arrangement had long been the stuff of ancient history.

The concrete club was certainly unique; but its demise did not mean the end of friendly relationships between general contractors and particular subs. There is a subtle difference between such understandings and organized bid rigging. Certainly during the period 1964–81, when Dic and then Dic-Underhill did all of our highrise work, everybody knew that this relationship was strong, based on long acquaintance and mutual reliance. Other concrete subs rarely bothered to give us a bid. I don't believe that KBF, or organizations we worked for, were hurt competitively by the arrangement. If a job had to comply with a government agency budget, Tony Bertone, Joe DePaola's longtime estimator, knew where his price had to be; and if we were in a competitive bidding situation, we always felt that the concrete bid we were given by Tony was helpful.

In some of the other key trades we had good friends, and doubtless their competitors knew it. Yet inevitably competitive forces would enter into the picture, and we would end up awarding contracts to a variety of firms. No one other than Joe DePaola had a monopoly on our work, or expected it.

THINKING back, perhaps our friendship with Joe DePaola helped insulate us from Mafia attentions. Yet I'm absolutely convinced that Joe himself was not a Mafia man. Anybody who ever attended an early morning meeting at the offices of Dic Concrete in Elmont, Long Island, could testify to Joe's total commitment to every detail of the work of the day. When it came to concrete he was fierce, energetic, and brilliant. He could never have achieved what he did if he had been engaged with the mob in criminal enterprise. Did he play ball with crooks and connivers of all sorts, corrupt politicians and unscrupulous union officials? I guess he did what he felt he had to do to make his way as a large concrete contractor in New York City in the second half of the twentieth century. In the end, after numerous investigations and trials, he was never accused of committing a crime, and rather than get into the business of being a mobster, he retired from the business he loved.

* * *

BUT let us assume that Joe was on friendly speaking terms with several members of the mob. Truth be told, I sometimes fantasized about what I would do if I was ever approached directly by the Mafia, and one possibility I considered was going to Joe for help.

Another possibility was presented to me as early as 1977, when Anthony Scaffidi, owner of Majesty Contracting Corp., made me an interesting offer. Tony had done several demolition jobs for us during the 1970s, being especially adept at clearing out the interiors of old commercial buildings that we converted into modern apartments. Unfortunately, Tony proved to be somewhat casual in the way he paid his men, a number of whom seemed to have recently arrived on these shores from abroad. This presented a problem on one job in particular where contract requirements included the submission of wage reports certifying that "prevailing wages" had been paid. Tony's reports ranged from incomplete to incomprehensible and promised to present serious problems. Somehow I was able to persuade the officials in charge—after half persuading myself—that the problem stemmed from the inadequacy of Tony's bookkeeping, that apparently the guy wasn't able to cope with red tape, that his contract was a tiny part of the whole, that nobody meant any harm, and so forth. This was the sort of bureaucratic battle that I invariably lost, but in this case, under the pressure of the agency wanting to close out the job, I managed to win. Tony was delighted. "Oh man," he said, "you done good." He put a hand on my shoulder, seemed to think for a moment, and then continued. "Look, Sammy boy"—"if you ever need help with one of the guys"—"if ya know what I mean"—"I did seven hard years in Danbury because I wouldn't snitch on nobody and they owe me." I thanked him and didn't think further about the offer—except occasionally when I would hear a chilling tale about the Mafia and wonder what would I do—if?

After that discussion with Tony, our firm didn't have any more jobs that required demolition, and I lost track of him—except for an unexpected encounter several years later. I was serving as an arbitrator, as I did occasionally for the American Arbitration Association, opting for small cases where only one arbitrator was involved. The hearing was ready to get under way when suddenly Tony walked into the room and sat down. He smiled and waved. I couldn't help smiling back, but immediately announced to all present that I knew this gentleman, Mr. Scaffidi, and in fact our two companies had done business together. The two parties discussed the matter briefly with their attorneys. Then the attorneys conferred and agreed on moving ahead, that Mr. Scaffidi was merely an acquaintance of the plaintiff's, that he played no important part in the case, and all present were confident in my ability to remain unbiased. So proceed we did. The plaintiff was a contractor who did small alteration jobs, claiming that he did work for the defendant but hadn't been paid. The defendant said that he considered the work unsatisfactory, and during his testimony pointed toward Tony and said that, by the way, that man had greeted him in the street one day when he was leaving his apartment house, backed him against a wall roughly, very roughly, and said that if he didn't pay up he'd be in big trouble. I couldn't help looking at Tony, who was grinning broadly and nodding his head. I was relieved when, during the lunch break, the parties reached a settlement. There were handshakes all around, Tony and I said our mutual "hi nice to see you," and that was that.

Some years later I was talking with a friend about Tony and wondering whether he was really connected with the Mafia or whether he had been making up his story in order to impress me. Subsequently this friend sent me an article from the *Newark Star-Ledger* making mention of Anthony Scaffidi—not my Anthony but his son. Apparently in 1983 the younger Scaffidi had pleaded guilty to a fourth-degree charge of conspiracy, served six months in jail, and was banned from working in the trash industry in New Jersey. The article minced no words: "He is a mobster, according to authorities, a known associate of the Genovese crime family." Does the son's crime reflect on the father? All I can say is that I now do believe that my Anthony, back in 1977, made an offer that did not come out of thin air.

* * *

THE individual who ranked number one on my secret mental list of those from whom I would have sought advice, or even help, if ever seriously threatened by the Mafia was my wife's uncle, Murray Gurfein. Murray was a distinguished federal judge, appointed to the United States District Court for the Southern District of New York in 1974, just in time to gain national prominence by rejecting the government's motion to enjoin *The New York Times* from publishing the Pentagon Papers. His ruling, initially reversed by a court of appeals, was ultimately reinstated by the Supreme Court. But it wasn't his legal accomplishments and fame that attracted me. Uncle Murray in his younger days had served as a top aide to Thomas E. Dewey, when Dewey was making his reputation as a special state rackets prosecutor, and Murray was instrumental in having the notorious Lucky Luciano put in jail. Then, during World War II, having served as an intelligence officer at the headquarters of the Supreme Allied Command in Europe, Murray returned to this country to negotiate with none other than Lucky Luciano. The objective was to gain Mafia help in protecting the New York City docks from sabotage, and purportedly, through the Italian branch, to support the American invasion of Sicily. As a reward for his cooperation, Luciano received a pardon from the then governor Dewey on the condition that he return to his native land. After the war, Murray Gurfein was an assistant to the United States chief counsel at the Nuremberg war crimes trials. Following successful years as a practicing attorney, he accepted the judgeship that capped his fabulous career.

On becoming a judge, Murray and his wife, Eva, bought a house near our woodsy retreat in Putnam County, where most weekends Murray would retire to work on his legal decisions. It was there that we spent a few social evenings together, and it was then that he entered my thinking as a potential counselor. Murray was reluctant to discuss his activities as an intelligence officer during the war and also as a so-called racket buster under Thomas Dewey. But I figured that anyone who had represented the government in negotiations with Lucky Luciano would be a good person to seek out if I ever got into difficulty with practically anybody in the world. Sad to say, Murray Gurfein died in late 1979, a loss for family, friends, and society as a whole. When, in the 1980s, Cosa Nostra's role in New York construction became the stuff of daily headlines, I could not help thinking how reassuring it would have been to have Murray nearby on weekends.

AS it turned out, I had no occasion to seek advice on dealing with the Mafia. After reading about the criminal trials that ended the careers of most of the mobster leaders, I rounded out my education by obtaining a copy of the Organized Crime Task Force report, the final version of which was issued in 1990. It was shocking to read that one of the city's outstanding construction firms carried on its payroll Harry Gross, a Teamsters racketeer, and Phillip Doran, a Teamsters business agent convicted of extortion. I didn't take this to mean that the reputable contractor was involved in unsavory business dealings but rather that the tentacles of the Mafia seemed to reach everywhere. It was even more alarming to learn that Frank DeCicco, underboss of the Gambino crime family, who was murdered by a car bomb in April 1986, had a no-show job with another major firm. The real power basis of the mob was proved by names and statistics showing that more than a dozen of the construction trade unions were controlled by made men or their underlings. And the Mafia-dominated cartels—not just concrete but also plastering, drywall, and painting—included firms who had performed work for my firm. Just by showing up for work in the morning I was entering a world rife with criminal activity.

The report had a statement that seemed directed especially toward me: "General contractors and construction managers responsible for general supervision of large construction projects sometimes acknowledge their awareness of racketeering, but claim to be ignorant of specific illegal activities." Yes, by 1990 I was certainly aware that Mafia racketeering was rampant in our industry, but could truthfully say that I had no knowledge of specific illegal acts. Is it possible that one or more of the laborers or teamsters on our payrolls had shady connections? Of course. It was widely known that several trucking firms who collected our trash and debris were owned by wiseguys; but it is common knowledge in many residential neighborhoods that their garbage collectors are a shady bunch, and nobody seems to make an issue of it.

The authors of the Goldstock report, as well as other people in law enforcement, politics, and in the general population, deplore the way the construction industry accepts the powerful Mafia presence, even seems comfortable with it. Never having been tested, I suppose that I have little right to speak out on the subject. Yet I'm quite certain that I would not ever willingly enter into any close connection with criminals. I do not claim to be a hero and cannot see myself taping conversations and turning them over to the FBI. If need be—at least this is how I have imagined things ever since I heard Joe DePaola say that he didn't want to go to jail and Walter Goldstein say that he didn't want to end up in the trunk of a car—I would have given up my business. Not being in a position to retire, I would have sought employment. Remembering the words of Jacques Kreisler, Sr., I was always reassured to have "a trade in my hands."

I may not be a stalwart crusading citizen, but neither do I make common cause with those who defend the situation as it is. "If people have a problem, they shouldn't build here." So said the late Lewis Rudin, a prominent real estate developer and cofounder of the Association for a Better New York, when questioned by a writer for *Fortune*. "Arrest us if we're corrupt. If there's something wrong with what I'm doing, put me in jail." I can understand this good man's exasperation, but I can't defend the status quo.

What to do? Support law enforcement; approve court-supervised oversight of certain labor unions; work toward rational improvement in municipal codes; subscribe to high-principled behavior by leaders in the building industry. Mundane, common-sense stuff, easy to shrug off yet important to pursue.

Progress has been made. The old leaders of the Mafia families have either died or been incarcerated for life, and many other members of the mob continue to be pursued through the courts. "The Mob in Decline: A Battered and Ailing Mafia Is Losing Its Grip on America"—thus was headlined a 1990 report by Selwyn Raab, a *New York Times* investigative reporter who covered mobster activities for three decades. Yet thirteen years later a headlined article appeared in the *Daily News* reporting a citywide caper:

February 27, 2003

Two Mafia bosses and their sons were busted yesterday with dozens of construction union officials for allegedly running a no-show job scam at every major building site in the city. Prosecutors charged the mob had a piece of the renovation of the Museum of Modern Art, the Mets and Yankees minor-league stadiums and even the building of a new Brooklyn federal courthouse. One group of wiseguys was busted after a bug was planted at a MoMA construction trailer.

The Genovese and Colombo families took control of two union locals, collecting the money through no-show deals in which mobsters and associates were paid for construction work they never did, prosecutors said.

"These unions are at every major job site in the city," said Deputy Inspector Brian O'Neill, commanding officer of the NYPD's Organized Crime Investigation Division. "It would be impossible to complete a job in New York without these unions."

CLEARLY much remains to be done. Yet now in the second decade of the twenty-first century, as police and FBI forces are increasingly concerned with the threats of international terrorism, the effort to eradicate Mafia domination of the construction industry will inevitably seem less critical. Of course, the five families have suffered serious setbacks, and through the passage of time and changing patterns of immigration and population resettlement, the Mafia may well wither away. Admittedly, as Selwyn Raab has written in his book, *Five Families,* "America's wiseguys have retained a precious asset that contributes to their survival. It is the media's romanticization of mobsters, subtly encouraging acceptance of the Mafia as just another aspect of the nation's culture." Yes, and this phenomenon goes beyond images reflected in the media. Consider the sentiments of Joseph O'Brien and Andrew Kurins, two FBI stalwarts who achieved one of the greatest anti-Mafia successes of all, the bugging of Paul Castellano's home. In their 1992 book, *Boss of Bosses,* they tell of observing the family leaders—those who were not already in prison—departing, in orderly, almost formal procession, from a meeting of the commission:

> Here they were, these mobsters, reduced to meeting in a dowdy little house in a frumpy little neighborhood, beset, archaic, at times almost comically inept; yet they also had this courtliness about them, this decorum it was all but impossible not to admire.

Even this Old World behavior may be vanishing. In a curious fashion, the decision of the United States Attorneys' Office in January 2010 to discontinue prosecution of John Gotti, Jr., after a hung jury ended their fourth failed attempt in court may have marked the end of what has been termed the mob's "celebrity era." After the abandonment of the Gotti prosecution, Robert Henoch, a former prosecutor, was quoted in *The New York Times* opining that a career in the Mafia is "much less glamorous than it was before."

I know that these men have been, and still are, criminals, murderers, brutes. But what will be the gain if the Italian mob goes into decline only to be replaced by Russians, Mexicans, or other gangs of thugs and desperadoes? And even if the Mafia were to be wiped from the face of the earth tomorrow, and likewise all the other immigrant gangs who follow, we would still be left with the criminality that seems to be deeply embedded in our industry. Violence isn't the only sin. In some ways the corruption of privileged citizens, people of education, financial advantage, and "respectability" is more distressing than the crimes committed by members of the underclass.

SIXTEEN | *Corruption*

BACK IN 1954, my then boss Joseph Blitz gave me an assignment that he said would help round out my education. We had recently completed a building in Queens, and I was to go to the New York City Department of Buildings to pick up a certificate of occupancy. "We usually have someone else who handles these things," Joe explained, "but he's away, and it will be a good experience for you." Construction was complete, final inspections had been conducted, and the papers were ready for distribution. He then told me exactly where to go, how I should ask for Mary Mulligan (I make up the name since I have long ago forgotten the real one), introduce myself, and Mary would tell me what to do. I would make the rounds, stopping at several desks, signing papers, and picking up documents along the way. And, oh, incidentally, here were some five dollar bills for me to drop into the people's desk drawers when they opened them. A few individuals were to get two of the bills, and Joe would give me a detailed list before I left.

"Joe," said I, aghast, "you're asking me to bribe city officials." "Oh, no," was his answer, "it's just a tip." "It's against the law, isn't it?" I protested. "Oh, come on. It's against the law to tip the mailman at Christmas time, but everybody does it. You're living in the real world now, kiddo."

In the end I did as I was told, and ever since have been expecting a law enforcement official to come knocking at my door carrying handcuffs. Although, after more than fifty years, it's beginning to look as if I'm not going to be punished for my misdeed.

Or perhaps all those years ago, dropping five dollar bills into opened desk drawers was really accepted as common custom. With the police, as I've already noted, before Serpico, monthly handouts were standard. And, as I rationalized at the time, those small payments to office clerks were not given in exchange for granting improper approval of unacceptable work. It was just what one did. I don't think that things are so casual anymore, but I can't say for sure. For many years now, our firm's permit processing has been delegated to recognized "expediters," the way other specialized work is assigned to lawyers and accountants; and we hope and expect that everything is done appropriately. How subcontractors handle their inspections and approvals I do not know. And what owners go through, along with their architects, to get plans processed through many complicated bureaucratic layers I also do not know. I suppose it could be said that I do not choose to know, yet I do not by any means assume that there is impropriety around every corner.

And yet there is. Simply by reading the newspapers I can see that scandal and malfeasance have been part of building department history forever. In 2008 a *New York Times* article about the New York City Department of Buildings was headlined "Agency with a History of Graft and Corruption," and examples were given dating to 1871. In "the latest debacle," according to the article, a review of the second fatal crane accident within three months revealed a faked inspection report plus violation of four local zoning regulations that should have prevented a building permit from being issued in the first place. The commissioner was forced to resign, although she had been doing her darnedest to improve efficiency, promote honesty, and all other good things.

Readers of newspapers come to take these things for granted. Oh, crooked building department inspectors: what else is new? Yet when we stop to think of it, some of the statistics are truly astonishing. In 1996, forty-two elevator inspectors were suspended, eighteen of whom pleaded guilty to federal charges, including extortion.

In 2002, nineteen of the city's twenty-four plumbing inspectors—including the chief inspector and the top supervisors in Manhattan, Brooklyn, Queens, and the Bronx—were charged with extorting hundreds of thousands of dollars to approve projects throughout the city. At one point nearly two-thirds of the plumbing inspectors who work for the city were under arrest. All nineteen of the accused eventually pleaded guilty.

And just when everything seems to have reached rock bottom, the situation gets worse. In 2009 three Luchese crime-family associates were found to have infiltrated the Department of Buildings, climbing to midlevel inspection jobs and according to officials, pocketing bribes of "tens of thousands of dollars a pop" according to the *New York Post*. The bribes were purportedly for granting building permits, expediting inspections, and overlooking building violations. Oh, great. Now we've got the Mafia setting up house within the building department.

LIKE most people, my interest is particularly piqued by scandals that are close to home, shocking events that involve people I know or know about. In this vein, I was intrigued to read, back in 1994, that the U.S. attorney charged several present and former New York City Board of Education employees with bribery, fraud, and other crimes connected to the award of school contracts and payments owed to contractors. Six years earlier the state and city had stripped the Board of Education of its responsibilities for contracting and created the New York City School Construction Authority (SCA). Everybody agreed that this was a good and necessary move, since the board's record was abysmal, new schools being constantly late in completion and way over budget in final price. I personally was pleased, since I had long been convinced that the board's personnel were totally ineffectual or, more probably, corrupt. One company in particular—Mars-Normel Construction—submitted bids so low that they must have known large change orders were sure to follow. And here was vindication. The owner of Mars-Normel had pleaded guilty to submitting fraudulent invoices totaling $4.5 million. Board of Ed. officials were implicated, and various plea bargains were negotiated. Yes, there was some small satisfaction in knowing that I had been right in my suspicions—but all in all, cold comfort.

IT is reassuring to learn that the illegal payments—be they extortion or bribery or, as is often the case, a mix of both—only rarely entail the knowing cover-up of defects that imperil the public. This may happen from time to time in places like Egypt, Nigeria, or even China, where buildings fall down and faulty design and construction, approved by corrupt officials, have been found to be the cause. But that is not the case in the world with which I am familiar. Sometimes codes are skirted to add space to a building or otherwise evade design standards. But not to hide an overtly dangerous condition. The Engineering Performance Information Center at the University of Maryland has analyzed hundreds of disasters in completed buildings, and in almost every case the cause of failure is found to be ignorance, carelessness, faulty calculation, and the like. Corruption has many bad consequences, but serious accidents invariably are found to be caused by errors in design. It can be argued that incompetence, particularly if linked to laziness or negligence, is immoral. But that is not what we mean when we talk about corruption in the construction industry.

The big money isn't paid to save a few pounds of steel or a bit of cement in the concrete mix; it is paid to save interest on building loans or the idling of a working crew. Builders need to keep moving, and the main weapon possessed by criminals in the building department is the power to delay.

Safety violations, such as they may be, usually present a danger during construction and are more a peril for the building tradesmen than they are for the public. In this area the building department is only one of several oversight forces, and often not the most important one. Creation of the federal Occupational Safety and Health Administration (OSHA) in 1970 has accomplished much. Also, insurance companies support the imposition of safety standards, joining private enterprise to government oversight, often an annoyance to contractors, but in the end much to the benefit of all.

IN trying to combat corruption at the building department level, many developers and builders have proposed simplifying the system. Redesign the bureaucratic process, they say, so that there are fewer opportunities for scoundrels to frustrate honest effort to build speedily and economically. One idea that has been tried, and for which I personally have had high hopes, is the delegation of certain inspection authority to private organizations using professionally licensed engineers. When a change in the building code put the testing of concrete—both in the mixing plant and at the job site—in the hands of specialized testing laboratories run by licensed engineers, I thought it was a wonderful development. But I was doomed to disappointment. In early 2009 a grand jury indicted Testwell Group, the largest material-testing laboratory in the New York City area, for systematically falsifying test results and overbilling clients. The firm and its top executives were found guilty of enterprise corruption. American Standard Testing and Consulting Laboratories took Testwell's place in the city; but in August, 2011, its executives were arraigned on charges of fabricating virtually all of its work for the past twelve years. (They pleaded not guilty.) Good grief. I have taken such pride in being an engineer. Years ago I devoted much time and energy studying for the examinations one has to take in order to earn a professional engineer's license. I did this even though I knew that as a contractor such a license would be of little practical value.

Although I like to believe that engineers rank high on the morality scale, I have long known that they can go astray. Spiro Agnew, when he was governor of Maryland, oversaw a system in which engineering firms working on state construction contracts paid kickbacks that went 25 percent to the state official who arranged the deal, 25 percent to the official who brought the deal to Agnew, and 50 percent directly to Agnew himself. "In retrospect," says Richard

Cohen, who covered the scandal for *The Washington Post,* "you wonder how anybody got away with it because thousands of people knew what was going on." Agnew chose to resign the vice presidency as part of a plea bargain that allowed him to avoid going to jail for income tax evasion in connection with the kickbacks. "It was all kickbacks and bribes," continues Cohen. For a reporter "it was heaven . . . a golden age of corruption."

It is amazing how all of us, newspaper readers, citizens, just folks, can't help getting a kick out of political scandals, the derring-do of rascals. Not so different from the Mafia mystique. Yet what we really want is for honesty to prevail, and while we may pray that the moral tone of society can be improved, our immediate best hope must rest in law enforcement. Years after the Agnew scandal, newsman Cohen reported that "things have changed. It isn't what it used to be. What happened in Maryland is that you started to get strong U.S. attorneys and that made a big difference." The same sort of thing has happened in New York City, and while we still have a long way to go, there seems to have been some progress since Boss Tweed and Tammany Hall swindled $200 million from the city in the 1860s.

ALTHOUGH my main area of interest may be New York City, the Agnew scandal serves to remind us that the Big Apple is not the national center of corrupt public officialdom, not by any means. Just flip through a few past issues of *Engineering News-Record* and one sees that crooked politicians and state employees in other parts of the land may be even more creative than our local breed. In Washington, D.C., the branch chief of a Federal Highway Administration center pleads guilty to taking bribes for letting contractors submit fraudulent invoices totaling more than $200,000. A former head of the Connecticut Department of Transportation pleads guilty to charges growing out of alleged kickbacks, larceny, and bid rigging. A former member of the Texas Department of Housing and Community Affairs was sentenced to eighty-seven months in prison and ordered to pay $783,455 in restitution following her conviction for conspiracy, theft, and bribery. She was involved in a scheme to falsely obtain federal income tax credits for construction of affordable housing. In every corner of the land, government officials have participated in crimes connected with construction projects.

When we talk about corruption and politicians we inevitably stray into the gray area of influence and politics, favors exchanged, contributions solicited, activities that are legal but that tend to make us uncomfortable. Yet in a society where lobbying is a multimillion dollar industry and where real estate developers traditionally make enormous contributions to political campaigns, we have to be cautious about casting the first stone. Whatever is legal at the moment is—well—legal; and it is not my purpose here to wander into the never-never land of debating the law. We seem to have enough problems simply staying within the laws as they exist.

ALTHOUGH many of the most choice corruption stories feature the activities of government employees, private entrepreneurs have proved well able to perform criminal acts without the help of crooked politicians. The world of civil corruption is every bit as lively as the realm of political shenanigans.

A prime example is the scandal, culminating in 1998, of the half dozen firms headlined by *The New York Times* as "An Elite Who Build the Interiors of Offices." My introduction to this "elite" had come many years earlier during the cocktail hour that preceded a gathering of an industry organization. A stranger who had apparently downed a couple of drinks too many came up to me, studied my name tag, and chuckled. "Ha!" he said. "I've seen your sign on a couple of buildings going up in Midtown, big, beautiful stuff, and I want to congratulate you." Then, giving me a friendly poke in the chest, "Very nice having your sign in the sky, but what I do is just alterations to offices in a few classy Madison Avenue buildings, and I guarantee that I make a lot more money, quietly and out of sight, than you do with your fancy skyscrapers." Doubtless he was right. Working in the offices of flagship corporate America, on jobs designed by some of the world's fanciest decorators, profit margins must have been comfortable. What I didn't know was that his niche of the marketplace was rife with price-fixing, kickbacks, bribes, and every other slippery practice one can imagine. Profit margins were not comfortable; they were prodigious.

Our firm wasn't about to move off in a completely new direction, so I gave very little thought to interior office construction until, in 1975, a newspaper article caught my eye. An employee of H.L. Lazar Construction Company, one of the city's biggest builders of office interiors, had been caught paying bribes, not only to building inspectors but also to real estate owners and managers as a means of securing contracts at inflated prices. About thirty private-sector individuals, including the owner, Howard Lazar, had pleaded guilty to conspiring to commit a bribe and were fined and sentenced to serve a number of weekends in jail on Rikers Island. That's where I lost track of things until two years later, when Mr. Lazar's name was again in the papers, and this time with consequences most unusual and sad.

The construction part followed a familiar pattern. H.L. Lazar was hired by the JC Penney Company to renovate the firm's New York offices, and a Penney employee was found guilty of not paying income taxes on the $1.3 million dollars he personally skimmed from the project. Penney sued the Lazar firm for improper overcharges, and the litigation was settled when Lazar agreed to repay the astonishing sum of $2.5 million. That seemed to put an end to the matter; but unexpectedly, the audit committee, reviewing the figures to calculate the overpayments, found that Lazar had performed work in the apartment of Kenneth S. Axelson, Penney's senior vice president and director of finance and public affairs. Axelson had paid Lazar's bill of $807.85 for the work; but when the problems arose about overcharging on the office project, this amount was questioned. Axelson had an independent estimate prepared that indicated the work to be worth $6,423, and he placed the difference between the estimate and what he had been billed—$5,615.15—in an escrow account. The audit committee ruled that no impropriety was entailed and recommended that this escrowed amount be paid over to Penney. Questions were raised, however, not only about propriety but about the value of the work.

Kenneth Axelson was a man I liked and respected. Leaders of the city's financial community, most of whom had spent time with him during the year he spent as a volunteer deputy mayor during the city's fiscal crisis, thought him a prince. The outpouring of support was extraordinary, as noted in *The New York Times* piece, "Axelson's Friends Ponder His Fall from Grace." It all would have blown over except that Ken had been on the verge of nomination as deputy secretary of the Treasury Department, and the Carter administration, informed about pending newspaper disclosures of the Penney-Lazar matter, abruptly accepted his request to be withdrawn from consideration. The date was March 9, 1977. Within days JC Penney invited Axelson to return to his executive position, and Governor Carey asked him to rejoin the State Emergency Financial Control Board. But Kenneth Axelson went into seclusion in Maine. "It's my life," he said, "my career, my reputation, my dignity and my self-esteem."

Perhaps it was irrational for me to consider Lazar as the evil demon in this tragic fall from grace; but that's the way I felt.

Twenty years were to pass before I had occasion to think of Howard Lazar again. June 16, 1998, a featured story in *The New York Times* revealed that "five top executives and four companies in the construction industry have agreed to plead guilty to collecting kickbacks and rigging the bidding on billions of dollars in renovation work for many of the city's most powerful corporations during the 1900s." One of the executives was Howard Lazar.

The following year thirty-one architects, real estate brokers, and managers as well as twenty-four companies pleaded guilty to bribery charges relating to bid rigging on construction projects. It was announced that this was part of a continuing five-year investigation into corruption in the $6 billion interior construction business. Involved was work in the offices of some of the city's most prominent corporations, including Morgan Stanley and Sony. Most of the people who pleaded guilty were sentenced to probation and ordered to pay fines. One, an interior designer, was sentenced to three years in prison.

This was all very interesting, and dispiriting, but by this time my main interest in the interior construction business had shifted from Howard Lazar and his gang to another individual—and this person happened to be in jail. Ted Kohl was the son of Sam Kohl, founder in 1938 of Herbert Construction Co., and friend and coventurer with our firm on two projects, one in 1966, the other in 1985. Herbert had a wonderful reputation, mainly because Sam Kohl was a wonderful man and an excellent builder. Amongst his clients were several of the city's most elegant department stores. I can only imagine Sam's shock and dismay when, in the summer of 1995, Ted was arrested on charges that he had bilked several major corporations out of more than $7 million in an elaborate kickback scheme. Whoever prepared the indictment saw fit to include the fact that Ted, with his ill-gotten gains, had purchased a Porsche, a Land Rover, and a Mercedes-Benz, as well as a $46,000 wristwatch. Ted Kohl, at the age of fifty-three, went to prison. Eventually, in exchange for cooperation with government agents, he was granted a five-year parole destined to expire in the summer of 2005.

Shortly before the parole was scheduled to end, Ted Kohl was back in handcuffs. This time he and a partner were accused of taking $2.5 million from a high-end retailer; then, instead of paying subcontractors, they pocketed the money and put their firm into bankruptcy. The name of the firm, incidentally, was IDI, standing for "I Deserve It." Pleading guilty, Ted Kohl returned to prison under a sentence of four to ten years. I felt it was a blessing that his father, Sam, did not live to see this second moment of disgrace.

I tend to think of the interior construction scandals in terms of Ken Axelson's shame and the dishonoring of Sam Kohl's legacy. But occasionally I recall my own passing contacts with that cesspool of corruption and shudder at what might have been. In the mid-1980s, just before Borg and Florman took in a new partner and CEO, we seriously considered the possibility of selling the company or merging it with a going entity and taking a less active role. The likely prospects included large and successful companies who were doing interior alteration work but who might consider branching out by taking on a conventional builder such as us. Among such prospects, the most plausible was Sam Kohl and his Herbert Construction Co. In 1986 our two firms were completing a joint venture, and I took advantage of the occasion to mention the possibility to Sam. As far as the future was concerned, Sam said, he was out of the picture and Ted would be the one to contact. This we did, and Ted seemed to take the idea quite seriously, at least to the extent of sending one of his top financial men to our office to review figures and discuss possibilities. Questions of honesty and business practices were never considered, our long-standing relationship with Sam being all the reassurances needed on both sides. (Ted's problems with the law were almost a decade in the future.) There followed two or three in-depth reviews and discussions; but it soon became clear that on the question of dollar value there was no meeting of the minds. With friendly assurances on both sides, the matter was dropped.

What would have happened if a deal had come to fruition? Would we have found ourselves in partnership with a criminal? Or, not quite as bad but still a grim possibility: would we have sold our company only to find its name associated with illegality and scandal? I shudder to think.

As the years seemed to fly by, the principals of KBF found themselves considering, with increasing seriousness, the possibility of sale or merger. One day in late 2008 an accountant friend called to say that the owners of Lehr Construction Corporation, a big interiors firm, might well be interested in adding a new-buildings division, and the possibilities might be worth exploring. A get-together was arranged, but when I learned that the principal with whom we were scheduled to confer was named Gerald Lazar, I heard the faint and distant buzzing of alarms. "Lazar," I asked. "Wasn't he in prison?" No, I was reassured; you're thinking about this man's brother. A different firm altogether. Oh, OK. A meeting occurred, and then another two or three exploring real possibilities. As we had come to expect, the value placed on an aging construction company by potential buyers didn't seem to measure up to anything that we found worthy of consideration, and that seemed to be the case here. So with the exchange of pleasantries, that was the end of that.

However, on a subsequent day, as I was engaged in research for this present book, I checked out several *New York Times* articles relating to Howard Lazar's plea of guilty to bribery and the prison sentence that followed. In a June 18, 1998, article I came across this statement: "His brother, who pleaded guilty to the same charge, was given a suspended sentence and is expected to continue to run the family's contracting firm, Lehr Construction." In an article describing a trial the following year, it was revealed that the owner of a design firm was to be sentenced to three years in prison for taking more than $1 million in bribes from two contractors, one of which was—Lehr Construction. And then, a decade later, in March of 2010, another bombshell, this time a *Times* headline: "District Attorney Raids Office of Construction Company." *Raids office!* Who? And why? "The Manhattan district attorney's office raided the offices of Lehr Construction early Wednesday, seizing project records, bidding documents and other records as part of a growing investigation into the interior construction industry." In February 2011 the firm filed a voluntary petition under Chaper 11 of the bankruptcy code. I try to avoid playing the fruitless game of "what if?"; but sometimes it's difficult to resist.

THE field of interior office construction, with its big-ticket scandals and big-name clients, may dominate the headlines in the real estate pages, but there are many allied fields that also warrant attention. For example, apartment managers, overseeing maintenance work on co-op and condo buildings, have been found working closely with contractors in bid-rigging and kickback schemes. Investigation of the "waterproofing" specialty—which encompasses costly roofing and brickwork repairs—has uncovered improprieties of startling extent and sophistication. In 1994 more than seventy-two managing agents—at some of Manhattan's most exclusive apartment buildings— were indicted on charges of extorting millions of dollars from seven maintenance contractors; and the contractors, of course, were found to be boosting their prices to cover the kickbacks, as well as conspiring to inflate prices. In 1999 there was another round of indictments, this time aimed at managers of middle-income housing projects. Several waterproofing companies were found to have changed their names in anticipation of the legal assault; but it appears that the problem, and the assault, will be part of the city scene forever.

Waterproofing is often a building's most expensive single maintenance cost, and apartments the most numerous type of structure. But the illegal practices are not limited to any construction specialty or any single kind of building. The director of maintenance operations at a college was indicted on charges that he took more than $25,000 in kickbacks when he helped a contrator get two maintenance contracts worth more than $1 million. A short time later the college announced that the gentleman in question had resigned his position.

I could go on listing individual instances of corruption in the field of building maintenance and repairs; but let me sum up with the testimony of a single individual whose company installs air conditioning units in existing buildings. This casual acquaintance told me in an offhanded way—as if I knew what everybody knows— that he paid fees, that is, bribes or kickbacks, to management officials in every type of building I could name: apartments, schools, hospitals, theaters, factories, army barracks, even churches. And then he paid substantial "tips" to workers in the buildings: superintendents, elevator men, handymen, and all the rest. The bribes were an essential element in obtaining work, the tips an essential feature of performing the work with a minimum of unnecessary delay. And, oh yes, of course, there were payoffs to any and all inspectors from government agencies whose approval was required.

I do believe that this individual, for dramatic effect, was overstating the case. But maybe not by much. It's almost enough to make a general contractor feel virtuous. We don't hide away in existing buildings, working in the clutter of dark recesses, cutting and patching, doing work that nobody can readily evaluate, making deals in hidden corners. We are out in the open, erecting new structures, in plain view, proud of what we do and who we are, announcing our presence with large signs (when the owners allow). For the most part we are the good guys, with reputations to maintain, good names to uphold.

Yet no sooner do I start to think along these lines than I read that a manager at Turner Construction Company has pleaded guilty in state supreme court to grand larceny by extortion because he sought out subcontractors the firm supervised on city agency contracts and coerced them to perform work at his home. Turner suspended the man and subsequently fired him. One of the biggest, most reputable construction companies in New York, in the nation, in the world.

But large companies—Turner has about five thousand employees—are bound to have an occasional embarrassment. At KBF some years ago we discharged an individual for improper handling of funds, and we may well have had other ne'er-do-wells among our small force that have gone undetected. How about other industries?

Perhaps we ought to challenge the assumption that construction is a special focus of corruption. Yes, we have the Mafia, tainted building departments, crooked unions, conniving contractor cartels, and all the rest. But maybe our corruption is simply more colorful, more out in the open than that of other fields. In a survey of construction industry people (including owners and architects) conducted in 2004 by the management consultant FMI in conjunction with the Construction Management Association of America, 84 percent of 270 respondents encountered or observed "unethical" behavior in the past year, 50 percent "yes, but on less than three occasions," 34 percent "yes, many times." Those figures are troubling, to be sure. Yet that one survey is not definitive, and it tells us nothing about the business world in general. When we think of financial scandals, what comes first to mind? Enron, Tyco, WorldCom, savings and loan, Billie Sol Estes, Robert Vesco, Global Crossing, Boesky, Madoff . . . a long, long list before we come to construction companies.

Even the large manufacturing corporations, the sort that I always thought were immune to unlawful intrigue, seem not to be prim and proper at all. I was naive to assume that crooked schemes could only be cooked up by small groups of piratical conspirators. When, in 2004, the former chief financial officer of the Boeing Company pleaded guilty to a felony, having secretly offered a job to an air force official while she was overseeing billions of dollars in contracts and, by her own admission, favoring Boeing, he—the former chief financial officer of Boeing—signed a remarkable document. "Members of the company's senior management," he confessed, "discussed the possibility of employing" the air force official. He had then sent an e-mail message to senior Boeing executives saying he "had a 'non-meeting'" with the official and suggesting that another Boeing representative follow up, which was done. The Boeing CFO who confessed was given a four-month prison term, and the air force official was sentenced to nine months. After lengthy and delicate negotiations, Boeing agreed to "accept responsibility" and pay a substantial fine but managed to avoid criminal charges. When one considers that the deal being discussed was for tanker planes worth $23 billion, all construction corruption pales by comparison.

And of course, as we struggle to recover from the recession of 2008, the real villains of the marketplace seem to be not the hardworking builders but rather the financial institutions.

EACH of us has favorite business scandals to discuss, those we've read of in the press and those we know about through personal experience or gossip. But is there any way to approach the topic of corruption with statistical rigor? Not really. Since corruption is in its very essence secret, it is impossible to "measure" statistically. In a *New York Times* op-ed article entitled "Counting Corporate Crooks," Stacy Horn complains that in the United States we don't keep even the most basic statistics on white-collar crime, such as counting such crimes or even recording numbers of arrests. Police departments must report to the FBI regularly every "serious" crime committed in their jurisdiction along with arrest statistics, all published annually in a report called *Crime in the United States*. But nothing on bribes, kickbacks, extortion, accounting tricks, and all that stuff, much of which, Ms. Horn acknowledges, is difficult to classify, legally speaking.

Transparency International evaluates nations on a corruption ranking; but the organization admits that its findings are based on "perception," mainly the way employees of multinational firms and institutions assess the behavior of public officials and politicians. Traditional leaders in the "least corrupt" listings are New Zealand, Denmark, Singapore, Sweden, Switzerland, Finland, Netherlands, Australia, Canada, and Iceland. The United States usually ranks about fifteenth, not too bad, all things considered. As one would expect, the less developed nations dominate the ranks of the most corrupt. However, Transparency International qualifies this finding with the note that "industrial countries that succeed in keeping a clean profile at home may be bribing officials abroad and thus bear a much higher burden of responsibility for corruption than the ranking can indicate."

OF all the transgressions I've encountered in the construction industry, the one that I find most offensive is an act that is hardly ever exposed to the public, something that I hear about in quiet asides, in whispers, in gossip. Certain individuals, working for certain general contractors, are rumored to extort money, secretly, from subcontractors, pocketing the money in exchange for awarding inflated contracts. They do this not only on cost-plus contracts, where the victim is a client, but also on fixed-price contracts, in which case they are deceiving—really stealing from—the people they work for or with: their employers, their partners, or, if there is a profit-sharing plan, their coworkers as well. Legally, I suppose that a kickback is a kickback, a crime is a crime, and I seem to be asking for honor among thieves. But no, I decry the corrupt act wherever it occurs and regardless of the identity of the parties. Yet I cannot help feeling worse where deception of close associates is involved.

★ ★ ★

WE are all against evil but are constantly judging human frailty by capricious emotional standards. If, in *Les Misérables*, Jean Valjean steals a loaf of bread to feed his starving family, we find it difficult to condemn him. How about the contractor who, bitter but resigned, pays a few dollars to obtain a document that he has earned and now desperately needs? I cannot condone; but I can empathize. And someone who accedes reluctantly to threats of violence? Who will presume to play the hero? As for the undisputably bad guys? Well, they're the bad guys; but how many of them are there?

Is it possible that reading so many reports about thievery we get carried away and lose our sense of proportion? How about the many decent, honorable people we meet in our industry? I cherish the trust that I have felt for partners, employees, fellow workers, and clients.

So what do we do?

Sermons and mutual pledges of virtue are to be applauded. At the same time, in the mode of "praise the Lord and pass the ammunition"—a chaplain's exclamation at Pearl Harbor—we would do well to rely on, and support, energetic law enforcement efforts. Ambitious and efficient attorneys general and government agents, encouraged by a free press and a politically active public, have proved to be effective.

As for ourselves, as individuals, I think that Maimonides had it about right. Moses Maimonides, the great Torah scholar of the Middle Ages, suggested: "One should see the world, and see himself, as a scale with an equal balance of good and evil. When he does one good deed, the scale is tipped to the good—he and the world are saved. When he does one evil deed, the scale is tipped to the bad—he and the world are destroyed."

SEVENTEEN | *Affirmative Action*

THE CIVIL RIGHTS MOVEMENT, as it burst forth after World War II, caught me by surprise. Like many northeasterners, I found it exhilarating and alarming in almost equal measure. In New York City we had no blatant discriminatory laws to be challenged, so the early part of the drama we watched from afar. But when the battle for legal rights was followed by a campaign for equal economic opportunity, our town was affected perhaps more than any other place in the nation. The struggle for "affirmative action," much of which was centered on the construction industry, brought with it some of the most memorable experiences of my professional career.

Born and reared in a New York City cocoon, I had blithely assumed that our nation was heading irresistibly toward the end of racial discrimination. At the Ethical Culture Fieldston School, founded by Felix Adler as the Workingman's School in 1880, our education was imbued with the pursuit of "social justice, racial equality, and intellectual freedom." In our weekly ethics classes the topic of equality was always high on the agenda, and I remember a particular day when Walter White, executive secretary of the NAACP, came to speak with us. He discussed how African Americans were not able to find jobs as salespersons in the city's major department stores, and how an effort was under way to gain access to such employment. I was surprised to learn that discrimination of that sort existed, but satisfied that the problem was being worked on and would soon be solved. I had only the vaguest idea of what life was like in the South.

New York was very much a city of immigrants and ethnic variety. Differences were part of the atmosphere. When I went to see baseball games at the Polo Grounds I walked comfortably through Harlem, although never giving much thought to why all the major league players were white. During my senior year in high school (1941–42), I spent many weekend evenings at the jazz clubs on Fifty-second Street, where the prominence of black musicians seemed natural. At Kelly's Stable, Red Allen on trumpet and J.C. Higginbotham on trombone, two of the outstanding black musicians of the day, played great Dixieland music alongside Pee Wee Russell, a white clarinetist, and nobody thought anything about it. In 1935, Benny Goodman, leader of the most popular big band, had asked the noted black pianist Teddy Wilson to join his trio, and the following year Lionel Hampton on vibes to form the Benny Goodman Quartet. At his epochal 1938 concert in Carnegie Hall, Goodman was joined by several famous black musicians. This was integration in the world's cultural temple. I didn't stop to think that Marian Anderson, the first African American to sing at the Metropolitan Opera, was not welcome on their stage until 1955. And as for Benny Goodman, it never occurred to me that if he had dared tour with his band in the South he would have been arrested, if not physically assaulted. In other words, while I was relatively free of prejudice, I was also relatively oblivious to the separation of the races and the prevalence of injustice in the nation.

When, in 1947, Jackie Robinson broke the color line in baseball, I thought "great," and when the following year President Truman ordered the integration of the armed forces I thought "fine, about time." In 1954 the U.S. Supreme Court, in *Brown v. Board of Education,* outlawed public school segregation, and I took this for granted as another step in an orderly and inevitable process. But, as it turned out, this was just the beginning of a crusade, more intense and filled with drama than anything I could ever have imagined.

The definitive event in my awakening was when, in September

of 1957, Governor Orval Faubus of Arkansas ordered out the National Guard to prevent nine African American students from entering Little Rock Central High School, and President Eisenhower, after federalizing the National Guard and ordering them to return to their barracks, deployed elements of the 101st Airborne Division to protect the students from hostile crowds and to enforce the federal court order authorizing their admission. This was a war, I could see, with elements of hatred and fear that were deep-rooted.

The rest of the Civil Rights Movement unfolded before my opened eyes, mostly seen through the gauze of television and newspapers, but starkly defined nevertheless. Beginning in 1960 there were a series of dramatic sit-ins against segregated lunch counters throughout the South. In May of 1961 the first Freedom Riders gathered in Washington and set off on a fateful journey. Their mission was to challenge the southern Jim Crow laws, but their scheduled trip to New Orleans was terminated in Jackson, Mississippi, because of violent counterreactions, the savagery of which shocked the nation. However, the rides continued, as did the violence. Gradually, the atmosphere seemed to calm somewhat, aided by the 1963 March on Washington, when Martin Luther King, Jr., delivered his "I Have a Dream" speech. There followed the Civil Rights Act of 1964, the Voting Rights Act of 1965, and the Civil Rights Act of 1968, all passed by Congress and signed by President Johnson.

The war was won, legally and constitutionally. But hostility continued to simmer, culminating in the murder of Martin Luther King, Jr., April 4, 1968. It soon became apparent that the struggle for equality and social justice would be ongoing.

THE protection of civil rights by banning discrimination, while a crucial step forward, did not guarantee equality in the world of commerce. Achieving full citizenship quickly loses its luster if it is not accompanied by an equal opportunity to earn a living. Thus affirmative action—the effort to help minorities get an equitable share of jobs and business opportunities—followed hard on the heels of the civil rights movement. In 1961, three years before the Civil Rights Act, President Kennedy had established the Committee on Equal Employment Opportunity and subsequently issued an executive order using the term "affirmative action" to refer to any measures generated to achieve nondiscrimination. In 1965 President Johnson issued an executive order requiring federal contractors to "take affirmative action" toward prospective minority employees. "We seek not just freedom," he said, "but opportunity." (Gender was specifically included in 1968.)

Perhaps most remarkable, on March 23, 1973, the Nixon administration's Department of Justice, Department of Labor, Equal Employment Opportunity Commission, and Civil Service Commission issued a joint memorandum titled "State and Local Employment Practices Guide." The guide pointed out that the administration "since September of 1969 recognized that goals and timetables . . . are a proper means for helping to implement the nation's commitment to equal employment opportunity." While strict quotas were not encouraged, goals based on specific timetables were.

Before long, as could have been predicted, a counterreaction set in. Passionate objections were raised to purported "reverse discrimination." In 1978 the Supreme Court ruled in *Regents of the University of California v. Bakke* that, while race was a legitimate factor in school admissions, the use of quotas was not constitutional. A 1989 Supreme Court ruling in *City of Richmond v. Croson* held that a program setting aside 30 percent of city construction funds for black-owned firms violated the equal protection clause of the Fourteenth Amendment. In 1997 the voters of California approved Proposition 209, which banned all forms of affirmative action. And so it has gone, with the courts and with the voters, back and forth, continuing into the twenty-first century.

The executive branch of government, as well as the courts, grappled with the problem. President Reagan (1981–89), in a backlash against affirmative action, cut funding for the Equal Opportunity Commission and the civil rights division of the Justice Department, drastically reducing federal action against job discrimination and segregation in schools and housing. President Clinton (1993–2001) bobbed and weaved a bit: "When affirmative action is done right, it is flexible, it is fair, and it works." However: "It should be changed now to take care of those things that are wrong, and it should be retired when its job is done." President Obama, debating as a candidate, said: "I still believe in affirmative action as a means of overcoming both historic and potentially current discrimination; but I think that it can't be a quota system and it can't be something that is simply applied without looking at the whole person, whether that person is black, or white, or Hispanic, male or female. What we want to do is make sure that people who'd be locked out of opportunity are going to be able to walk through those doors of opportunity in the future"—a statement that *The Boston Globe* called "intriguing but vague."

OF course, I had a special interest in New York City, which had its own calendar of events. In the postwar years, as the city started to lose its manufacturing base, just as there was an influx of southern and Caribbean minority workers, construction jobs became especially attractive. In the summer of 1963, Mayor Robert F. Wagner (1954–65) found protesters occupying his office, demanding more construction jobs for blacks and Puerto Ricans. He allowed them to spend the night undisturbed, then met with them to discuss their grievances. John V. Lindsay (1966–73) made repeated efforts to appease minority militants, whereas Ed Koch (1978–89) chose to downplay activism. (I've skipped over Abe Beame because in his short term, 1974–77, he was so overwhelmed with the city's financial crisis that he hardly had energy for anything else.) Koch's successor, David Dinkins (1990–93), the first and so far only African American to hold the office, set a new standard for aggressive action, directing city agencies to not only set aside jobs for minority workers but also to award 20 percent of the city's $3 billion in contracts for goods and services to companies with black, Asian, female, or Hispanic owners, even when their bids were as much as 10 percent higher than those of other companies. When running for reelection he claimed that the city had nearly doubled the value of contracts going to such firms, ending a long-standing pattern of discrimination. But a detailed analysis of the program by *The New York Times* showed that his claims were vastly overstated. Then along came Rudy Giuliani (1994–2001), announcing that he would eliminate altogether the Dinkins affirmative action program for minority contractors. His reasoning, according to his chief economic adviser, was the following: "What this program says to minority contractors is that they don't have to be efficient and City Hall will absorb the extra cost." As an alternative, Giuliani suggested an investment from the city's pension funds by small development banks in poor neighborhoods, an idea that never got very far. In 2005 Mayor Michael Bloomberg signed Local Law 129, creating a new Minority and Women-Owned Business Enterprises (M/WBE) Program. Based on this the New York City Department of Small Business Services built a program dedicated to promoting fairness and equity in city procurement processes. Unfortunately, in August 2011, *The Wall Street Journal* reported that the plan was "failing." Three-quarters of city dollars paid to contractors participating in the program went to companies owned by either Asian Americans or white women. Businesses owned by Latinos received 15 percent of that pool of money, black-run firms 7 percent.

While the word from City Hall varied wildly, sometimes from day to day, most city agencies moved steadily forward, putting into effect programs of their own. Richard A. Kahan, who from 1978 to 1982 served as president of the New York State Urban Development Corporation, stated: "The one place we made history here is not the Convention Center, it's not Battery Park, it's affirmative action in the construction industry, in every aspect of it."

IT is illuminating to review the history of affirmative action as it evolved—and continues to evolve—in the world of legislation and court decisions, the world of politics and legal theory. But, just as the Civil Rights Movement began with protests, marches, and sit-ins, so did affirmative action—at least in construction in New York City—begin with picketing and protests, in the streets and on the job sites. In the evenings I followed with interest the news emanating from the White House, the Supreme Court, and City Hall; but during the day I lived in the midst of the real revolution. I was only rarely on the dangerous barricades, but our office became in effect a small command post where economic peril was very real; where reports of physical violence came in from job sites all over the city, occasionally our own; and where difficult decisions had to be made.

In June of 1963, when minority groups picketed the construction site of a large annex to Harlem Hospital, the situation threatened to spin out of control. Demonstrators blocked the passage of trucks, scuffled with the police, and chanted, "If we don't work, nobody works." City authorities ordered the work stopped. For a day, then a week, and then for five months, the project remained idle. Finally, Mayor Wagner announced that he had been assured by the contractor—who happened to be my old boss, Joe Blitz—that the work would resume with "a very substantial number of minority-group members" on site. The mayor further promised that the city's Commission on Human Rights, the Labor Department, and other agencies were engaged in "a wide range of undertakings designed to provide more jobs for qualified craftsmen and more apprenticeships and other opportunities for untrained but otherwise qualified youths."

This announcement called attention to the fact that "prejudice" was not the only problem being confronted. Union members were jealously protecting their turf, excluding minority members from training programs as well as membership, fearful of new competition in the trades that were their livelihood. "Who says unions are public property?" demanded one business agent bitterly. "Our conditions and wages weren't given us by decree—they were fought for."

This book is not intended to carry a political message or reveal a political bias. But when I hear right-wing radio commentators demanding that "we take our country back" from the government, do

AFFIRMATIVE ACTION

away with the welfare state, and generally let free market forces rule, I think of those hostile demonstrators at construction sites, wielding crude weapons and shouting, "If we don't work, nobody works!" And I wonder.

When, in May 1964, white union plumbers refused to work alongside a black and three Puerto Ricans hired on a job at the Terminal Market in Hunts Point and hostile forces started to trade threats, President Johnson asked his labor secretary to "see what could be done," while George Meany, president of the AFL-CIO sent his two top civil rights troubleshooters to investigate. When the president of the United States and the top official in the nation's labor movement become personally involved in a dispute among a handful of plumbers working in the Bronx, one has to conclude that the matter is important and is being taken seriously. I found it reassuring—and still do—that, in an atmosphere of anger and distrust, amid a clash of legitimate interests not readily reconciled, with violence constantly brewing and occasionally boiling over, Americans found a way to keep moving on. The political game was played, along with threats, promises, accommodations, deals of every sort. The process defies analysis. No "solution" has been reached. People cannot even agree on what a satisfactory solution might be. Yet in the half century since "affirmative action" became a term, and a cause, a lot of good things have happened. Minorities have achieved many objectives—not all, not nearly all, particularly since the goal is to gain business opportunities as well as employment. Yet despite friction between the classes and the races—the New York construction industry has made progress on many fronts.

AS for KBF, all through the 1960s we moved ahead, under the radar, just as we did in the heyday of the Mafia. We weren't very big as New York contractors go, and we weren't engaged in projects that were especially newsworthy. Also, we did our best to play by the rules. We followed whatever guidelines were laid down by the agencies or institutions for whom we worked, and we used subcontractors who were accustomed to operating under the same rules and expectations. We contracted with the "recommended" local people for watchman service and waste removal. John Cricco, overseeing our field operations, used his personal touch to good effect with community leaders, local merchants, and such minority people who had any connection to our projects. Being a good guy doesn't solve every problem; but on and around a construction site it can be very helpful. Besides, we believed in opportunity for all, while at the same time recognizing the wrenching changes that established union workers were being asked to accept.

Finally, in early 1971, we lost our knack for moving smoothly, almost invisibly, through the world of community action. It could hardly have been otherwise as we prepared to break ground for Grace Towers, a 168-unit apartment project funded through the HUD Model Cities Program, sponsored by the Grace Baptist Church, and located in the heart of East New York, a section of Brooklyn occupied mostly by minority families. We were just getting settled at the site when our superintendent, Jerry Kreiger, was visited by a group of community people. This visit was a memorable moment in the annals of our company, since the group's leader, Moses Harris, was dressed in a tribal robe and hat and carried a shepherd's staff. Politely but gravely he told Jerry that our firm would be expected to hire a full-time person, a community representative who would see to it that an appropriate number of local people would be working on the job.

I later read in the newspapers that some contractors were objecting to having to hire an individual with the title of community coordinator. They considered this to be an outrageous tactic, nothing more than a shakedown operation. I suppose it could be considered that, if the individual lounged around all day and caused trouble, or certainly if it was a high-paying no-show job. But from the start we thought of the idea as potentially advantageous for all parties. We preferred the term "community representative"—an assistant for the superintendent, someone who knew the neighborhood and could give us sound advice on how best to make our way, someone to assure the local people of our good intentions and of the benefits accruing, not only from jobs, but from the creation of a handsome new residential building in their area.

As it turned out, the community-representative activity proved so successful that Bob Borg suggested we enrich it with an educational component. We had long had a company policy to subsidize business-related education that any of our long-term employees chose to pursue, and Bob's thought was to offer this to young minority men with good, rudimentary education who would learn construction from us while working as field clerks and also take night courses that we would pay for. John Cricco proposed the idea to Jose "Lucky" Rivera, president of Positive Work Force, which at the time had become the most prominent citywide job-placement organization. After discussions at several meetings, Lucky endorsed the plan enthusiastically. It was put into effect with great success and subsequently adopted by other construction firms.

BUT that was several years in the future. When, in 1971, Moses Harris, waving his shepherd's staff, presented to us a representative from the East New York neighborhood, we didn't know quite how to react. From Jerry Kreiger's tone on the telephone it was obvious that he didn't think we had much of a choice. John Cricco agreed, but since I was the watchdog on project expenses they asked for my approval. Well, all right, I said, but for a young guy with no experience we can't pay more than $150 a week. Silence for a few moments at the other end and then a response: the demand was for $200. Too much, I replied. What Jerry said next remains etched in my memory. "Mr. Florman, are you comfortable in your Scarsdale office? I'm out here in the middle of East New York, there's a bunch of people gathered around me, and they're saying $200." So $200 it was.

The man was Donald Wallace, in his forties, not exactly the young guy we had expected, but trim and well-spoken. When I saw the first job report he prepared I was impressed by his excellent gram-

mar and spelling and by the beautiful penmanship. When I compli-
mented him on this, he told me that he had benefitted from classes
while serving an eight-year term in prison for second-degree manslaughter. Needless to say, I was taken aback. However, as it turned
out, acquaintance with Donald Wallace was one of the highlights
of my many years in the construction industry. On the job he was
punctilious, ever courteous, devoted to the well-being of the project
and of our company, and pleasant to be around. When neighborhood
kids stole some construction materials, Donald recommended that we
buy them back at a nominal price, after which he gave those young-
sters a lecture, and there were no further incidents. We were working
in the midst of one of the most troubled, violence-prone neighborhoods in the city, but the project was trouble-free. When Donald
received word that violence was threatened in the neighborhood on
the anniversary of Martin Luther King's assassination, he insisted
that Jerry Kreiger go home, while he took responsibility for safety on
the site. I enjoyed my job visits, not least because of the chats I had
with Donald. When he left our employ at project's end, to engage in
some "neighborhood affairs," Donald wrote me a long letter over-
flowing with affection and signed "Your loyal employee, your devoted friend, and your loving brother."

Unfortunately, a few years later we received word that Donald
had been arrested for carrying an unlicensed gun. John Cricco and I
went to his trial as character witnesses, but he was sent back to prison,
where, we learned later, he died. An unhappy ending to an unforgettable interlude. Speaking of unforgettable, before going on the
witness stand at Donald's trial I was questioned, I should say grilled,
by an assistant DA—How did I meet Donald Wallace? Who were the
people who recommended him? And so forth. I can only imagine what it must be like to be involved in criminal proceedings with
the aggressive defenders of the law. Good for the DAs I thought later.
But thoroughly shaken is how I felt at the time.

Venturing to build in the depths of East New York at a time
when violence was pervasive in the construction community; having Moses Harris greet us in his tribal garb; coming to know Donald

Wallace, spend time with him, then later testify at his trial—that's more than enough adventure to experience in connection with one project. But I haven't even gotten to the truly explosive incident that is forever associated with Grace Towers. We achieved substantial completion on March 9, 1972, about fourteen months after breaking ground, not bad for a 168-unit project, and we were very pleased with ourselves. But oh, how pride goeth before a fall. Eight days later the project was occupied by squatters. Or, looked at another way, the project was taken over by outraged citizens who felt they had been wronged. Let me put it in the words of the El Nuevo Mundo Tenants Association:

> The residents of the East New York and Ocean-Hill Brownsville areas were forced to take over a building of the Grace Towers Apartments Development on Friday, March 17, 1972.
>
> This action was taken due to the graft and corruption which exists in the Central Cities Model Cities Program and its sponsoring agencies.
>
> There are 86 Puerto Rican and Black families inside the building at this moment. They are many of the families which paid the $200-$500 gratuity to the Model Cities workers to secure apartments. The reason they did this was to insure that they would get the apartments because they are tired of living in sub-standard housing where rats and roaches run rampant. However, after having paid the money they found that they had been literally robbed, and left without any hope of a clean apartment or a refund of the money.
>
> They then decided to form an association and take action. There are approximately 500 people, 300 of which are children. We need the full cooperation of this community at large to combat the dereliction of our community and drive away political and poverty pimps.
>
> We therefore appeal to you as brothers and sisters and people who are either going through the same thing or who

will someday be forced into the same situation, to unite. You must help these people and yourselves by giving staunch support to these people who are fighting to make a better future, not for themselves, but for EVERYONE.

The occupation was reasonably orderly, but of course totally illegal. We consulted with people at Model Cities, with officials at the pertinent city and federal housing agencies, and with Reverend Underwood, pastor of the sponsoring church. Everyone said call the police. OK, we called the police. But there then ensued two months of bureaucratic dancing around while everyone agreed that action should be taken but nobody wanted to take it. Finally the police received orders from city authorities to go ahead and move the occupiers out, but—only after somebody filed a formal complaint. More bureaucratic dancing. The final decision? The contractor would have to file the complaint. We weren't happy, and we didn't think it was fair; but we decided to bow to the pressure. John Cricco was the individual who signed whatever the police told him to sign, and the building was emptied without violence. During the interim some behind-the-scene negotiations had taken place, and the final allocation of apartments included some families from the aggrieved group.

This sit-in brought to the surface an underlying problem: the festering conflict between Puerto Ricans and blacks in East New York and throughout the city. Today there is, in New York and throughout the nation, a very large and diverse population of Hispanic immigrants. But in the late 1950s, with unemployment in Puerto Rico hovering around 25 percent, there was a great tide of immigration from that one island, and Manhattan was the destination of many. They settled in some of the poorer areas of the city, where they mingled with, and inevitably competed with, the African American community, competing for both housing and jobs. The rivalry grew to be intense, often violent. As late as 2002, the United Hispanic Coalition set upon the Positive Workforce Coalition at a construction site on Lexington Avenue and Eighty-seventh Street.

The two groups had fought in Times Square in 1998 and in Chelsea a year later, but this incident was particularly violent, with the attackers wielding bats, rocks, and metal pipes and also a handgun. Three workers were critically injured. Police Commissioner Raymond W. Kelly announced that his department would be taking serious measures to prevent a recurrence. "There's been a long history of this," he said. "I'm told that this has waned in the last few years, but we don't want this to be a precursor of more violence."

Fortunately, there was no violence at Grace Towers. Once the squatters, or occupiers, were removed, we cleaned up the mess, which could have been a lot worse, the designated tenants moved in, and KBF moved on.

JUST as we were bidding farewell to East New York in the spring of 1972, we were breaking ground for Lionel Hampton Houses on 130th Street between Eighth Avenue and Saint Nicholas Avenue in the heart of Harlem. This was an attractive addition to the neighborhood, 355 apartments, financed by the Urban Development Corporation and private investors. I remember this as a happy job, beginning and ending with gala groundbreaking and dedication ceremonies featuring Lionel Hampton playing his vibes with great gusto and good humor. As for affirmative action, we and our subcontractors were primed, and in an article in *The New York Times Magazine,* titled "The Bricks and Mortar of Racism," a Workers Defense League troubleshooter was quoted by the author as saying of the job, "We get good cooperation here."

Which is not to say that the project was without its quota of action and excitement. The site seemed to fall within the territory of a local bookmaking operation, and this led to an unusual arrangement for job security. In order to be on the alert for possible police intrusion, the group had a widespread surveillance team, who they said would make any hired watchmen superfluous. So this was, for a while, our free security operation. One night our trailer was broken into, although nothing appeared to have been stolen. The next morning the lookouts apologized for the intrusion. A bloodied piece of copper pipe outside the trailer door gave evidence of the way they had handled the matter. The site was secure and the service was free, but it made us uneasy. The problem solved itself in a dramatic way. One morning, Spanish Raymond, the leader of the bookie operation, was found dead in the trunk of his car in a nearby parking lot. That was the end of bookmaking on our block. The group either disbanded or moved to a different location. We hurriedly arranged for a conventional watchman service and added one more episode to our memory book of adventures.

Our community representative on Lionel Hampton, recommended by the locals but not involved with the gambling crowd, at least as far as we knew, was Danny Dekind, a bright young man who served us well. I remember Danny most especially for one particular evening when he drove my wife and me around Harlem and showed us "his country." It came about under unusual circumstances. Our longtime housekeeper, Ellen Lindsay, suffered a terrible loss when her daughter unexpectedly died. The funeral was scheduled for nighttime at a large church in Harlem, and my wife and I wanted to be there. I had no particular fears about Harlem, but this was not the prewar Harlem when my parents went to nightclubs, nor the Harlem of today with yuppies moving in. Nor were we to go to a nightclub or an individual residence but to a church, I knew not where. Rather than take a cab to the church and then hope for the best, or order a limo, I asked Danny if he was free that evening. He was, and we struck a deal: he would drive our car, take us to the church, wait around, pick us up, and bring us home. As it happened, we were early starting out and Danny drove us around Harlem, giving a tour guide's lecture that I wish I had captured on tape. He delivered us on time to the church, and we found ourselves to be the only white people among a congregation of several hundred. The singing was beautiful, the eulogy eloquent, and, when a line formed to move down the aisle and pass the opened coffin, we took our place and followed. After the service we, along with other friends, joined Ellen and her husband at their apartment. Danny drove us there and waited for more than an hour as we drank and dined. After a suitable interlude we left with emotional farewells. Danny seemed somewhat bemused by it all.

DONALD Wallace and Danny Dekind were the two community representatives with whom I had the closest contact. But there were others who did good work, assisting the job superintendents as well as providing liaison with neighborhood people. Fortuitously, the program that had started in minority communities blossomed as we took young black and Hispanic trainees into other parts of the city where we were building luxury housing. It was especially satisfying to see the progress of those who took advantage of our offer to support educational enterprise. Looking through the files I see that Danny Gonzalez took courses at the New York City Technical College of the City University; Joshua Nunez completed the Site Safety Manager course at the NYU School of Continuing and Professional Studies; also at NYU, Manuel Torres completed courses in blueprint reading, construction methods, and fundamentals of building systems; Steven Brown took the Site Safety course offered by the Building Trades Employers Association; Dion Rivera studied at the Mechanics Institute. Most exciting of all, Johnny Garcia, who was with us for seven years, studied drafting, building construction, and estimating at Mechanics Institute; became a project manager; and went on to found his own company, Solera Construction Inc. That firm became certified as a minority business enterprise by the New York City School Construction Authority. Upon leaving to embark on his new enterprise, he wrote a note that said in part: "Thank you for always being a staunch supporter of your employees and their needs."

We believed we were doing good, and we weren't above taking credit for our actions. Yet admittedly we were also responding to the pressures of the times, most particularly to the programs and incentives emanating from the various city agencies.

In 1993 we were awarded a contract under the New York City

School Construction Authority Mentor Program, the mission of which was "to increase, facilitate and encourage the participation of Minority, Women-Owned and Locally-Based Enterprises by providing a flexible framework for eligible firms to develop and grow within the construction industry." We were given oversight for the Borough of Queens, and our task was to assist small, prequalified firms in the performance of minor alteration jobs in numerous schools. Bidding, preparation of trade-payment breakdowns, contract documents, scheduling, job meetings, safety—all were subjects for review and instruction. In the words of one of our people: "Through our mentoring, many of these small businesses successfully climbed the ladder of success, moving into the mainstream to become a capable, bondable, insurable, and financially sound organization." At one point we had a staff of as many as forty, and our partner in this remarkable program was Bill King, owner of Hannibal Construction, an honest-to-goodness, long-established, capable minority-owned firm. (Women entrepreneurs, discussed in the following chapter, were also involved.)

At about the same time as the mentor program, and also with Hannibal as co-venturer, we embarked on a five-year program for the New York City Housing Authority, rehabilitating three thousand apartments in Harlem. This was a particularly challenging undertaking since the extensive alterations had to be performed with tenants in occupancy. I had feared that it might prove impossible to work where people were living and that this project would see us entangled in a morass of hostility and resentment. I was delighted to be proved wrong. Our people, with considerable contributions by Bill King's people, were able to carry the day, not only with a skillful sense of scheduling but also, even more important, a wholesome dose of diplomacy. Local workers were given jobs, local merchants were given business, and tenant leaders were given respectful hearings. Troubles were few and far between.

To round off this pleasant period of fraternity and good feelings, Bob Borg and I agreed to meet with a group of Harlem-based contractors to talk about the ins and outs of working for public agencies. As I recall, the idea for the meeting came from a housing authority official. The get-together was very friendly, with wide-ranging discussion, and we agreed with a request to tape the proceedings. At one point, however, someone asked a rather ticklish question about the building department. I hesitated with my answer and, before proceeding, suggested that for this part of the meeting we would be well advised to turn off the tape recorder. There was an outburst of laughter, and it was some time before we returned to serious business—and resumed recording the proceedings.

I have some pleasant memories of those days, but it would be misleading to imply that the era of affirmative action was a time of fun and games. Grace Towers and Lionel Hampton Houses, built in the early 1970s, went smoothly (despite the squatter incident at Grace), largely because of the efforts of Donald Wallace and Danny Dekind. The mentor program and Housing Authority rehabilitation were not likely targets for the coalition groups. And after we came to terms with Harlem Fight Back and started working together with Positive Workforce on our education program for community representatives, there were few hostile forays. But few doesn't mean none. A partial list of the groups that we encountered: Black and Puerto Rican Coalition of Construction Workers, Black Economic Survival, United Tremont Trades, Brooklyn Community Construction Workers, and Chinatown for Construction Workers. Also, there were several who were nameless, simply engaged in extortion racketeering.

Then there was Jimmy Simms with his "Black Economical Survival"—that's what his business card called it. Jimmy was a friend, but he associated with a rough crowd, and we never knew what to expect when his people showed up. One day in mid-1993, two yellow buses brought a gang of about thirty men to Belmont Boulevard Apartments, a building we were constructing in the Bronx. Leading the group was Jimmy's younger brother, and while he was negotiating job openings with John Cricco in the trailer, a gunshot was heard outside. When John learned that a bullet had gone through the window of an adjoining building, narrowly missing a mother and child, he sent one of our men over to make sure everybody was all right and also to give the woman a hundred dollars to pay for replacing the shattered glass pane. At the same time, John told the young Simms that the meeting was over. He then called Jimmy to say that his brother was to be kept out of our sight and to emphasize that another incident like this would end our relationship. There were no more such incidents, but that single gunshot has continued to reverberate through our corporate memory.

AS early as 1978 the newspapers had started to report that contractors were accusing community groups of shakedown operations. Increasingly, it became difficult to tell the legitimate job-placement organizations from the criminals. In 1991, according to the police, there were 542 reported incidents of violence, and the following year many more. Finally, in 1993, thirty-one individuals were indicted on charges of running eight groups that violently extorted thousands of dollars from New York building contractors under the guise of obtaining construction jobs for black and Hispanic workers. If workers were actually hired by the harassed contractors, they were found to be kicking back part of their pay to the extortionists. But often finding jobs was not an objective at all; rather, the objective was payoffs to avert violence and work stoppages.

Isn't this the nastiest turn that a well-intentioned movement can take? Well no, not at all. A final layer of criminality was revealed in 1998, when, in conjunction with the conviction of six coalition leaders, a Mafia presence was identified. A defector testified that the Gambino crime family and two major coalitions had, several years before, agreed to work together. The coalition leaders would stage disruptions at construction sites, and Gambino family members would step in, promising, for a fee, to stop the harassment. What a perfect arrangement between malevolent forces!

On December 16, 1998, a federal jury in Manhattan convicted

four leaders of Brooklyn Fight Back and United Construction Labor Coalitions on charges of extortion conspiracy. On the same day, in federal district court in White Plains, two leaders of the Black and Latin Economic Survival Coalitions pleaded guilty to extorting money from a company that had a state contract for repairs on the Grand Central Parkway in Queens. Jim Haughton of Harlem Fight Back was quoted as saying that the "teaming up of these convicted coalition people with organized crime has discredited legitimate efforts to bring about fair play for blacks, Latinos and Asians in this industry."

Law enforcement, the press, and public indignation have all played a role in reducing these crimes—at least for the moment.

THROUGH it all, my firm mostly managed to stay out of trouble. Still, when occasionally one of those yellow buses, filled with potential demonstrators, pulled up to one of our job sites, nerves instinctively jangled. Usually, a friendly palaver or a well-placed phone call would settle things down; but the experience was never without its emotional downside. I rarely was out in the field when these events occurred, although once I was, and the outcome was, in retrospect, mildly amusing. I was in my car, pulling up to a job site in East Harlem just as one of those ominous school buses appeared. More curious than fearful, I started to get out of my car only to have two very tough-looking hombres come charging over to confront me. "And who the hell are you?" one of them shouted in a not-friendly way. Now more fearful than curious, I blurted out the only thing I could think of to say: "I sell refrigerators." "Well we don't want any," came the answer, and I was only too pleased to get back in the car and take off, maintaining such dignity as possible. I made the mistake of reporting on the event back at the office, and for the next few weeks would occasionally be asked by some fearless employee: "How is the refrigerator salesman today?"

* * *

CRIMINALITY also tainted another aspect of the affirmative action movement: the effort to funnel work to minority business enterprise. Noble efforts were made to help M/WBEs (Minority and Women-Owned Business Enterprises) get a fair share of the contracts and subcontracts awarded, at least on publicly funded projects. Guidelines were established by the various agencies, and reputable contractors did their best to measure up to them. Unfortunately, this facet of the affirmative action effort, while it did not lead to violence, became plagued by fraud. As spelled out in the 1990 report of the New York State Organized Crime Task Force:

1. A prime contractor sets up a phony MBE, to which he purports to subcontract work. In reality, the prime contractor does all the work and supplies all the labor. Frequently, the phony MBE lists as its president one of the prime contractor's minority employees.

2. A member of a qualifying minority group sets up an MBE, allowing his "firm" to be hired as a subcontractor. In fact, he performs no work, and may be not more than a shell company through which billings are processed.

In 1984 the New York State Commission of Investigation concluded that illegitimate minority-business-enterprise contractors outnumbered legitimate ones. Outnumbered! There have been indictments and convictions for such misrepresentations, but nothing commensurate with the number of offenses. And even where, technically, firms do meet the qualifications for special consideration, a very large percentage are flimsy fronts for clever people who are taking improper advantage of the well-meaning programs. As late as 2011, Skanska USA and Schiavone Construction Co., two of the nation's largest construction firms, each paid a $20 million fine for using a "front company" to meet required minority participation on government-financed projects. According to *The New York Times,* "Law enforcement and construction industry officials say such schemes are widespread."

So be it. Illegality and just plain chicanery are newsworthy. Violence even more so. But in the midst of all the excitement, we should not forget that affirmative action is about obtaining a fair share of jobs for all deserving workers and a fair share of opportunities for all deserving businesses. There have been difficulties and setbacks, many of which had to be expected. Yet much has been achieved.

AND beyond the world of large unionized construction projects— the world in which my firm has made its way—there is a turbulent universe in which, without the benefit of affirmative action programs, people are making progress in ways that defy measurement. Only about 15 percent of our nation's more than seven million construction workers are members of unions. In every city, in every suburb, there are individuals and small groups digging, welding, and wiring—building, renovating, and tearing down.

If my wife and I need some snow plowed or a trench dug at our weekend cabin in Putnam County, fifty miles north of New York City, we call on Fred Adams. Robert is our plumber, John our electrician, Bob a jack-of-all-trades. They're white Yankee types who work alone or sometimes bring a son along as a helper. For ethnic variety there is Frank the landscape guy, whose crew defies classification. In the nearby town of Brewster, a large group of Guatamalans shape up on a street corner each morning and are hired for the day, as may be needed, by small building contractors who come by in pickup trucks. This is the ultimate in free enterprise, with all the system's advantages and shortcomings played out daily. I read that in 2009 the state attorney general sued a contractor for illegally paying his white workers $25 per hour, blacks $18, and Latinos $15. The article doesn't spell out exactly what law was broken, but the case makes it clear once again that all is not sweetness and light in the rough-and-tumble construction marketplace.

Still, for all the imperfections that we see and live with, the Civil

Rights Movement and the affirmative action efforts that followed in its wake have contributed to making what most of us will conclude is a better world. One feels this in the construction industry at least as much as anywhere else.

EIGHTEEN | *The Women*

"WOMEN'S LIBERATION." The words may not evoke images of hostile confrontation and high drama the way the term "Civil Rights Movement" does. Yet in the flow of human history, it represents a truly unique revolution. Anatomical distinctions between male and female, rooted in billions of years of evolution, are not subject to significant change. As for the roles of the sexes, largely defined by the phenomenon of childbearing—woman the mother and home-maker, man the hunter—similar patterns have evolved in practically every human culture.

Thus the feminist movement, although it started relatively quietly in the eighteenth century among mostly middle- and upper-class Western women, has to be recognized as truly earth-shaking. First came the demand for suffrage and political equality, with American women winning the right to vote in 1920. A "second wave," usually dated 1950s–1980s, featured protest against an array of cultural and political inequalities such as property rights and no-fault divorce. And a "third wave," seen as both a continuation of the second and a response to its perceived failures, has moved energetically on a variety of fronts: access to university education, broad employment opportunities at equitable wages, independence in sexuality and reproductive rights, gender-neutral language, reconsideration of participation in housework and parenting, and, in general, elimination of patriarchal dominance in the professions, in politics, and in the business community.

I first became aware, vaguely aware, that momentous societal changes were pending back in the 1930s when I heard my mother express regret about not having gone to college even though her parents had the means to send her. Then, when she enjoyed the experience of working as a volunteer with the Red Cross during World War II, she wistfully wondered what it might have been like to have a career. But these were just passing thoughts. Basically, she believed that her role of managing home and family was the way things were and the way they were intended to be. The girls I went to school with began to see things differently, and suddenly everything had changed. My wife and her friends, and then my daughters-in-law and theirs, seized opportunities and somehow combined working and parenting, although mostly in special fields, with interruptions and rarely on lifelong career paths. Now, with my granddaughters, after only four generations, the sky appears to be the limit.

I exaggerate; the sky is not yet the limit for women everywhere in all respects. We know that in many parts of the world ancient customs prevail. And even in the United States there are "glass ceilings" or their equivalent all over the place. Traditions, social conventions, and mysterious "networks" present hurdles that legislation cannot readily remove. Nor are protest marches and other such activities suited to the current situation. More useful are the efforts of organizations that seek through scholarship and advocacy to improve the lives of women, and the many groups, formal and informal, that are seeking representation for women in various industries and professions.

CONSTRUCTION fits into this general scene of ferment, although in many ways it is unique. This is particularly the case with the most basic part of the industry: work in the field.

During the 1950s and 1960s I visited dozens of building sites hundreds of times, and I don't recall seeing a single woman hardhat. In the trailer, yes, a few secretaries, timekeepers, and the like, but precious few; and none among the tradesmen. Starting in the late 1970s I would occasionally spot a female worker, still very few and far between. If I did come across one I wasn't shocked, elated, or alarmed; I simply considered it an oddity. In April 1978, the Department of Labor, responding to political pressures of the day, set goals and timetables for hiring women on federally financed construction projects, aiming to see female representation rise to 6.9 percent of the workforce in three years. The hope was that by the turn of the millennium, women would make up close to a quarter of the construction-trades workforce. This did not happen. In the early 1980s women's share of the construction force rose to just over 2 percent and ceased growing. Even in the early twenty-first century the figure stands at about 3 percent. The National Association of Women in Construction (NAWIC) claims that women workers make up nearly 10 percent of the construction industry, a figure very close to that of the Department of Labor. But this figure includes engineers and project managers as well as workers in the trades. So the 3 percent ceiling for women field workers seems to be holding. Checking KBF jobs on a typical day, I find that our figure is a little bit higher, but not much, and our operation doesn't provide a significantly large sample.

IN the past, whenever anyone mentioned affirmative action and minorities in the workplace, my mind would leap immediately to the arena of African Americans and Hispanics, a place where my time, energy, and concern were fully engaged. I was interested in women's rights, surely; but since the issue didn't arise on any of our projects, I tended to leave well enough alone. Then, in early 1998, I was asked by *The New York Times* to review a book titled *We'll Call You If We Need You: Experiences of Women Working Construction*. It was, putting it mildly, an eye-opener. The author, Susan Eisenberg, told of the dramatic experiences of the first women who had showed up on construction sites in 1978. Ms. Eisenberg was herself an apprentice with Local 103 of the International Brotherhood of Electrical Workers, and she tells the story through interviews with thirty women—carpenters, electricians, ironworkers, painters, and plumbers. Gaining entrance to unions and apprenticeship programs was difficult, and after successfully doing so came the need to learn the ropes on the job, a strange and unwelcoming environment. Then the women had to contend with blatant, fearsome sexual harassment compounded by the loneliness of not having a female support system. Special nastiness was faced by women of color and by lesbians. There were elemental problems relating to sanitation facilities on site; and much of the work was arduous and dangerous, made more so by male "partners" who were often uncaring or outright hostile. This grim story modulates into a cheerier key when it reports on the help and support of a few "exceptional men." And it ends on an up note by reporting the pride and delight many of these women found in their work: "You have this thing you can touch and see and experience." "I get a high off of it just unbelievable." What a story!

I wrote an enthusiastic review, which the *Times* captioned "Hard-Hatted Women," and that, in the way of our fast-moving world, was that. There were other matters requiring attention. However, three years later I was interested to see that *Engineering News-Record* carried a "Viewpoint" essay by Ms. Eisenberg, under the headline "Misogyny Hurts Craft Labor." According to this bitter piece, women on construction sites continued to be abused, and "amazingly, contractors let this situation fester."

Two years further along—bringing us to October of 2003—*ENR* ran a cover story on the "women's movement" in construction and noted that Susan Eisenberg had given up working as an electrician because she had become "weary of her lonely crusade." An editorial was titled "Crummy Conditions in the Crafts Keep Women Away." Attempts to enforce hiring goals had proved to be fruitless. The editorial concluded that pay and benefits should be increased and sexism should be aggressively attacked. "Tolerating it is not only illegal, it is unfair and bad business. Zero tolerance is the ticket to success."

In the past few years conditions in the field have indeed improved, not only because of management's efforts but also because of the attitudes of a new generation of men. Yet a troubled economy and an industry with a "last hired, first fired" tradition adds to feelings of uncertainty. Even with the continuing efforts of public agencies and the special efforts of certain contractors and developers of large projects, one hesitates to predict near-term growth in the number of female hardhats.

IT is equally difficult to predict the fate of newly formed woman-owned construction businesses. As noted in the previous chapter, a large number of these were hastily put together to take advantage of government programs and turned out to be fraudulent. Even those that are honest and well-intentioned may be ill-equipped to succeed as a newcomer in a complex, inherently risky industry. It is important, of course, that opportunity be there for all. But how much enticement and support is appropriate? There are several organizations working actively to educate, encourage, and sustain a pioneering effort, including a bit of astutely planned lobbying. Yet in an *Engineering News-Record* article titled "Women Take on Construction," a female contractor who questions the political approach is quoted: "I am not a person who thinks the government should give me or set aside anything."

WHATEVER my doubts about prospects for field labor and newly formed woman-owned firms, there is one thing that I do know: women are perfectly capable of running a successful business in the construction industry.

Miller Druck Specialty Contracting is a leading stonework subcontractor with whom KBF has worked for many years on large and complex projects. The firm's president, Barbara Cohen, is a well-known member of the construction community. She is shrewd, competent, knowledgeable—everything one could wish for in a field that is technically demanding.

When our firm built a dormitory for Columbia University in 1997, we worked under the supervision of Patricia Lancaster, assistant vice president of planning, design and construction, as smart as they come, and as tough as any man one can think of. A registered architect, she was in 2002 appointed by Mayor Bloomberg to be commissioner of the Department of Buildings. She was doing an excellent job with an impossible agency when, in 2008, she felt obliged to resign in the wake of two dreadful crane accidents. Trapped in the hard, cruel world of construction politics. One can be sure that she will go on to a successful career.

Speaking of construction politics, and the wonderful, humane role it can sometimes play, who can forget Clara Fox? Clara was an advocate of subsidized housing for poor and moderate-income people and the founder, in 1969, of the Settlement Housing Fund, a nonprofit organization that played a sponsoring role in forty-four buildings in New York City. She also served as cochairwoman of the New York Housing Conference, a coalition of more than seventy organizations representing developers, bankers, architects, housing advocates, and owners of nonprofit buildings. Along with her assistant and eventual successor, Carol Lamberg, she played a role in many of the projects we built, and I don't recall ever attending a luncheon or dinner related to housing at which she was not a leading presence.

I've previously mentioned Linda Hoffman, the president of the New York Foundation for Senior Citizens, another do-good organization. I have to mention her again as I list just a few of the many competent, energetic women who are successful leaders of construction organizations, private and public.

And if we want to make our standard the close, personal supervision of the construction process itself, including the technical and financial details, there is nobody better at it than Carole Pittelman. As I noted in the chapter on developers, Ms. Pittelman, the daughter of Leonard Litwin, owner of Glenwood Management, is considered by our KBF people to be one of the best construction administrators they have come across. Big buildings, fine quality, on schedule, under budget, and a well-organized operation. What more can one ask?

I could go on and name others, some with whom KBF has dealt, and many I've heard about but never come across. A large number compared with men? No. But my point is that women who come to construction through a natural progression of events: family, education, social concern, social connection, or even serendipity can be, and have been, successful. There are many interesting points of entry, as we have just seen, and as I observe with pleasure looking back over the history of my company.

IN the chapter "A Happy Family," I gave full credit to Virginia Crowley, who came to us as a teenage secretary and eventually became our office manager and corporate secretary. There is no job description to fully encompass what her skills are or define what she has meant to our company.

Barbara Brandwein spent fourteen years with us before retiring with her husband to Florida. She started as a plan clerk and left as a project manager; but I remember her best as an expediter extraordinaire. A critical part of the construction process is getting men and materials to arrive on a job site at the time they are needed. Cajolery, pleading, implied promises, and veiled threats—whatever it took, Barbara had it. Construction is a very complex business, and one can spend a lifetime trying to learn the technical side of things, plus the financial, political, and personal. But the basic knowledge of what goes into a building, and where and when, is not rocket science. Barbara quickly grasped the essential facts and had a combination of brains and disposition well suited to our needs.

Serda Urganciyan joined KBF in 1995, bringing with her a bachelor of architecture degree from the New York Institute of Technology and, interestingly, in addition to excellent English, a fluency in Armenian, Turkish, and French. We couldn't take full advantage of her language skills, but we certainly benefitted from her ability to work well with people of all sorts, particularly in jobs that we did with the New York City Housing Authority, doing extensive alterations to apartments that were occupied. Her professional skills were useful not only in technical application but also in gaining respect from city officials overseeing the work. After ten years Serda left us, with much regret on both sides, to travel west with her gentleman friend. That is a potential problem in hiring young people in this increasingly peripatetic world.

When, in 1992, we joint-ventured with Hannibal Construction to run the School Construction Authority Mentor Program in Queens, as well as other work for city agencies, Grace Malcolm took over as the project's office manager. I suppose it helped our image on these particular jobs to have a black woman in a leadership position; but the real benefit came from Grace's intelligence, her ability to efficiently track a multitude of complex projects and to handle her responsibilities with firmness leavened with a pleasant nature. This may sound like an advertising promotion, but the words come from those who worked most closely with this amazing woman. After six wonderful years, Grace left us for the state of Florida. Climate is almost as big a hazard as romance for those who want to keep a good organization whole.

Incidentally, coming out of the mentor program, there were at least two women who continued on their own managing successful businesses: Andrea Phillips of Annandale Contracting, a GC, and Monica Foster of F&R Contracting, window specialists.

FOR a success story about women in construction, it is hard to top the career of our own Joan Ulbrich. Her college background was in the arts, but as a single mother living in Westchester with two small children, she came to KBF mainly because of our proximity to her home. She started as an aide in the accounting department; but one thing seemed to lead to another, and pretty soon she found herself in the construction end, expediting and assisting project managers. The most exciting part of the chronicle, at least as I see it, began when Joan, taking advantage of KBF's offer of assistance, embarked on a most extraordinary journey of learning. Studying civil technology at Westchester Community College and construction management at New York University, she applied her new knowledge to her work, advancing through the ranks to become a project manager. As the years went by, she obtained a license as a New York City site safety manager, and many other certifications including OSHA "10 hour" safety, asbestos supervisor, lead manager, torch operations, and fire watch. She topped it all off in 2009 by earning designation of "LEED AP building design and construction" from the Green Building Certification Institute. LEED stands for "leadership energy and environmental design." I should not forget to add that along the way Joan was named a KBF vice president.

DURING the 1990s, the YWCA in White Plains inaugurated a program called Salute to Women of Westchester. They presented awards to "recognize extraordinary women in the work force and to honor Westchester companies that promote the advancement of women in business." Among the honorees were KBF's Joan Ulbrich, Grace Malcolm, and our corporate secretary, Virginia Crowley. The festive luncheons at which the awards we're presented invariably lifted my spirits and made me feel proud—for them and for us.

I wish I could end the chapter on this high note. But there is more that must be told, not to detract from the wonderful things that have happened, but simply to face up to the difficulties that do exist.

Some thirty years ago, a woman worked for us who was, in effect, our chief financial officer. She had started with us as a bookkeeper and, very good at her specialty, had reached the top rung in our very small and rather informal bookkeeping department. All was well until 1990, when accounting bills for the previous year were found to have risen to incredible heights, totally unacceptable for an operation such as ours. We called in our accountants and raised the roof about the escalated costs. The explanation given was that our bookkeeper was unable to keep the records in a way that would minimize the work required by the auditing firm. If we replaced our top bookkeeper with an honest-to-goodness CPA the problem would be solved and large sums of money would be saved. After considerable deliberation we decided to make the recommended change. We called in the woman in question, explained the problem, told her that we admired her and what she had accomplished yet felt we had no choice but to follow the advice of our accounting firm. The job market was good, and with our strong support and recommendation we were certain that she would find a position at least as good as her present one. To make sure that she had ample time to find a suitable situation, and to show our appreciation of her good service, we gave her a payment equal to six months' salary. Although well pleased with the parting bonus, she was naturally not delighted to be terminated. Yet with our hearty support she soon found a position very much to her liking and had most of the half year's pay to do with as she willed.

A year or so later, she lost that job, had problems finding another one, was introduced to a lawyer who specialized in sex-discrimination litigation, and, bang, we found ourselves sued. Since the CPA we had hired was not only male but a young male, her lawyer tossed age discrimination into the mix. We sought and received vindication from some local government panel, but that couldn't stop the court proceedings. After venting our anger and lamenting our stupidity, we settled for what our lawyer said would be the cost of fighting, even if we won. Something like $50,000, if memory serves.

That was about what we paid a few years later when a woman based in our Queens office brought suit because one of the men there didn't show her the proper respect in a meeting with public officials present. This matter was spiced up a bit when she added claims of improper sexual advances, all very subtle as far as I could tell from the recorded testimony. Our decision came down to settle or incur substantial legal expenses, and we paid.

Following this second episode, one of our lawyers suggested that, in order to avoid future trouble and expense, we authorize an educational program for our entire organization. Feeling somewhat abashed, we agreed. The therapy consisted of lectures to the staff in groups of various sizes, from an expert in the field of discrimination law. I recall the talk given in the office, in which we were told that we had to change our ways. It's a shame, said the speaker, since he knew that we felt like a family and acted with free and easy ways. But from now on we had to be careful: say nothing that will in any way shock or scandalize an employee or even a visitor. No swearing or off-color jokes; no ethnic remarks; no sexist references; nothing that might be offensive to anybody. This might be a drag, but the world has changed, and we had to change with it. We were thoroughly intimidated, and for a week or so we did as we were told. Ginny even stopped swearing at her computer. Then one day somebody—maybe it was me—said, "Aw, fuckit." We went back to our old ways, but apparently haven't offended anybody in a long time. At least not enough to get sued.

ONE last word about women in construction. Through the years, I have followed the evolution of the engineering profession, thinking about it, reading, writing, and lecturing. I know that not everyone in construction is an engineer, not by a long shot, but I can't help feeling that the experience of women in construction is related to their experience in engineering. I've been particularly struck by the fact that participation of women in the engineering profession has—through their own choice—leveled off at an implausibly low figure. While women now exceed men in the numbers of college degrees earned and have attained parity in law school and medical school, also making notable gains in some of the sciences, for engineering majors there appears to be a fixed ceiling of 20 percent. Starting from close to zero in the 1950s and 1960s, the figure passed 10 percent in the 1970s, 15 percent in the 1980s, then disappointingly slowed to 18 percent in 1996 before reaching the 20 percent level that has prevailed for more than a decade. And that 20 percent of the student body has so far translated into only about 10 percent of the practitioners. Every imaginable effort has been made by professional organizations, academe, industry, and government to attract women to engineering, but without significant results.

Perhaps there will be a breakthrough, particularly now that the concept of humanitarian service—which studies have shown has a particular appeal to young women—are increasingly becoming a feature of the profession. Engineers Without Borders, an international aid organization, was established in the year 2000, thirty years after the founding of Doctors Without Borders, but better late than never. In American engineering schools the concept of "service learning" has taken hold. Engineering Projects in Community Service (EPICS) was established at Purdue University in 1995 and has served as a model for comparable programs in many other institutions. EPICS engages engineering undergraduates in team-based, multidisciplinary design-and-build projects in their communities, typical ventures being school playroom facilities for handicapped students and an environmental monitoring system for an art museum.

Many reasons have been propounded for the reluctance of women to opt for a career in engineering—early stereotyping of gender roles, lack of peer support, and so forth. But looking at the breakthroughs in so many other fields, these explanations begin to seem inadequate. Back in the spring of 1977, I was invited to visit Smith College to speak about engineering as a career and to meet with some of the very bright young women who were studying the sciences there. I came away with the conclusion, which I set forth in an article in *Harper's* (February 1978), that these talented female students thought engineers were not appropriately respected in our society, certainly not compared with doctors and scientists. In other words, *if you're smart enough to be an engineer, you're too smart to be an engineer!*

I responded by quoting from the statement of purpose of the National Organization for Women (NOW). That manifesto speaks of bringing women "into full participation in the mainstream of American society *now,* exercising all the privileges and responsibilities thereof in truly equal partnership with men." I concluded my remarks, and later my *Harper's* article, with the suggestion that the ultimate feminist dream would never be realized unless women become engineers and participate in building the world we share.

THAT declaration could logically be broadened to apply not only to engineers, but to all constructors of buildings. Yet perhaps the notion needs to be rethought.

If, at this time, for whatever combination of reasons, women do not become full partners with men in the construction industry, that is no great tragedy. Their participation, at any percentage, is welcome and can be fruitful. We just have to make sure that opportunities remain open to them. Perhaps in one more generation the picture will change.

Incidentally, in 1999—more than twenty years after my visit— Smith College instituted an engineering program, already dynamic and very well regarded.

NINETEEN | *Danger*

"CONSTRUCTION MEANS DEBRIS; Gravity Means It Falls." Thus did *The New York Times,* in a somewhat lighthearted headline, choose to tell its readers, in mid-September 2007, about a happening to which New Yorkers had become almost inured: a shower of materials falling from a building under construction. In this case, I believe that a more serious tone would have been appropriate. At the fifty-three-story Bank of America tower being constructed near Bryant Park, a huge steel bucket, struck by the cable of a crane, fell from the roof, shattering windows on its descent and sending twisted metal and shards of glass in all directions. People ran for cover, and several cars swerved onto the sidewalks. This was the seventy-fourth such incident of the year—undoubtedly the most spectacular—but simply keeping pace numerically with the previous year's reported total of 101. Eight people suffered injuries, fortunately none of them serious.

In mid-December gravity struck again, this time at the site of the new Goldman Sachs headquarters being built a block north of Ground Zero, and this time the consequences were more grave. A crane dropped a load of metal studs, weighing roughly fourteen thousand pounds, on top of the project trailer, and an architect visiting the site was critically hurt, incurring injuries that left him a paraplegic.

The construction year ended with these two distressing mishaps, but this was simply a prelude to 2008, a "plague year" if ever there was one, borrowing the title of Daniel Defoe's fictionalized account of the year 1665, when the Great Plague struck the city of London.

On March 15, 2008, in one of the city's worst ever building-site accidents, a crane collapsed at 303 East Fifty-first Street. Seven people were killed, six construction workers and a woman visitor from Florida. Twelve other individuals were injured, some of them seriously, and three hundred tenants of seventeen adjacent buildings were evacuated over a period of several days. On Fifty-first Street portions of the top floors of a nineteen-story building were destroyed by the falling crane mast. A block away, on Fiftieth Street, two floors of a six-story building were demolished; a four-story building was completely collapsed, crushing the female visitor; and a steel beam, sent flying, penetrated two small residential structures. Pandemonium reigned.

Incredibly, on Friday, May 30, two and a half months later, another crane collapse—this one at Ninety-first Street and First Avenue—killed two workers, injured a third, and sheared off balconies on an apartment house across the street from the building site.

In a predictable aftermath, the city council passed tough new crane regulations, the buildings commissioner resigned, and the Department of Buildings announced it would hire sixty-three additional inspectors, and more than fourteen thousand stop-work orders were issued, a 50 percent increase from the previous year.

Neither the public nor the politicians were mollified by reports that crane accidents had within the year occurred in twelve other states. Nor did anyone seem interested to learn that when a construction worker in Las Vegas was killed in a recent crane collapse—the eleventh death on Strip projects in eighteen months—the incident provoked a general strike and a demand for safer working conditions. For New Yorkers, the local disaster scene was what counted. A jungle of cranes was making their streets perilous, and guilty parties had to be found.

Various agencies, including the district attorney's office, got to work. The owner of a crane service admitted bribing the former chief inspector of cranes to certify cranes that had not been inspected and to license crane operators who had not passed the operators' exam. Both the briber and the chief inspector, in plea agreements, received sentences of two to four years in prison. William Rapetti, master rigger on the March 15 collapse, the most lethal, was indicted on multiple charges of manslaughter, criminally negligent homicide, assault, and reckless endangerment. As outlined in the report of OSHA, who imposed a fine of $220,000, he was accused of improperly overseeing the use of nylon slings during a crane "jump." Mr. Rapetti, who was one of the heroic leaders of crane operations during the post-9/11 Ground Zero cleanup, pleaded not guilty and, waiving his right to be heard by a jury, opted for a trial before a judge. On July 22, 2010, he was acquitted on all charges. Criminality was no longer in the picture, but Rapetti was subsequently stripped of his operator license and there still loomed years of litigation concerning potential liability.

In a lamentable coda, another worker died in September when he slipped off a working platform attached to a crane at the fortieth floor. He was wearing a safety harness, but it was not attached to anything. The licenses of two crane operators were suspended because they had cut a guardrail on the platform in what a buildings department official called "a shortcut gone terribly wrong."

During the plague year of 2008 there were nineteen construction-worker fatalities in the city. In all of 2009 only three such deaths were recorded. This improvement was clearly related to the recession that brought an abrupt halt to New York's building boom. However, the Department of Buildings commissioner chose to credit increased enforcement by his department as well as better supervision at work sites. Implausibly, official records showed that the number of construction accidents jumped from 151 to 224. The commissioner attributed this to better reporting by contractors.

EVEN when nobody is hurt, construction accidents can have serious economic and political consequences. Tishman Construction, one of the biggest and busiest builders in the city, was not involved in the lethal accidents of 2008, but the firm had to endure continuing embarrassment at the Goldman Sachs headquarters project near Ground Zero. At that site, shortly after the two horrendous crane disasters, a fluke gust of wind blew a steel plate, thirty inches square, off a hoist eighteen stories above the street. The plate arced through the air and knifed into a field about twenty feet away from a ten-year-old boy who was playing in a Little League game. "I was really scared," said the youngster, according to the press. One can only imagine what an uproar there was, not only from the community and the building department but also from Goldman Sachs, a firm that was concerned with other problems in the midst of a developing Wall Street crisis. A perfect alignment of newsworthy events.

Stop-work orders were issued, meetings were held with community people as well as with city officials, and special precautions were ordered. A senior Tishman executive was assigned full-time to the project and directed to give regular briefings to the Goldman Sachs CEO. Plastic safety netting that had enwrapped the building to a height of sixty inches on each floor, according to code, was now carried to full ceiling height allowing no open space at all.

Still, the fates had not had their fill. On April 1, 2009—April Fool's Day indeed—as a carpenter was boarding an exterior hoist at the seventeenth floor, the gate bumped against a hammer in the worker's tool belt, flipping it out into the air. The hammer slipped into the three-inch gap between the hoist and the building, then bounced free, dropping to the street, where it shattered the back window of a taxicab. To add to the drama, children were walking by on their way to school. No injuries, but oh my goodness, the fallout! More stop-work orders, more public uproar, more bad publicity, more stringent procedures introduced.

I mention Tishman not because of any particular failure on their part, but only to ponder: there but for the grace of God go I. What happened to this experienced, professional, well-regarded company could happen to any general contractor, no matter how good his intentions or how well-designed his safety plans.

* * *

GOOD GUYS, WISEGUYS, AND PUTTING UP BUILDINGS

MY firm, doing only a minuscule amount of work compared with the giant contractors, was statistically much less likely to suffer an accident. But I was concerned nevertheless because in 2008 and 2009 we were construction manager on the Beekman, that seventy-six-story tower in lower Manhattan designed by Frank Gehry and sponsored by Bruce Ratner, both high-profile names. As the superstructure rose in the midst of crowded downtown streets, we held our collective breaths. When the disastrous May 30, 2008, crane collapse occurred, the concrete subcontractor was the same one who was working on our job. As a large number of his crew rushed uptown out of concern for their fellow tradesmen, it flashed through my mind that it might well have been the other way around with workers rushing to our site.

As it happened, we topped out the concrete safe and sound, in November 2009, and as that year came to an end, enclosure of the building with stainless steel panels was well under way. We were in high spirits.

Then came January 25, 2010. The story of that day's events is told in a January 26 letter addressed to KBF's president by the borough president of Manhattan:

> Dear Mr. Zelazny:
>
> I am writing to you regarding the incident on January 25, 2010 at the Beekman Tower construction site at 8 Spruce Street. Around 8:00 a.m., netting being used to secure materials became loose and debris was sent crashing to the ground. The Department of Buildings immediately placed a "stop work order" on the site, and the Fire Department instituted a "frozen zone" around the area to prevent pedestrians from being put in harm's way.
>
> Debris should not come loose and fall from a construction site under any circumstances, even when abnormally high winds occur. It is unacceptable for residents' sense of safety to be jeopardized in this way, particularly in Lower Manhattan where traveling past construction sites is a daily reality.
>
> We must all work together to ensure future events like this do

*not occur. I urge Kreisler Borg Florman to send a representative to
the next Community Board 1 Seaport/Civic Center Committee
meeting to speak to concerned residents about the incident and
how site safety can be ensured.*

The law of averages had caught up with us. It was tremendously
scary to have heavy steel turnbuckles—that was the nature of the
"debris"—raining down on the streets. But it could have been worse—a
lot worse. As can be gleaned from the moderate tone of the borough
president's letter, we were victims of extremely unusual circumstances,
everybody behaved appropriately, and blessedly nobody was hurt.
What happened was that on a stormy day, winds at the upper levels of
the tower were estimated to have reached one hundred miles per hour.
Those winds buffeted the safety netting installed on the floors not yet
enclosed by exterior walls and tore some of the netting loose. This
would have been harmless enough, except that the netting was fastened
to the building by metal turnbuckles embedded in the concrete. This
was all done according to code and best practices. But in a once-in-
a-million circumstance, a few of the turnbuckles were joggled savagely,
actually torn out of the concrete, and sent flying. To quote from a
report issued by the inspecting professional engineer: "The exact cause
of the turnbuckles coming undone is unknown, but it is not difficult
to imagine that in winds of 100 mph there were extreme forces and
oscillating motion that can wreak such havoc."

The affected turnbuckles were replaced—with special wire ties
added to secure against rotation—the safety netting was restored,
and the building department authorized work to proceed. The meeting with the community board went smoothly, the borough president was pleased, and our client, Forest City Ratner, seemed well
satisfied with the way everything was handled. As for public relations, this was one instance in which we did not at all resent seeing
news releases that identified the building as "Gehry's Tower," and
that neglected to give the name of the construction manager.

★ ★ ★

WE'VE experienced one other event associated with bad weather, equally frightening, even more bizarre, but again with a happy ending in that nobody was injured and our anonymity was preserved. The anonymity stemmed from the fact that the accident took place on a site where we were scheduled to put up a building, in fact were just days away from signing a contract, but had not yet done so. We could honestly tell inquiring reporters that we were not the builder. The incident occurred one rainy March day in 1979, on the East Side of Manhattan's Third Avenue at Thirty-first Street. We had agreed with an owner/developer to build an apartment house, and, pending final agreement on contract details, this entrepreneurial gentleman had obtained a building permit, signed up an excavation contractor, and authorized work to proceed. A hole was dug, and then the rains came.

Adjoining the site stood a very old structure with three floors, one apartment on each floor. The excavator had a pump but couldn't keep up with the inflow of water, and soon the future basement area began to look like a large swimming pool. Would I have managed things differently if I had been in charge? I like to think that I would have insisted on additional pumps, but I can't be sure. It is not unusual to see a temporary accumulation of water in an excavation pit, and in this instance the water was not deep enough to present a danger to passersby, the area was properly fenced, and there was a watchman on duty. What nobody realized was that water was seeping, then flowing, under the foundations of the very old adjoining building.

The rain continued heavily through the night, and in the early dawn the entire front facade of the three-story structure suddenly collapsed—slid right off like a theatrical curtain abruptly removed. Indeed, the building suddenly looked like a stage set, the three apartments exposed, startled tenants—panicked tenants—looking out at the wide, wide world. It would have been amusing except for the horrifying thought of what a more total collapse would have meant. Even now I find it hard to believe what happened except when I look at the article, including photo, that appeared in *The New York Times.* The excavator's name was mentioned, but ours was not.

There was another incident that received extensive newspaper notice. During the summer of 2002, on what must have been a very slow day at the *Daily News,* we were dismayed to see the headline: "Buried Man Is Dug Free." The article relates somewhat breathlessly how a worker was "trapped at the bottom of a 15-foot hole . . . buried up to his waist" until rescued and "hospitalized with leg injuries in stable condition." No name of a contractor is given, but the job was ours, alterations to a school in the Bushwick section of Brooklyn. Unlike other accident stories, however, this one has a humorous element, not as described in the paper, but as related with guffaws in our office. According to our own in-house eyewitnesses the hole was not nearly as deep as described by the reporter, but rather a simple ditch less than shoulder high, and the victim was not buried up to his waist but barely to his knees—"to his ankles," said one of our men. The man's shouts of surprise brought an army of rescuers, bystanders, and people with telephones calling 911. Also a safety inspector who appeared from nowhere and seemed happy to find an incident to write up. The *News* reporter correctly noted that the man was "a Pakistani immigrant" but failed to add that he obviously hailed from a part of Pakistan where English was not the native tongue. Despite cries intended to say that he felt fine and wanted to be left alone, he was pulled about, jostled, and dumped into an ambulance that appeared on the scene. The following day KBF representatives had to appear at hearings and accept warnings and notices of a fine. Only the presence of the "victim," unnerved by the excitement, but clearly fit as a fiddle, saved us from lord knows what sort of penalties.

I suppose that accidents and humor should not be linked, but in the hardhats' world, as long as the end result is not tragic, this sometimes happens. On the East Midtown Plaza project, built in 1973, while pouring concrete for the third floor, one of Dic Concrete's workers drove a concrete buggy off the rampway and fell, buggy and all, onto the debris piled below. The man suffered a broken leg and some cuts and bruises but recovered and returned to the job. His fellow workers started to call him Flapper, citing his gestures during the fall. He claimed that he just yelled "whoa" and didn't wave his arms. But eyewitnesses disagreed, and the nickname stuck.

MY mood turns quickly from humor to melancholy as I recall a weekend in November 2002. It was a Saturday afternoon, on the northwest corner of Third Avenue and Ninetieth Street, when our concrete subcontractor's crane, with all proper permits in place, was using a rope to hoist a heavy steel cable to the top of the crane's boom. After the cable was attached to the crane, the rope broke, leaving the cable to dangle to the street, where it started to swing back and forth, whipping about like a giant snake. Workers shouted warnings, and people started running every which way, some even taking refuge under a truck. A young bystander was quoted as saying that "one man was older and couldn't move fast enough." Sure enough, the older man was struck across his legs and felled, seriously hurt. The incident was recorded in the *Daily News* and *New York Post*, New York's tabloids. This time our name was mentioned; but somehow that seemed to be of little consequence.

I suppose it is only human for contractors, when accidents occur, to think of ways to avoid responsibility, minimize expense, and in general ward off blame. In this case legal and financial consequence were disregarded, as sympathy took over. A couple of days after the event, Arman Boyajian, our project manager, along with the owner of the concrete superstructure firm, visited the injured gentleman in the hospital. I didn't know how the project's various insurance companies might have felt about this, but I approved of the gesture. Arman reported in a memo that the injured party—who happened to be a registered nurse at Beth Israel Medical Center—had suffered a broken leg, and, in surgery, a rod had been inserted. The man recalled that he tried to run when he heard people yelling but that he couldn't get away. After being hit, he didn't remember anything until he was in the emergency room. Arman's memo ended with a simple sentence: "He thanked us for coming to visit." Insurance claims were settled without complications.

STRANGE the memories that come to mind, not only accidents that occurred but also, even more vividly sometimes, those that almost did but didn't. The roof of Tilden Towers is one such instance. On that sixteen-story apartment house that we built in the Bronx back in 1967, the roofer had stored large bags of gravel in preparation for completing his work. One evening an unidentified intruder—some people said it was a kid who lived in the neighborhood—gained access to the building, climbed all the way to the roof, picked up one of those heavy bags, and threw it out over the parapet. Whether by intent or by accident, the bag crashed through the roof of a two-story house below and landed on a bed—a bed that was to have been occupied within a half hour by a young child.

VIVID memories, and yet the one I should remember most clearly is so vague as to be practically nonexistent. Our one fatality. In more than half a century one man was killed on a KBF job, and there was nothing known except that a man had died. It was the Lionel Hampton Houses project in 1972, long before the passage of most of the safety laws that now seem so much a part of how we build. For example, we had no safety netting surrounding the open floors, simply a couple of ropes, and often on recently poured floors not even that. The fatality came without a story, unobserved and very little discussed. A man simply fell off the side of the building, and nobody could say how it happened. He worked for the carpentry subcontractor, and he seemed to have no friends on the job, at least as far as I could learn, and there were no details about family. We heard rumors about political unrest in the carpenters union, and the more questions we asked the more our field people reported that the carpenters had gone into the "three wise monkeys" mode: see no evil, hear no evil, speak no evil. So, for a short time, the event appeared to have a sinister aspect. However, the police investigated and called it an accident. Nothing further was heard from any quarter. And that seemed to be that.

I say that this was our one fatality, but I don't want to forget to mention George Farole. He was one of our good men, and on a Saturday he was cleaning debris on one of the upper floors at Soundview Estates, an apartment house for the elderly that we built in New Rochelle in 1979. The watchman was bringing a cup of coffee to George and found him lying down. He had not been doing dangerous work or even particularly arduous work. He had simply died of a heart attack. We grieved because we had lost one of our own. But in my thoughts I cannot include this with the accidental deaths that occur on construction jobs.

THERE comes a point when we find ourselves dealing not with individuals but with statistics. That, in fact, is what the study of construction safety is basically about. And while a sense of personal involvement and concern about particular people is essential to our humanity, mathematical analysis is essential to our efforts to solve problems of large scope, efforts to improve conditions for the multitudes.

The basic facts about construction safety—and danger—are well known to most people whose profession is building. As I have noted previously, in the United States, more workers are killed in our industry than in any other, the annual number of fatalities averaging between 1,000 and 1,300. The *rate* of fatalities is not quite the highest, but construction remains up there as one of the top three or four occupations in that statistic. The rate has decreased gradually from 13 per 100,000 full-time workers in 1990 to about 10 per 100,000, where it seems to linger. Nonfatal injuries and illnesses are down to about 5 cases per 100 full-time workers, much improved from what *Engineering News-Record* characterized as "that dismal period in the late 1970s when you could count on 18 out of 100 suffering some type of job-related injury or illness."

Falls from heights are the most frequent cause of death, and cranes are currently the hazard most discussed and analyzed, at least around New York City. Other leading sources of danger are scaffolding, ladders, trenches, objects dropping from above, forklifts and other mechanical equipment, as well as exposure to live electrical wires and harmful chemicals.

Safety standards—federal, state, and local—are constantly being proposed, enacted, and revised. We think of these as coming from humane instincts; but looked at historically, such instincts have not been the main force bringing about change. Early government efforts, relating mainly to mining and railroads, had minimal public support. Meaningful and effective government legislation—the Occupational Safety and Health Act of 1970—appeared, as can be seen from the law's title, very late in the day.

The most effective motivation appears to have been the arrival of workers' compensation insurance. First conceived in Europe, this form of insurance provides compensation medical care for employees who are injured in the course of employment, in exchange for mandatory relinquishment of the employee's right to sue his or her employer for the tort of negligence. In the United States the first such law was passed in Maryland in 1902, and by 1949 all states had followed suit.

Since employers were required by law to carry such insurance, and since rates could be affected by experience, accidents began to carry cost. Once industrialists realized that accidents were no longer cheap, or even free—as they had been in the past, when injured workers had the often very difficult burden of proving liability—interest in safety seemed to intensify. Unions and progressive organizations also showed ever-increasing concern for safety. Some workers resented the loss of the right to sue for negligence—except in extremely unusual circumstances—but by and large the trade-off is considered good for all. Of course, the worker does not relinquish the right to sue third parties, and general contractors—KBF definitely included—carry a portfolio of claims against them by subcontractor employees. For example, if a worker is injured because the general contractor has left a floor opening uncovered, he or she may seize the opportunity to pursue a complaint outside the workers' compensation format.

In addition to industry and labor, the public and politicians have taken action to address concerns stemming from particular events. In New York City, in 1911, fire broke out on the upper floors of the Triangle Waistcoat Company, resulting in the deaths of 146 of the 500 employees, mostly young women. In the wake of this horrific event, new rules were issued, among them requirements for standpipe and siamese connections bringing water to upper floors for fire department use.

In May of 1979 falling masonry, coming loose from an old building, fatally injured a Barnard College student. The accident led to New York City Local Law 10 of 1980 (modified in 1998 by Local Law 11), which compels building owners to inspect and repair facades. This created a whole new industry and changed the face of the city forever. With all sizeable buildings having to be inspected every five years, and then repaired as recommended, an army of engineers was put to work, and hundreds of caulkers and patchers of masonry found steady employment.

In the early 1980s, four serious crane accidents resulted in one pedestrian killed and seventeen injured, plus several workers hurt. This led to Local Law 45, which required a licensed rigger to erect and dismantle tower cranes, allowed stop-work orders to be issued if a sidewalk shed was not in place when necessary, and required a designated safety coordinator for all projects over fifteen stories in height.

In May of 1985 a woman was trapped for six hours under a collapsed crane, a drama that played out on local TV channels. This set in motion strict certification requirements for site safety managers, outlining specific responsibilities including record keeping.

In June of 1987 a steel beam fell off the edge of a building and killed a pedestrian. Before the end of that year Local Law 61 addressed rules relating to storing materials close to the perimeter of buildings under construction. It also brought about the requirement for the black and orange safety netting that now surrounds all floors not yet enclosed by the building's facade.

A series of scaffold accidents in the late 1990s led to new rigging safety rules.

And so it goes. The catastrophic crane accidents of 2008 have naturally led to changes in rules and, more important, should result in more careful attention to abiding by procedures already required.

MY company's safety record has been a good one. Workers are hurt on our jobs, but usually bumps and bruises, scrapes and cuts—and, in recent years, for some unexplained reason, a noticeable increase in wrenched backs. An occasional passerby will complain about having tripped on an irregular sidewalk. I shouldn't tempt the fates by saying this, because disaster could strike tomorrow. Our people are well trained and well motivated, but so are those employed by firms that have suffered catastrophic mishaps, and Lady Luck is known to be fickle.

We are covered by insurance, of course, although occasionally one hears of an accident that blows away the protection of insurance like a hurricane sweeping away a flimsy tent. When Texstar Construction Corp. in 1987 was performing lift-slab work for a project in Bridgeport, Connecticut, the superstructure collapsed, killing twenty-eight workers. The firm filed for bankruptcy, claiming that they faced liabilities far beyond anything that they could muster.

Then there are occasions when insurance might cover the dollar losses, but nothing can compensate for intangible side effects. George B.H. Macomber Company, a century-old Boston contractor, suffered a devastating accident in April 2006 when a self-climbing platform lift collapsed off the side of a dormitory building under construction and landed on heavily trafficked Boylston Street, in the heart of downtown Boston. Two subcontractor workers and a passing motorist were killed. The Macomber firm had been undergoing a difficult financial stretch, but executives appeared to be solving their problems when the accident occurred. "It shattered us emotionally," said CEO John D. Macomber. "Once something like that happens, it makes it difficult to win new work because of the extra scrutiny." In early 2007 the venerable company closed its doors.

This is not to imply that accidents are a major cause of contractor failure. As noted in the first chapter, financial disaster is endemic in our industry. According to the Surety Association of America, construction company failures usually have multiple causes. A master list features unrealistic growth, performance issues (inexperienced or inadequately trained personnel), changes in ownership or key staff, accounting and financial management problems, and "other factors" (economic downturn, high inflation, weather, onerous contract terms, owner's inability to pay), and so forth. Safety on the job site is apparently not a major factor in contractor failure.

Still, everyone agrees that worker safety is a tremendously important concern of every right-thinking person in the industry. And the fact that, independent of worker safety, construction is a financially hazardous business, simply points up—not that we need any reminders—that risk plays a prominent role in our lives.

REALISTICALLY, thinking about workers on a construction job, what can we hope to achieve by way of keeping them from harm?

I have on my office wall, framed, the cover of a publication called *Leslie's Illustrated Weekly,* issue of August 29, 1907. The work of art—for that is the proper term for it—shows three workmen standing at the edge of a building under construction, one reaching out with his right hand to guide into place an enormous piece of cornice stone being hoisted from above while holding on to a steel column with his left hand. One of his fellows, standing beside him, is casually holding on to the back of the leaning man's overalls. There are no safety harnesses, no netting, no scaffolding, nothing that gives the slightest indication of concern for safety. Two of the men are wearing beat-up fedoras, the third is bare-headed. The drawing, which was given to me by my sons on some festive occasion, is captioned "The Risky Work of the Sky-Scraper Builders."

Leslie's Illustrated Weekly, published from 1852 to 1922, was known for its patriotic fervor and for its cover pictures of soldiers and other heroic Americans. It is clear from the picture that hangs before me that construction workers of a hundred years ago were considered—at least by the publishers of *Leslie's*—to be heroes, gallantly building a new nation, and willing to expose themselves to danger in the process.

When, as a young boy, I watched ironworkers riveting beams and columns outside my apartment window, the men seemed to climb about on the steel framework, not recklessly, but with a comfortable self-assurance, the way I used to climb on the jungle gym in the local playground. Freedom of action is vital to the hardhat at work, and that, combined with the inescapable requirements of the job—reaching, hoisting, moving, concentrating—and the rugged terrain that even the neatest construction site presents, make it inevitable that there will be occasional tripping, loss of balance, touches of carelessness. Human nature being what it is, the inclination to take a shortcut is always present, along with the streak of independence that leads the strong-willed worker to believe that sometimes rules are made to be broken. Finally, from time to time, there are sure to be imperfections in the machines and materials with which the hardhat lives, making it impossible to eliminate risk. Which, of course, does not mean that we should slacken our efforts in this endeavor.

As for the public, the numbers of injuries and fatalities caused by construction jobs are very small, amazingly so if you consider what actually goes on when enormous towers are erected in the midst of crowded cities. Naturally, we want that number to be zero, and we work assiduously toward achieving that goal.

The more serious danger to the public lies in the finished structures. And in that regard, disasters are invariably found to lie in the work of the design engineers. The most notorious disaster in recent years was the 1981 collapse of a walkway in the Hyatt Regency hotel in Kansas City, killing 114 people and injuring more than two hundred others. The fault was found to lie in the design of steel rods supporting the crucial walkways.

OF course, nobody in their worst nightmares could conceive that twenty years after the Kansas City catastrophe, more than 2,700 Americans would die in the collapse of two 110-story towers in lower Manhattan. The cause: two large jet-powered passenger planes.

TWENTY | *9/11*

MOST PEOPLE REMEMBER where they were and what they were doing at nine o'clock on the morning of September 11, 2001. Certainly
New Yorkers do.

I was just walking through the door at Michael's, a barber shop on
upper Madison Avenue. Usually I get my haircuts at Henry's in Scarsdale, convenient to my office, and more reasonably priced than Manhattan establishments. But occasionally, for old times' sake, I used to
drop by Michael's, where I had often taken my sons when they were
young. Although there was an adult clientele, the shop catered to kids
and featured a number of small elevated cars that served as seats, an
attraction—along with toys and lollipops—for the younger set. The
cheery, somewhat circuslike room was a bizarre place in which to
witness a horrific, historic event.

I know that I arrived a little before nine, since the first plane had
just hit the north tower, and as I was getting settled into a chair, a
second plane struck the south tower. History tells us that the times
of impact were 8:46 and 9:03. The first TV reports were aired by
CNN at 8:49, and all stations were reporting on the situation within
minutes after that. The TV was on in Michael's, and confusion reigned
among the few people present. Everybody assumed that the first plane
crash was an accident, but the second one, accompanied by increasingly alarmist commentary, quickly gave rise to a mood of anxiety.
By 9:30 it was generally presumed that a terrorist attack was under

way. I got my haircut—perhaps the speediest one ever—and hopped into my car, determined to get to my office. I somehow felt—being totally irrational—that I ought to get to my desk, a control center of sorts. But first I called home to ask my wife if she had heard anything about our daughter-in-law, who worked for Merrill-Lynch, right across the street from the World Trade Center. She was fine, I was assured, having taken one of our granddaughters to nursery school for opening day. Good. Well, I'm off for the office. I suggest you come home, said my wife. After a few moments' reflection I took her advice, which was fortunate, since all tunnels and bridges were soon closed to incoming traffic, and I would have been stuck in Westchester County overnight.

I arrived home shortly after 10:00 to learn that the south tower had just collapsed. The north tower followed at 10:25, and we were left staring at a scene of smoldering ruins. The personal tragedies being played out before us were horrifying. Troubling news had come in from the Pentagon and from a field in Pennsylvania. Added to the appalling loss of life and destruction of property was concern for the nation, and worry about the implications of terror from abroad.

But as the hours passed and the initial shock abated, I found myself starting to think as an engineer. How could these huge structures, built in accordance with the strictest design codes, have been totally destroyed in such a brief moment, and by just a couple of airplanes? I recalled that back in 1945 a B-25 bomber, lost in a fog, had crashed into a high floor of the Empire State Building. It was a terrible accident, the plane crew and a number of workers in the offices most directly impacted were killed. Yet the building, overall, was scarcely affected. Here, more than half a century later, two of our most splendid towers, a landmark known throughout the world, had been destroyed, totally, in a scene that didn't seem real even when viewed again and again in replays.

In the days and weeks that followed I, along with many other builders, engineers, and interested citizens, read the reports of various study groups and acquired knowledge from several sources about the buildings that had so spectacularly collapsed. No fault could be found, no designer blamed, for what had happened. In fact, the buildings' sturdiness, their strong outer frame and central core, had resisted the impact very well. The use of lightweight trusses, spanning the area between the core and the perimeter, somewhat unusual in an office tower, was the subject of some questioning. But, overall, the design was deemed sound.

A few days after the incident I received a phone call from Lewis Lapham, editor of *Harper's,* for whom, as a contributing editor in years past, I had written a number of technology-related articles. Lewis, an intellectual gadfly and shrewd critic of the establishment, wanted me to write an appraisal of the Twin Towers' structural design, pointing out its glaring shortcomings. I suppose what he really wanted was something of an exposé, with intimations of ineptitude, if not outright scandal. I was always attracted by Lewis's enthusiasm, and I liked the idea of entering the arena of journalistic battle. I demurred, however, on the basis of lack of knowledge. Yet I told Lewis I would get back to him if I found some information relating to a cover-up or malfeasance. This never happened; and as a number of studies were conducted in the ensuing months—and years— particularly the exhaustively complete work of the National Institute of Standards and Technology (NIST), I was pleased to have resisted the temptation. The publication of that treatise would have made any snide comments of mine seem unprofessional, to say the very least.

The report's key findings are presented with impressive authority: "Some 200 technical experts—including about 85 career NIST experts and 125 leading experts from the private sector and academia—reviewed tens of thousands of documents, interviewed more than 1,000 people, reviewed 7,000 segments of video footage and 7,000 photographs, analyzed 236 pieces of steel from the wreckage, performed laboratory tests and sophisticated computer simulations of the sequence of events that occurred from the moment the aircraft struck the towers until they began to collapse."

Some lessons were learned and put to use—for example, in the design of exit stairs in tall buildings, in the number and location of stairwells, and in the materials used for the walls of stairwells. But the idea of blaming the collapse on the design engineers never took root.

WHILE I, on that fateful morning, was seated at home, mesmerized, brooding about human tragedy, international hostilities, and technological uncertainties, other engineers and construction people were galvanized into action. It's not that I didn't think about what help I might be able to render; but as an individual, and even with the forces of my small company, I couldn't conceive of a useful contribution. The situation called for courage, intelligence, engineering knowledge, and something more—a most important ingredient—leadership. Effective leadership could only come from people who had an element of authority, and as the fates would have it, the right people were at hand.

In New York City the fire department is designated to take the lead in rescue operations, the sanitation department normally handles debris removal, and the city's small Office of Emergency Management educates the public about preparedness and works to coordinate activities in crisis situations. But clearly the challenge of the 9/11 disaster was far beyond the capacity of these agencies. Representatives from the Federal Emergency Management Agency (FEMA) and the U.S. Army Corps of Engineers headed for the site, as is usual in large-scale disasters; but on arrival they found organized activity already under way.

Serendipitously, Kenneth Holden, commissioner of the city's Department of Design and Construction (DDC), along with his deputy, Michael Burton, happened to be attending a meeting near the World Trade Center on the morning of 9/11. DDC, charged with oversight of the city's building-construction programs, had many competent people on staff, but nothing like an organization intended to handle an unparalleled cataclysm. Yet when disaster struck, Holden and Burton simply moved in and started to act. As Holden is quoted by William Langewiesche in his book, *American Ground,* "None of us wondered, 'Should we contact the state? Should we contact the feds?' . . . We had the equipment. We had the connections. We could handle it. We just went in and did what we had to do. And no one said no."

Holden still had an agency to run, so it fell to Burton to take charge on-site at what quickly became known as Ground Zero. Michael Burton, executive deputy commissioner of DDC, was at the time of the 9/11 event thirty-nine years of age. An engineering graduate of Manhattan College who had joined DDC in 1996, he turned out to be the right man in the right spot that fateful morning. As Holden had said, "we had the connections," so Burton started to make phone calls. He recruited the LZA/Thornton-Tomassetti firm to provide engineering advice, then asked several leaders of major construction firms to join him on an initial survey of the site and surrounding buildings.

Burton and the DDC took on the vital leadership role; but, just as important, the construction community of New York City came forward in a magnificent wave of energy, talent, and determination. The job to be done was overwhelming in scope. Rescue operations were a first priority, although they quickly turned into careful recovery of remains. Tons of debris (1.6 million) had to be removed, the Hudson River kept at bay, the site stabilized, general cleanup attended to, infrastructure repaired, adjacent buildings inspected . . . the list of urgent tasks was long and daunting.

Before anything could be done, engineers had to inspect dangerous conditions—including a seventy-foot hole in the seven-level basement and a 240-foot-tall jagged remnant of one of the tower walls—evaluating what was stable and what was not. A representative of Mueser Rutledge, geotechnical engineers, explored hazardous underground caverns to check on the structural integrity of the slurry-wall foundation that was keeping the Hudson River from flooding the site. Engineers from the Port Authority, owners of the destroyed buildings, contributed their detailed knowledge of the structures and surrounding utilities. Safety engineers were brought in by FEMA, and numerous volunteers stepped forward from the three-hundred-member Structural Engineers Association of New York. Many of these engineers took great personal risks inspecting the rumbling, burning, tottering heaps of debris. Then they demonstrated a different sort of courage—perhaps even more impressive—by recommending what actions to take.

Speaking of courage, the firemen, who had shown a surplus of that before the collapse, soon swarmed over the site searching for lost comrades. And, from the earliest news of the disaster, construction tradesmen came in droves, bringing tools, actually adding to the chaos as their numbers increased into the first night and beyond. Sandy Perotta, one of our company's senior field men, who had risen through the years from laborer to punch-list specialist to superintendent, joined the hundreds of hardhat volunteers, bringing with him an acetylene torch for cutting steel. When I heard about the rush of construction workers anxious to help, I thought instinctively about the large number of workers, oldsters as well as youths, who joined the Seabees in the early days of World War II. I don't know what there is that makes construction workers seem to be more patriotic than average citizens. I will leave it to others to provide theoretical support for this phenomenon; but I am ever impressed by it. Even after order was restored at the site, with the National Guard controlling entry to the work area and the crowd of volunteers reduced to an organized workforce of fewer than 2,500—mostly ironworkers, equipment operators, carpenters, and laborers—flag-painted hardhats were very much in evidence.

BY the third day Burton and his staff had decided to divide the site into four quadrants, each to be managed by a contractor. The four firms selected were large and well established: Bovis Lend Lease, AMEC, Turner (with Plaza as coventurer), and Tully. (This team arrangement was modified in January, with Bovis Lend Lease given approximately 60 percent, AMEC 40 percent, and Tully becoming a subcontractor responsible for most excavation and trucking.) The contractors were selected without competitive bids and given authority to select subcontractors also without bids, based on ability to perform.

Burton got under way by calling on the "establishment," the people and firms he knew. He maintained a semblance of order by chairing twice-daily meetings in a kindergarten classroom adjoining the site. At times there were close to a hundred participants representing as many as twenty different organizations and government agencies. At those meetings, again to quote from the Langewiesche book, "there was a new social contract . . . All that counted about anyone was what that person could provide now." Permits and other bureaucratic hurdles were overcome with unprecedented speed. A marine contractor was retained to move the tons of debris across the river to a landfill site—where the material was carefully sifted for human remains and belongings of the deceased. Chaos gradually gave way to organized progress.

JUST two weeks into the job there was a slight whiff of scandal when word circulated that Bechtel had breezed into town and was scheduled to take over the whole operation. In the November 27 issue of *The Village Voice* it was alleged that "Rudy Giuliani is moving to award the city's biggest-ever emergency contract to one of America's most politically connected corporations." Bechtel was about to be given "the lucrative job of cleaning up the World Trade Center site." But two weeks later a Bechtel spokesman announced that the DDC would remain in charge. *Engineering News-Record* reported that the Army Corps of Engineers had praised DDC's management and had concluded that "continuity is the key at this juncture, to retain corporate knowledge, lessons learned, and strategic relationships." Local 375 of the municipal employees' union also endorsed the decision.

As could have been expected, the always cynical public and the always inquiring media were not satisfied with the no-bid procedure under which the work was proceeding. One evening I received a telephone call from a reporter at CBS asking if I wasn't suspicious, and resentful as well, because my firm had not been given an opportunity to submit a proposal. I replied that this was an emergency; that the four firms selected were large, well regarded, and of proven competence; and that I fully supported the action. Of course, I added, cost controls must be established and appropriate audits conducted. But the important thing was to move ahead with forces able to muster the workers and equipment needed. The reporter was clearly not satisfied with my response, but I meant it from the bottom of my heart.

In an effort to control costs and maintain public confidence, DDC had in fact retained "independent private sector inspectors general" to oversee operations of each of the four main contractors. The leader of one of these firms reported in a *New York Times* op-ed piece that "The result was that not one corruption scandal emerged—and this in a city once renowned for graft in its construction industry."

I fear that this was something of an overstatement, although the operations of the four major construction managers were indeed well controlled. My firm played a small role in this oversight when some of our office people—who were working on another DDC project at the time—were recruited to check Ground Zero bills for accuracy.

ALTHOUGH honesty prevailed at the top tiers of authority, there were no controls that could keep a few purported bad guys off the site. As the *Daily News* put it in a 2005 look backward, "the mob and corrupt contractors raided the 9/11 money pot." Among the *News*'s allegations: "AMEC's No. 1 guy on the ground was Vice President Leo DiRubbo, a reputed associate of the Lucchese crime family. At Ground Zero, it was DiRubbo's responsibility on behalf of the Lucchese crime family 'to ensure labor peace between organized crime and contractors' according to investigators' reports." And it wasn't just AMEC who brought in the so-called unsavory element: "Turner Construction hired Seasons Contracting, owned by Salvatore Carucci, a reputed Lucchese associate who was indicted in 1995 on charges of using a bogus minority-owned business to illegally win government work." (The charges were later dismissed.) The *News*'s revelation of "where the money went" goes on to list several of the longest-established New York City excavation contractors, all of whom are alleged to have made "payments to corrupt officials of Local 15 of the Operating Engineers, a local that prosecutors say long has been infiltrated by the Colombo crime family."

I fear that if there had been a ban on all firms accused of making inappropriate payments to union officials, access to the city's heavy construction equipment would have been severely limited. And at the end of the *News*'s exercise in journalistic innuendo, one realizes that, while the amount of money paid to each subcontractor is listed, no proof—or even accusation—of actual *over*payment is made. Still, I suppose we must assume that some money fell through the cracks.

Be that as it may, in the 9/11 cleanup the New York City construction industry, with all its blemishes, was on display. And the performance, almost everyone agrees, was remarkably successful.

Incredibly, there were no worker fatalities on the job. Unfortunately, many people who spent time in the vicinity of the wreckage, especially rescue and cleanup workers, were exposed to contaminants. As many as ten thousand individuals filed lawsuits based on health problems, or anticipated health problems, and in June of 2010 a settlement of approximately $700 million was reached covering most claimants, the funds to come from a federally financed insurance company that insures the city. Then Congress, in one of its final acts of that same year, passed a $4.3 billion bill to fund health-monitoring and treatment programs and additional compensation for job and economic losses.

OUR firm, aside from providing personnel to DDC for auditing invoices, played no part in the remarkable "unbuilding" of the World Trade Center. My only personal contact with the project came one afternoon in late January 2002 when I found myself on the thirtieth floor of the mostly abandoned American Express Building adjoining the site. Along with several other KBF people, I was scheduled to meet with officials of the DDC, and although the topics to be discussed related to other projects—mostly police stations and firehouses in other boroughs—if you wanted to speak with the agency's key people, they were invariably to be found not in their Queens office but "downtown."

The meeting was chaired by Michael Burton, and I still marvel that he was able to fit in other business along with the complex Ground Zero operation. Of course, more than four months had passed, the major decisions were long since made, and the work was very well advanced. Burton greeted us amiably, showing little evidence of the long days and nights spent under pressure. He disposed of our agenda swiftly, almost perfunctorily, and then led us to a window overlooking the work area down below. Clearly Burton was proud of what had been accomplished. The monstrous "pile" of debris had been converted into an orderly construction site. What had been a dangerously unstable, smoking, mountainous wasteland now had the look of an enormous building-excavation project. Numerous backhoes and bulldozers were efficiently at work, ramps provided access for trucks, and barges were docked nearby for taking materials to the landfill across the river. Provisions had been made for stabilizing the slurry wall that kept the river at bay, and plans were well advanced for repairing subway and commuter railroads, electrical systems, and many other complex underground facilities.

As Burton discussed details of the work, he gradually shifted emphasis from the mechanical to the human. He spoke glowingly of how cooperation among a multitude of organizations, public and private, had overcome bureaucratic obstacles that ordinarily would have thwarted progress for months, possibly years. Incidentally, he interjected, as just one small example of how formal protocols were being set aside, a writer from *The Atlantic Monthly* had been granted full access to the site, including attendance at key executive meetings. This was William Langewiesche, who had been living with the project night and day and would be in a position to tell a singularly insightful story, first for the magazine, then in a book.

This casual footnote to Burton's discourse evoked memories of a previous literary effort. Back in 1981, the author Tracy Kidder, also under contract with *The Atlantic,* had "lived with" a group of engineers who were designing and building a new computer at the Data General Corporation. Kidder wrote of his experience, first in the magazine, then in a book titled *The Soul of a New Machine.* It was my pleasure to write a review of his fascinating book for *The New York*

Times Book Review and later to meet him. After winning the Pulitzer Prize and the American Book Award, *Soul* became an international bestseller, and several of its real-life engineer characters became, at least for a while, culture heroes. I told Burton about this phenomenon and added a lighthearted bit of advice. "Play your cards right," I said to this young, energetic, obviously ambitious construction engineer, "and you, too, may become the hero of a book and eventually a culture hero."

Indeed, when the Langewiesche book appeared a year or so later, it was favorably reviewed, given the New York City Book Award for Journalism, and named runner-up for the general nonfiction award of the National Book Critics Circle, although it never did achieve the acclaim and wide distribution of *The Soul of a New Machine*.

As it happened, Mike Burton didn't need Langewiesche's book to achieve a quotient of celebrity. In April of 2002 he was featured on the cover of *Engineering News-Record* and given the magazine's prestigious Award of Excellence. He must have been very proud of the award and pleased by the citation: "For his grace under fire in carving order from chaos at Ground Zero, for guiding his team to a safe and successful conclusion despite so many obstacles, for being both a tough and compassionate decisionmaker and for allowing the construction industry to prove its mettle, the editors of *ENR* choose Michael Burton for the 2002 Award of Excellence."

All credit to Mike Burton; but I also like the line about allowing the construction industry to prove its mettle. The CEO of Turner Construction, Peter Devoren, was quoted in the *ENR* article as saying, "the city, primes, subs, unions, everyone put their best foot forward and it should enhance the perception of New York's construction industry."

I don't know about public perception, and it is certainly an open question whether the New York construction industry will ever gain the general esteem of our fellow citizens, but I do know that when I left the DDC makeshift office that afternoon in January 2002, I felt really good about what I do for a living and about the people with whom I do it.

9/11

★ ★ ★

IT is ironic, and perhaps a lesson in the elusiveness of lasting contentment, that back at my office a message from our lawyers was waiting for me, news about what was about to become the ugliest experience of my professional life, news about—the Job from Hell.

TWENTY-ONE   *The Job from Hell*

I CAN'T SAY we weren't warned.

"Don't work for those people!" our friendly subcontractor sputtered. "They have a lawyer who would rather sue you than say hello."

After all, our alarmist friend was talking about the Osborn. The Osborn, "Westchester's premier senior living community," as they advertised themselves, and as I knew them to be by reputation. And by more than reputation. I had friends who lived at the Osborn, and I had visited them on a number of occasions. The place was beautiful, the atmosphere delightful, and the residents totally pleased with the attentive service of the staff.

It is still a lovely place, well kept and well run. When I speak of the Job from Hell, the demons I have in mind are lawyers.

LIKE most horror stories the opening chapter is deceptively serene. In April of 1999, KBF entered into a preconstruction agreement with the Osborn to assist in the finalization of documents for construction of two residential buildings, four stories tall, containing ninety-four spacious apartments. Located on a picturesque fifty-six-acre campus in Rye, the project featured attractive masonry exteriors topped by a steep mansard roof that gave the buildings an Old World flavor and also served to conceal mechanical equipment on the flat roof behind. Perkins Eastman were the architects, Severud

Associates the structural engineers, both well-established, respected professionals with whom we were pleased to be working. The attorney was LePatner & Associates, headed by Barry LePatner, the dangerous individual about whom we had been warned. But we weren't worried about lawyers. In fact, we weren't worried about anything. We were good guys intent on doing a good job for good people.

After several months of preconstruction consultations, agreement was reached on a guaranteed maximum contract price of $39 million. Our bonding company cheerfully provided the needed certificates. On January 14, 2000, we signed a final contract based on completed drawings and specifications. The document contained a substantial completion date of April 15, 2001, and final completion of May 15. Fifteen months seemed like a pretty tight schedule for this $39 million project; but we were confident we could make it, and if we missed it by a few days, that didn't seem so forbidding. The penalty for missing the completion date (without appropriate extensions of time) was limited in the contract to a maximum of $350,000. This figure was deemed adequate to cover such additional costs as the owner might incur. So much for the happy first chapter.

THIS being an imperfect world, it happens from time to time that on a construction job unanticipated problems may arise. Well, in this case serious problems did arise, causing delays. I marvel to think that despite these we achieved completion just three months behind schedule. When tenants started moving in—including one couple who were my longtime family friends—everyone seemed to be in great good humor. The buildings looked beautiful, and we breathed a sigh of relief. Difficulties overcome and another job well done.

Of course, the unanticipated problems had resulted in additional expenses, and as these were presented, and the total cost of the project was seen to have exceeded the guaranteed maximum by a substantial amount, the atmosphere became considerably less festive. Even so, we had no feeling of impending crisis. If worse came to worst, differences could be resolved in arbitration. The contract, under a section called "Conflict Resolution," seemed to say so in soothing words.

I still find it hard to believe what happened. When compromise proved elusive, the owner's attorney, Mr. LePatner, appeared upon the scene. Rejecting first mediation, then arbitration, he took us inexorably on a journey through the courts, a trip of horrors for us, twenty-six subcontractors, the owner, and two design professionals, thirty parties in all, carrying along, by my best count, twenty-two law firms plus special consultants. This journey lasted for more than eight years, from the fall of 2001 until February of 2010, when a settlement was reached on the eve of going to trial.

WHAT was the nature of the conflict? I think all parties would agree that the delay and extra cost stemmed mainly from three major causes. First, the heating system was changed from two-pipe to four-pipe. The cost of this mechanical change was agreed to and was not an issue; but the heating redesign required multiple structural changes, and the essential details were not provided by the structural engineer when required by the job schedule. Thus, we were unable to proceed with pouring concrete beams and manufacturing pre-cast concrete plank. This presented a serious setback in the early stages of the project.

The second delay was also structural, stemming from an unfortunate error on the part of the engineer. The mansard roof, in effect a thin curved wall sitting atop the buildings, had to be designed to withstand wind pressure, and the engineer belatedly discovered that his design was based on a figure lower than that established by the current building code in New York State. He changed the design to conform to code, but not in time to prevent a delay in manufacture of the structure supporting the mansard roof. This in turn held up installation of the flat roofing, and prevented us from making the building watertight.

We were already behind schedule because of the first delay. Now, with the roof held up, and unable to proceed with interior work until the building was watertight, we resorted to a temporary roof. In a sad quirk of fate, this ended up costing time instead of saving it. Harsh winter weather took a toll on the temporary roof—or, let me argue for the enemy, was the temporary roof not properly maintained? In any event, leaks developed. The leaks dampened some of the drywall, which should not have been a serious matter, except that the drywall developed mold. Oh boy! Mold. The drywall was found to have been defective, and the cost of replacing it was covered by insurance. But the damage to the schedule was now beyond repair. To keep the time overrun to a minimum, we embarked on a program of acceleration. This entailed costs for overtime labor, which was authorized by the owner—or not, depending on who tells the tale.

So who was responsible for the delay and the additional costs? In the legal imbroglio that was to ensue, Mr. LePatner took a scatter-shot approach: his "Response to Demand for Expert Disclosure," submitted to all parties, stated that his expert witness would testify to the fact that "Perkins Eastman and its design consultants failed to provide complete and coordinated design drawings for the Project which led to delays . . ." etc., etc. in great detail. In other words, the architect and his structural engineer were at fault. Good news for the contractor, since the design professionals were employed by the owner. But wait. The expert would also testify that "as a result of KBF's overall project management, including KBF's acts, errors, omissions, negligence and breaches of the Osborn/KBF Agreement, the Project was substantially delayed causing specific and calculable damages to The Osborn." So, in the alternative, KBF was to blame. If we had been smarter, more diligent, more adaptable, we could have minimized the delays or at least reduced their adverse effects. And if the temporary roof hadn't leaked, the most serious delay could have been averted.

In dollars and cents the controversy revolved around our final requisition for approximately $9 million: roughly $3 million held by the owner as final "retainage" (owed under the contract), $3 million for replacing the defective drywall (paid for by insurance), and $3 million for the costs of delay, including acceleration overtime. The first $6 million was clearly payable. So we looked at this as essentially a $3 million claim. Admittedly, that is a large overrun; but, at 7½ percent, not a total disaster on a $39 million project that had run into serious problems.

Mr. LePatner rejected our claim in toto and subsequently prepared a counterclaim of approximately $5 million. This was purported to cover the owner's cost for a late opening, plus additional professional fees and paying in-house contractors to correct our inferior and incomplete work. For good measure, he added $1–1.5 million for "future corrective work," making his counterclaim $6.5 million.

As for the $350,000 limit we thought protected us in case of late completion, LePatner claimed that we hadn't given proper notice, or that we had abandoned the job, or been discharged or whatever—I never did understand the details. In any event, the protective limit vanished in a morass of legal phraseology.

CLEARLY, we were not going to collect all of our $9 million requisition. We and our subcontractors could not expect to avoid bearing some share of the cost overrun. A compromise was called for.

In the absence of agreement, we were anxious to proceed with mediation or, if need be, arbitration, which would doubtless result in a forced compromise. Would we end up with our $3 million extra completely wiped out by disapprovals and counterclaims? A little better? A little worse? This was the scope of the problem, as we discussed it with our subcontractors, our attorneys, with advisers, with kibitzers, with at least one judge who tried to persuade the parties to settle. The amount of the final settlement is confidential, although dozens of people know the nature of the dispute and the course of events. I mention the figures just to put the whole business in perspective and to reveal the absurdity of the cost in time and energy, as well as money.

Eight years of legal conflict. Eight years. KBF's legal bills exceeded $2 million. This I know because I signed the checks. Reliable sources, to use a journalist's term, have revealed that the owner's legal bills were more than double this figure. Add in the subcontractors' lawyers—twenty-two as I have noted—and the architect's and engineer's and surely the total amount spent on attorney fees exceeded $8 million, possibly $10 million.

I cannot say that the lawyers didn't work hard to earn their money. They spent hours—days—weeks—months—laboring over documents of every conceivable sort. And interminable conferences, phone calls, hearings, shuffling papers in a process called discovery, and perhaps the greatest time-waster of all: depositions. Osborn deposed five of KBF's people plus eleven subcontractors, the architect, and the engineer—that's eighteen individuals!—while we deposed four of the Osborn staff. In all, twenty-two question-and-answer sessions, some of them lasting more than a day, each hearing with stenographer, staff, and attorneys. Even in this computer age, there were reams of paper piled high, impossible to keep track of. The cost to all the private parties was only part of the shameful business. Consider the expense born by the greater society through use of the courts. Although we never went to trial, there were countless days spent in hearings with judges. Dozens of government attorneys devoted weeks to reviewing motions and writing lengthy opinions. There were multiple hearings before appeals courts—practically every motion was appealed—followed by the writing of tomes by many judges and their aides. And those palatial courthouses themselves: how expensive they must be to maintain. With the armies of guards and court officials and stenographers. (I won't count the jury, since a pool of jurors was on hand on the day of settlement, but I trust they found useful occupation elsewhere.)

IN January 2002, informal discussions having proved fruitless, we filed for mediation. A number of potential mediators were recommended by the American Arbitration Association, but Mr. LePatner turned down the entire list, complaining that none of them had experience representing owners in the legal arena. He followed this with a refusal to participate in mediation altogether.

Since LePatner turned down mediation, we took the next step provided in the contract and served a demand for arbitration. We consoled ourselves with the thought that this might prove to be more quickly conclusive in the long run. But no. Arbitration was also resisted by our opponent. Puzzled, our attorneys obtained an order from the court for an arbitration to proceed. LePatner reacted by filing a motion to stay the arbitration. He also commenced a lawsuit, indicating his determination to carry this matter into the courts.

Four months later the court denied LePatner's motion to stay the arbitration, and we thought that at last, the delaying tactics having been played out, we would be moving ahead. How wrong we were. The following week our nemesis appealed. We were to learn that in this new nightmare world, every decision would be appealed, making for more delay—and, of course, more expense. After a wait of seven months he argued his case before the appellate division, and two months later—now June 30, 2003, two years after substantial completion—received the ruling he desired: the Osborn "cannot be compelled to forego the right to seek judicial relief and instead submit to arbitration . . . The Supreme Court erred." Quite a shock.

Yet studying the papers, I could understand the appellate division's reasoning. The "Dispute Resolution" section of the contract does call for discussions, then mediation, and as a last resort arbitration; yet it specifies that each dispute of up to $150,000 must be subjected to arbitration as it arises. This, of course, taken literally, makes the whole clause useless; nobody is going to stop to arbitrate each small disagreement as a job progresses, and we didn't. The original Supreme Court judge was persuaded that the contract favors arbitration over litigation, and ruled accordingly. But in the end, the devil turned out to be in the details.

So, here we were, to repeat, two years after substantial completion, our requisition unpaid, a lawsuit commenced against us by the owner, subcontractors impatiently demanding payment—in other words, up the proverbial creek.

* * *

TWO years had been wasted simply trying to get to arbitration, and six more years of legal nightmare lay ahead. But let me stop at this crucial juncture. This was the moment of crisis, of tragedy, of comedy, of disbelief, of shame, of disgust. Why did LePatner resolve to proceed in a court of law, knowing from experience what this would mean in time and money and waste? Why did he not choose to proceed with arbitration, regardless of the judicial analysis of the contract language?

In turning away from an initial mediation, LePatner stated that none of the proposed mediators had experience representing owners in construction matters, so perhaps he felt the same concern about arbitrators. Yet given the very large number of experienced arbitrators available to the American Arbitration Association, it is not reasonable to claim that a panel of three with backgrounds satisfactory to all parties could not be found. And let me say parenthetically that I consider it a great insult to construction professionals who have served as arbitrators—including me—to imply that a contractor or an attorney who often represents contractors will not properly consider the rights and privileges of an owner. If anything, a contractor-arbitrator will look askance on improper behavior by someone in his industry, at any action that he knows from experience is not fair or professional. I find it hard to believe that LePatner based his decision on a belief that he would find understanding and fairness in a judge and a jury but not in a panel of arbitrators from the AAA. Perhaps he believed that dragging us and our subcontractors—and his design professionals—through a long and costly legal process would wear us out, break our will, possibly ruin us financially.

THE avoidance of arbitration was a great disappointment to some of us at KBF even before we realized how dreadfully extended the legal route would prove. I have always admired what seemed to me to be the most civilized way to address disputes: negotiation, mediation, arbitration in that order as required; and I served as an arbitrator for many years. John Cricco, after he retired from KBF, chaired

GOOD GUYS, WISEGUYS, AND PUTTING UP BUILDINGS

seminars for the AAA. And Bob Borg, most of all, dedicated years of ardent voluntary support for the cause of alternative dispute resolution. Having earned a degree in law as well as in engineering, Bob was particularly suited to participate in the crusade, and among his many activities he served as chair of the National Construction Industry Advisory Committee, later to become the National Construction Industry Dispute Resolution Committee. This organization, composed of fourteen prominent engineering, architectural, and business societies, endorsed the use of the Construction Industry Arbitration Rules of the AAA. It was sad to see Bob, near the end of his career, finding his company embroiled in wasteful, belligerent litigation, the very barbarism he had worked so hard to remedy.

I've thought long and hard about why LePatner chose to take the route he did; and after reading some of his writings in the press, plus comments on his firm's Internet site, and especially in his book *Broken Buildings, Busted Budgets: How to Fix America's Trillion-Dollar Construction Industry,* published in 2007, I begin to see a pattern to his thinking. As I see it, he would have his readers believe that when a building contractor has a dispute with an owner, the contractor is likely to be a predator guilty of unscrupulous conduct. This, then, would justify fighting the contractor to the death— speaking rhetorically—using any and all legal methods available. Not only does the victimized owner deserve to be protected; he suggests that society is well served if the villain can be destroyed.

"After work begins," LePatner declaims in his book, "construction contractors become de facto monopolies whose superior information and bargaining position enable them to take advantage of owners." He then continues, "Not all contractors use their market power to exploit owners, but many do, and unfortunately they are the ones most likely to remain in the business."

There are, as I have admitted earlier, contractors who bid low and hope to make their profit through change orders, contrived as needed to fit the occasion. But such contractors are, by their nature and reputation, largely restricted to public works, and, even in that world, government agencies work hard to blacklist them or otherwise control their underhanded ways. The important, indeed critical, fact that LePatner chooses to ignore is that private work is very different. In this field, where contractors are chosen by individuals or organizations not controlled by government low-bid restrictions, a good reputation—for honesty and fairness as well as competence—is all-important.

Consider the following statement that appears in the 1990 report of the New York State Organized Crime Task Force, a scrupulous work prepared by a group that is passionately committed to honorable performance in the New York City construction industry:

> A contractor on a private construction project has a strong incentive to please his client, whose satisfaction determines whether the contractor will be hired again and/or be recommended to other developers. Overcharging, waste and litigation will not endear the contractor to his private sector employer.

Like most contractors, large and small, our company tries very hard to develop the best reputation possible and to cultivate good relationships throughout the industry, with architects and engineers, with subcontractors, and with potential clients, private and public. This doesn't mean that we won't have occasional differences of opinion, or even disputes. But it does mean that we do the best we can, which is usually pretty good, and we have made our way with reasonable felicity and success for more than half a century. Doubtless someone at the Osborn checked us out before deciding to have us perform work for the institution.

Also, I have found that most owners are not innocent fools asking to be duped. They are usually intelligent, experienced executives represented by architects and other talented professionals. In any event, I find no merit in the LePatner hypothesis of contractor power and wicked intent. It was my bad fortune to run into an attorney with such a low opinion of our industry and such a venomous approach in his dealings with contractors.

Yet it was my good fortune, as a writer and would-be scholar, to spend eight years in the arena with "America's Construction Reform Guru," as his publisher refers to him. In a torrent of books, articles, speeches, interviews, and blogs—as well as in the way he practices law—Mr. LePatner makes his case. I take my stand in opposition to his arguments and his actions. In putting up buildings, there will always be an element of "the unexpected." Leaks, imperfections, miscalculations, delays and such, are part of life in the construction industry. This is not the realm of crime and punishment, freedom of speech, or civil rights. To carry such matters into the courts while actively avoiding Alternate Dispute Resolution is a distortion of our precious legal system. In my view such an approach is socially pernicious. Economically it is demonstrably irrational.

Cynical friends, after considering my analysis, say that I philosophize too much. They hold that in general, when lawyers drag matters out over a period of years—purposefully, ingeniously, gratuitously—they do it in order to maximize the fees to be generated for themselves.

I pick up the story again at the end of summer 2003, two years after substantial completion, arbitration now ruled out, and the way ahead dark and forebidding. There was, belatedly, a discussion between attorneys and a brief try at mediation; but that yielded not an iota of compromise from the other side, nor any move toward arbitration. With the backing of the appellate court's decision, our opponent was determined to litigate, and we had no choice but to follow.

The next stage was "discovery", that is, production and review of documents. I don't have the least idea how this massive exchange of papers, discs, and whatnots took place; all I know is that it took a year—November 2003 to the end of 2004—and was costly.

Three years now gone, and counting, it was time for depositions. At a court conference held in the spring of 2005, the depositions were scheduled to start in the summer of 2005 and run through 2006. This sounds like a long period of time, but as noted previously, LePatner elected to depose eighteen individuals while we deposed four—that's twenty-two mini-trial procedures.

In early 2007, discovery and depositions finally behind us, each side filed motions for summary judgment. Apparently this is an obligatory part of the ritual, even though nobody expects that a summary judgment will be granted.

At about this time it occurred to me that this pretrial activity, having started in September of 2001, more than five years earlier, could go on forever, while some of us weren't getting any younger. Half kidding, I asked Allen Ross, our attorney, if senior citizens couldn't be given some special consideration by the court. Much to my surprise, Allen said, well yes, under provisions of CPLR 3403(a)(4) trial preference could indeed be given to senior citizens. So Borg, Florman, and Zelazny had copies made of our birth certificates and filled out some forms. Appropriate papers were submitted to the court; but since we had allowed years to go by since the start of this whole mess, the application was rejected as untimely. LePatner's contribution was to formally oppose this request to expedite matters. What more blatant evidence could there be of our antagonist's objective to extend the time and increase the expense of the proceedings? As it happened, the principals survived, but there were those who did not. While the eight-year tragicomedy played itself out, death claimed three key role players: Aldo Rizzo, our project manager on the Osborn; Franklin Chan, our chief estimator, who knew every little detail in the plans; and Michael Pirraglia, the Osborn's chief of construction. A truly mournful feature of this deplorable tale.

Finally, on November 19, 2007, an "assignment conference" took place in the chambers of the Honorable Joan B. Lefkowitz at the New York Supreme Court in White Plains. The purpose was to set a date for trial and to select a judge to handle the case. But Judge Lefkowitz did what any practical, right-thinking person would do—and I loved her for it—she lectured the parties about the foolishness of carrying this matter to trial. A complex case before a jury: it would take weeks in court, nobody would understand it, at the end any decision would be appealed, and the matter would go on for more years with ever-mounting expenses. She knew practically nothing about the facts of the matter, but she talked sense to the parties, together and apart, and within a short time came up with a recommended settlement figure. It was a compromise figure, of course, very close to what we at KBF had been thinking of, and very close to what everyone knew a settlement figure would eventually prove to be.

The attorneys for the major subs and suppliers were either present in the court or on tap by telephone, as were their clients. News of the proposed settlement was greeted, as expected, with moans and groans, anger and disgust. "We've come this far," was one refrain, "let's stay with it and see the bastards in court." Those subs who were, however reluctantly, willing to talk settlement were divided into two camps: those who had nothing to do with the whole mess, having provided metal door frames, for example, and felt that they shouldn't be expected to share pro rata in any discount, and those who had everything to do with the whole mess and, having invested extra money on labor, felt that they were entitled to a bigger proportional share of any recovery. What followed in the next two hours was a thing of beauty. Joe Zelazny, with patience, humor, resignation, and good sense, convinced one and all to go along more or less pro rata. His message was: "Let's get on with our lives. We'll do other jobs together. Let's put this bad dream behind us." If the world worked like this, I mused, how wonderful that would be.

Of course, the world doesn't work like that. The other side flatly refused to accept the proposed figure.

We met again with Judge Lefkowitz two weeks later, December 3, 2007; but with no movement from our opponent, settlement was forgotten and work proceeded on selecting a trial date. At this point, one of the judge's assistants pointed out that there were a number of motions that had been made by the various parties—some more than a year previously—but never decided. Impossible, said the judge, such motions are supposed to be disposed of within a month of coming to the court. Impossible or not, that was the situation. It was a total mystery—and a total disgrace—that nobody, within the court or without, had taken action on this. But there we were: motions made, filed, but not acted on.

We had no choice but to see trial postponed pending decisions on the motions—a dozen or so, some rather complex—then of course appeals, argument before the appellate court, followed by a lengthy wait for final decisions. So instead of the trial being scheduled for early 2008, we ended up with early 2010, a further delay of two years. I can't believe some of these dates, but there they are in my notes, stark in their reality.

The only positive feature of this torturous experience was my visit to the Appellate Division, Second Department, in May of 2009 when the motions were argued. The questions asked by the judges were so sensible, pragmatic, and down-to-earth, that the lawyers, relying on the fine print in contracts, seemed to be on the defensive. I was pleased with the way the hearing went, and doubly pleased with the wording of the decisions when they were issued. There was nothing we could use to say we'd won the case; but I'm inclined to believe that the rulings, in the end, helped to bring about a satisfactory settlement.

The other significant experience of that two-year time of travail was a single day attempt at mediation. The lawyers had discussed getting the architect and engineer, who were also being sued by the Osborn, involved in the process. But these design professionals—irate at finding themselves in litigation with their client—refused to participate, effectively dooming the effort. Nevertheless, we were game to try anything, and a hearing was scheduled. The feature of the day was Mr. LePatner's showing of a screen production, intended, I suppose, to impress a jury, and incidentally to intimidate us. I must admit it was a professionally prepared epic. The pictures of moldy drywall were technically impressive. However, nothing substantive was accomplished that day, no compromise even hinted at.

The much-postponed trial was finally scheduled for February 1, 2010, a Monday. More than two years had passed since our meetings with Judge Lefkowitz, and eight years since we had filed a demand for mediation. In a world thirsting for sensible use of resources, what a waste of energy and talent—and money. In a world desperate for civilized management of quarrels, what a sorry example of stubborn vindictiveness. All during this time I had received assurances from veterans of such fiascos that this was the way things were done, and all would be settled "on the courtroom steps." The way things were done? It need not be the way things are done. It should not be the way things are done. It was a shameful business, and even though I felt like the helpless victim, I was ashamed to have been a part of it.

THE end came suddenly.

I happened to be out of town for several days, planning to return on the fateful Monday to observe selection of the jury. On Friday I telephoned the office and was told that, under the aegis of the Honorable William J. Giacomo, a settlement had just been reached. Joe Zelazny, canvassing our subcontractors again, had encountered the expected emotional outbursts but managed to come up with a result similar to what he had achieved two years earlier. LePatner did whatever he had to do. The terms of the settlement, and any negotiations leading up to it, are confidential. But it is not revealing any secrets to say that we at KBF were satisfied with the dollar figure agreed on. Not that this mitigated the disaster. There was no recovery of our $2 million in legal expense. Nor could we make up the eight years of crippled bonding and lost business opportunities. The long-sought settlement had been attained; but there could be no satisfaction in any of this. Ever.

On Monday a sizeable group—including most of the larger subcontractors and their attorneys—gathered in a courtroom. The judge perfunctorily recited the settlement terms and asked if the parties agreed. They did. (We found out several days later that Osborn's case against their design professionals was also settled.) His Honor then said, in effect, that's it—just another day at the office for him.

It was quiet. Suddenly I found myself thinking of T. S. Eliot's famous poem "The Hollow Men," which I had studied in school many years before. We were, all of us in that room, hollow men indeed, "Headpiece filled with straw. Alas!" And our world seemed to be ending, as Eliot suggested, "Not with a bang but a whimper."

TWENTY-TWO   *And a Happy Ending of Course*

ENOUGH OF GLOOMY T. S. ELIOT. The Job from Hell is not the end of the world. Risk and adventure are part of the game, and even when the outcome is not to our liking, there are always lessons to be learned and even satisfaction to be derived from holding up under pressure. "The fullness of life is in the hazards of life." That's from Edith Hamilton's *The Greek Way,* a quote that Robert Kennedy underlined in his copy of the book.

And, let us remember, there is another side to things, something not to be forgotten or taken for granted. Simply put: there has been much pure delight in being a builder. So, let us think about the good times. I put aside "The Hollow Men" and turn to Stephen Sondheim's opening number from *A Funny Thing Happened on the Way to the Forum.*

As the curtain rises—or, as I recall, unexpectedly collapses—the great comic actor Zero Mostel (in the original version, 1962) steps forward and assures the audience that there will be no tragedy in this evening's performance. The orchestra strikes up, and he sings out "Comedy Tonight," a song that has become part of Broadway history. Good cheer fills the theater, and my mood brightens as we are promised a happy ending.

No more thoughts of the courtroom, let me start this final chapter with a recounting of KBF's experience in showbiz—to be precise, in the moviemaking business.

WHEN John Lindsay was mayor of New York City in the late 1960s and early 1970s, he encouraged filmmakers to leave their Hollywood sets and to use the city as a realistic backdrop for some of their work.

One morning in 1973 I received a phone call from a representative of the mayor's office. It seemed that the city had granted a license to Paramount Pictures to film a scene at the site of a building KBF was constructing on the Upper West Side of Manhattan. I responded by saying that this sounded exciting and I assumed we would be paid a handsome fee for granting access to the Hollywood giant. Oh no, came the reply, you're building a city-financed project, and the mayor expects you to grant access as a courtesy, without reimbursement. Under the circumstances, I was not about to argue, although I did warn that the visitors should come prepared to satisfy the hardhats whose working day they would be disrupting, perhaps buy lunch or in other ways show their appreciation. This suggestion was understood and accepted, and two days later a crew showed up with cameras, lights, and miscellaneous equipment. What excitement! (I managed to fit a site visit into my schedule that day.)

Two scenes were to be filmed: First, a villainous-looking man comes running by the construction job, and a bunch of hardhats, suddenly alerted, go after the bad guy and pummel him. Then there is a close-up of one of the hardhats, standing in front of the half-constructed building, being interviewed. We didn't know it at the time, but the film was to be *Death Wish,* starring Charles Bronson as an architect turned vigilante after the murder of his wife and brutalization of his daughter. The vigilante spirit spreads throughout the city and is responsible for the determination of the construction workers to take justice into their own hands.

It was great fun to see the cameras set up, the crews busy with this and that, and the actors milling around. Finally, all was set to go, with the interview scene to be filmed first. However, as the actor stepped forward before the cameras, we KBF people were astonished to see that the costume designer had made a terrible mistake. The actor playing the part of the construction worker was wearing a flat helmet, reminiscent of a World War I doughboy, rather than the familiar hardhat of today, which is modeled along the lines of World War II headwear. (The flat helmet is worn by heavy construction underground workers—the "moles"—but never by building construction workers.) John Cricco rushed over to the assistant director, who was in charge, and at the last moment prevented what would have been an incredible embarrassment, or possibly considerable expense if they had to return for a refilming. Expressing great appreciation, the young man asked if we could lend him a helmet of the proper sort. "Of course," said John, smiling, as he handed over a helmet with the KBF logo emblazened on the front. This elicited a groan and an outburst: "Thanks, but you know we can't possibly use that helmet in a close-up. Don't you have a plain one?" A hushed negotiation took place, and a compromise agreement was reached. We provided a helmet with no logo on it, and for the next take, the running scene, a large KBF sign was positioned as a backdrop.

The movie, released in 1974, was a great box-office hit, and we started to receive phone calls from friends and colleagues. The sign appears for only a few moments about two-thirds through the film, but it is amazing the impact that it had. I must confess that my favorite call was the one that came from a competitor who said that we'd spoiled his evening at the movies.

THAT was our only direct participation in the entertainment business, unless I count working with the many stage and lighting specialists who designed the exhibits we built at the 1964 World's Fair. Their flamboyance gave me a taste of what life in the theater is like. Very different from the contractors' world. Although, when you come to think of it, in construction we have our own theatrical productions, festivities that have provided us with a lot of pleasure through the years. I refer to groundbreakings, topping-out parties, and ribbon-cutting dedications.

For me the most diverting of these were the celebrations at Lionel Hampton Houses, with Hampton himself, the world-famous vibraphonist, providing the all-star music and cheerful repartee. But there were many other notable occasions, some graced with band music and singing, and all featuring resounding speeches. On the podium I would often find myself mingling with celebrities, everyone in great good humor. In addition to the ever-present politicians, there were frequently the sponsors of projects, such as the Estée Lauder family at the dedication of the Adventure Playground in Central Park. And when we built for the Salvation Army, the New York City Mission Society, the Jewish Guild for the Blind, United Cerebral Palsy, White Plains Interfaith Alliance, and various hospitals and nursing homes, there were always officials and board members on hand, including business leaders and social luminaries.

Dedications of religious structures and buildings sponsored by religious organizations were special, graced by the music of choirs and the blessings of priests, ministers, and rabbis. And among the most special of the special was the dedication, in 1990, of Wyatt Tee Walker Senior Citizens Housing on 118th Street and Frederick Douglass Boulevard in Harlem. The ceremony began with a Sunday morning service at Reverend Walker's Canaan Baptist Church of Christ, at the conclusion of which the congregation, in a holiday mood and dressed in their finest, walked the few blocks to the apartment house, where a reception was held. What made the occasion especially memorable was the fact that Wyatt Tee Walker was a historic figure, one of the great leaders of the Civil Rights Movement. He had been chief of staff for Dr. Martin Luther King, Jr., and in 1958 had become an early board member of the Southern Christian Leadership Conference. The apartment project we dedicated that day was only one small example of the many community-improvement activities for which, in recent years, Dr. Walker had been responsible.

INEVITABLY, the good fun at these events is transmuted into good feelings of a deeper sort, as compliments are distributed liberally to one and all, to community leaders, owners, lenders, architects in their moment of glory, and finally the contractor. It is pleasant to be given credit for good work, and really nice to see project managers, superintendents, and foremen given verbal pats on the back.

Finally, attention shifts from people to the building itself. Sometimes there are tours. But even without actual exploration of the premises, the architectural radiance of the structure makes itself felt. The creativity of the architect shines forth. The majesty of the building impresses: so large and imposing a physical object compared with the simple humans who made it. And most of all there is the satisfaction evoked by noble purpose—to shelter, educate, heal, and inspire. It has been my good fortune to work mostly on projects that are deemed socially worthy. Not that this makes me a superior person. Our firm has built luxury housing, and we doubtless would have been pleased to take on resort hotels or any other legitimate construction project that might have come our way. Yet housing for low- and moderate-income people and for the elderly; hospitals and clinics; schools and university buildings; places for worship and religious education—it is satisfying to be able to say to oneself, "hey, we built that."

The ceremonies punctuate our lives and are memorable. Yet even after the music fades and the speeches are long forgotten, our relation to these buildings is lasting. I asked John Cricco, several years after his retirement, what experiences came to mind when he thought back to the good old days. Responding by e-mail, he wrote:

> January of 1984. Casabe Housing for the Elderly, sponsored by a non-profit organization providing assisted living opportunity. Tenants were beginning to move in. A small pickup truck arrived with an elderly Spanish-speaking lady accompanied by two strong young men, her grandsons perhaps. The pickup held the lady's meager belongings: a cushioned chair, a small table with two kitchen chairs, a TV, a bed, a chest of drawers, and a few boxes. As she walked through the bright, clean lobby, which still smelled of fresh paint, the new tenant dropped to her knees, made the sign of

the cross, kissed the floor, and began to cry. With the help of the two young men, she rose, thanked the nearby workers, and went up to her apartment. We had no way of knowing what kind of living conditions she left behind. But those of us who watched her, could only have more incentive to do a good job.

Heartwarming memories. They come upon me unexpectedly as I find myself in different parts of the city. I can't go anywhere near Hudson Street without thinking about the Village Nursing Home, an icon of Greenwich Village, the interior of which we completely rebuilt in 1982, including new elevators, kitchens, and mechanical systems, with the residents—incredible as it may seem—maintained comfortably and safely in the building. The institution had been on the verge of closing in the 1970s when a "Save Our Nursing Home" campaign was waged, money was raised, and a nonprofit corporation, Caring Community, was formed to buy and refurbish it. Robert Lott, a young Catholic priest, was co-founder and first chairman of the organization, and there has never been a more saintly, good-natured "owner." In fact, everybody in that building, or in any way affiliated with it, seemed to be endowed with a sweet nature. This made working on the project a pleasure but was not necessarily good for business. This was a group to whom it was impossible to say no.

While I'm still in lower Manhattan, my mind drifts toward the Chinatown Planning Council for whom we built three apartment houses—Hong Ning, Chung Pak, and Everlasting Pines—and a health clinic. The projects went smoothly, and we coped well with narrow and crowded streets. But what I remember most vividly are the Chinese New Year celebrations I attended, grudgingly at first, just to please a client, and then with increasing enthusiasm, enjoying the feasts and the pageantry. Working in the Chinese community some thirty years ago, one got a sense of the energy and creativity that has become such an important factor in the world of today.

Another memory comes from downtown. For a private developer we built a nice apartment house in the Chelsea area. After completion, our superintendent informed me that the building was filling up rapidly and seemed to appeal to gay couples. That did not surprise me, given what I knew about the neighborhood, and I was pleased to learn that the project looked like it was going to be a financial success. But what I found especially touching was the experience of one of our punch-list workers. The man had been retained by a few of the tenants to work weekends putting in shelving and extra trim. Apparently all parties were well satisfied with his craftsmanship and jovial personality. As for the grizzled hardhat, he reported to me that talking with a gay couple was something new in his life. To his surprise, he found "that they're pretty nice guys." Two worlds meet, and the result is mutual admiration.

On my way uptown, most mornings on the Henry Hudson Parkway, as I pass 250th Street I catch a glimpse of the Conservative Synagogue of Riverdale. When we completed the project in 1962, I thought that Percival Goodman's design made this the most striking building on which we had worked. It seemed to have about it the feeling of ancient desert civilizations, an aura related somehow to the concrete facade with Hebrew letters inscribed. Unfortunately, the forming and pouring of that special wall ran way over budget and almost led to a serious falling-out with the building committee. In keeping with the biblical setting, we had a Solomon within our midst, Bernie Axelrod, chairman of the committee, whose sermon on fairness and charity—and suggestion of compromise— saved the day.

AS I am reminded of the cost overrun on that concrete wall, it occurs to me that when I think of our happiest jobs, I rarely recall the financial outcome. I remember the structure and the bulding process, the people we worked with and the people who used the finished facility, but not the bottom line. Yet contractors work for profit, don't they? At KBF we've certainly tried hard to maximize our earnings, always. This brings to mind a very special book, *Roll Back the Sea,* by A. den Doolaard, which tells about the rebuilding of the dikes in Holland after their destruction during World War II. The story starts with the urgent needs of people whose homes have been destroyed and progresses through the work of politicians and design engineers. Finally, contractors appear on the scene, absorbed in estimating how much money they will earn from the project. But den Doolaard makes the point that their true purpose, whether they recognize it or not, is to play a vital role in this life-enhancing enterprise. As for profit, writes the author, "profit is merely the bait that destiny has offered to these calculators."

The bait that destiny has offered. A profound thought. An unforgettable phrase.

I mustn't overlook the attraction of technical challenges. If we accept Darwin's theory of evolution, we know that humans are drawn to technological creativity by instincts hardly less basic than hunger and sex. Just spend a few moments looking at children playing with blocks. As a contractor I don't get to share in the satisfaction of doing work with my hands. Nor do I participate—except peripherally—in the design of the structures that I build, even though my engineering education was largely a preparation for such endeavors. But I do plan, compute, schedule, supervise, and in a variety of ways create the structures that I contract to build. And those jobs that present unique technical or organizational challenges are often especially satisfying.

Take, for example, the Lyric, in some ways just an ordinary apartment house, but in other ways one of the most extraordinary buildings with which I've been associated. The story starts with Symphony Space, a small theater on the corner of Ninety-fifth Street and Broadway known for its productions of Gilbert and Sullivan operettas and assorted, sometimes delightfully quirky, concerts, plays, readings, and lectures. Many ambitious real estate people had, through the years, sought to develop the entire blockfront, but the owners of the theater, built in 1915, refused to consider altering it in any way, or even to close it down for more than their summer recess. Steve Ross, the smart, energetic, and venturesome developer, was undeterred. He resolved to meet the challenge by building an apartment house over and around the theater, acceding to every requirement of the owners.

Our firm was selected as construction manager, and we found ourselves participating in discussions about how best to approach this unusual technical challenge. Basic design was the province of the structural engineer; but practical concerns for constructability, cost, manufacture, transportation, and erection presented us with challenges we relished. A scheme was developed featuring five enormous steel girders, each 109 feet in length—more than half a city block—spanning the theater and supporting the building above. On a Saturday morning in July, 1999, the girders, which had been fabricated in Pennsylvania, were loaded onto flatbed trailers, composing a caravan nearly a quarter of a mile in length. Pursuant to special permits, the procession came rumbling over the George Washington Bridge just as the sun was rising. The girders were in place by nightfall, the operation being observed by a friendly crowd and written up in the newspapers of a city not usually impressed by feats of construction. The apartment house, when completed, quickly filled with satisfied tenants, and Symphony Space continues to provide its wonderful assortment of entertainments.

Another project that presented us with unusual tactical challenges was the construction, in 1968, of an underground radiology laboratory for New York City's Mount Sinai Hospital. Building underground in the center of the hospital campus we had to deal with two challenging problems. First, although it would have been prohibitively expensive to use a tunneling technique, open–cut excavation made it impossible for fire engines to reach certain locations that had to be accessible. The solution was to construct, as the excavation proceeded, an elevated timber roadway capable of supporting the necessary fire-safety equipment. Second, since the excavation required the blasting of rock, a comprehensive communications system had to be installed so that we could be in constant contact with all parts of the hospital, particularly the operating rooms. Blasts had to be scheduled with great care, and then confirmation received from all concerned parties just before detonation. For construction people used to rough and ready ways of working, these unusual requirements could have caused tensions. Strangely, the great responsibility and our success in measuring up to the demands of the moment were the source of high morale and considerable pride.

High morale and considerable pride. That sort of sums it up. We had good times and did good work.

AND what of the future? Of one thing we can be sure: construction is an activity that will remain a vital center of human enterprise. What particular exciting developments are on the horizon?

By all indications, the wonderful world of BIM (building information modeling) shows promise of perhaps not revolutionizing our industry but certainly carrying it to new levels of creative efficiency. This new technique begins with the generation by computer of a 3-D model of a building. "Imagine," said a lawyer I met at the theater one evening, "you have the whole building complete before you begin construction. Just think of it: all the mechanical systems laid out. No more conflict with pipes or conduits or ducts bumping into one another. How wonderful! This will be the end of construction litigation!" I fear that he was being a bit simplistic about what generates lawsuits in construction. Nevertheless, the BIM concept does sound exciting, and the 3-D model is apparently just the beginning. Elevations and sections can be generated from the model, and information, either graphical or nongraphical, can be added without limit. Ah, the information age! And what else?

"Green construction" and "sustainable building": using processes that are environmentally responsible and resource-efficient throughout a building's life cycle.

And materials. We can look forward to improvements in steel, concrete, glass, and other traditional elements of a building, plus new composites and a host of magical substances developed by the chemists of the future.

And of course there is the eternal pursuit of "productivity."

DURING my own working years, construction efficiency—productivity—has seen considerable improvement. *Engineering News-Record* articles in 2004 and 2005 reported that according to the analysis of Preston H. Haskell, chairman of a large design-build firm, the cost of building per square foot (comparing similar types of buildings in current dollars) declined more than 13 percent from the mid-1960s to the middle of the first decade of the new millennium. At the same time, more than 16 percent in new expenses have been added to buildings by way of improvements: fire- and life-safety protection, seismic and wind resistance, life-cycle cost expectancy, accessibility, security, and energy efficiency. Thus we come up with a total increase in productivity of approximately 30 percent over a period of forty years. Haskell's conclusion: "We are receiving more building for less money than we did 40 years ago, and moreover, the product is qualitatively superior."

According to *ENR,* Thomas Gilbane, Jr., chairman and CEO of Gilbane Building Company of Providence, one of the nation's largest, oldest, and most respected firms, has, in reviewing his own organization's work, confirmed the Haskell conclusions. I, and other contractors with whom I've discussed this, agree, based on empirical evaluation. This is not as spectacular an improvement as some of the leading manufacturing industries, but I think it's pretty darned good considering what it is that contractors do and the difficult, unalterably primitive, conditions under which they work.

There is, be it admitted, a contrary view. Paul Teicholz, a civil engineering professor from Stanford, maintains that the construction industry's productivity from 1964 to 1998 declined by an average of nearly 0.5 percent per year while productivity in other industries was increasing 1.7 percent annually. This sounds dreadful—and almost unbelievable, until we learn that his analysis is based on what *ENR* calls the "Teicholz metric." This metric consists of eight magic words: "hours of field work per dollar of contract." Since this figure has been increasing, Teicholz concludes that productivity has been declining. Along with Haskell, Gilbane, and other established builders, I am more impressed by the total cost per square foot of completed buildings than I am by "hours of field work per dollar of contract," the importance of which I find rather elusive—particularly when *ENR* reports that Teicholz admits that his figures include the large proportion of construction done by individuals and small firms and "do not show what the best in the industry can do." I have great respect for the several million workers who do alterations, repairs, and the like, but I don't see how they can be included in a productivity study along with firms that construct large buildings.

At the start of this chapter, I vowed to put aside all gloomy thoughts. But I find that my *bête noire*, Barry LePatner, attorney at law, relies on the Teicholz metric in his broad-ranging critique of the construction industry, making comments that demand a hearing—and a response. In a widely read article published in *The Boston Globe* in 2007, Mr. Le-Patner asserts that construction is "the most wasteful, least productive industry in America . . . a bastion of waste and inefficiency." Then, for comparison, he extols the progress made by the automobile industry, oil refining, and steelmaking.

Let us admit that the construction industry, like everything else in this world, can be better than it is. But I believe that the Haskell figures, endorsed by numerous reputable contractors, show that improvements in productivity have been achieved and that intemperate accusations of waste and inefficiency are unwarranted. I also believe it is misguided to seek improvement in imitation of the assembly line.

It does make sense to take advantage of factory-type economies wherever doing so proves possible. But it is the burden—and the glory—of most construction that each building is unique. This is true even for most housing. Yes, we should draw on precedents and accepted standards. Yet each design is special—and who would have it any other way? And building design has to be made a reality, not on some clean factory floor but in a very special, one-of-a-kind location, often in the center of a pulsing, heavily trafficked, overcrowded city. The Associated General Contractors of America reports that a large number of contractors complain that traffic adds 11 percent or more to their cost of doing business. Traffic congestion is one of the curses of our society, and negatively affects productivity in countless ways. But there are no traffic problems within any factory that I know of.

Can't we nevertheless take advantage of prefabrication? Yes, certainly, but not by forgetting old lessons learned. In the 1970s, we had Operation Breakthrough, sponsored by George Romney, a noted automaker, when he was appointed secretary of HUD. I visited one of the newly built factories and was enthralled to see prefab bathrooms, kitchens, and other manufactured units ready to be plugged together like a LEGO set. But even with union cooperation and grudging consent from architects—and disregarding the complexities of transport and handling these large units on site—the experiment didn't work. Paradoxically, it was defeated by the dynamic, creative free-enterprise system of which we are so rightly proud. One project would be in a rush to get started, another delayed by financial problems, still another put off for months because of political difficulties or perhaps technical complications in the foundations. There was no sure way of determining when each particular project would commence and according to what schedule it would progress. Change and uncertainty was an inescapable element of the process—not construction problems as much as the business and political forces that controlled the construction. Without an adequate degree of continuity the factory bogged down—and eventually had to close, as did all of the nine Operation Breakthrough sites. The need for continuity is crucial to factory operation. Keeping this in mind, I do not doubt that new approaches to prefabrication will be devised and prove successful. In the spirit of entrepreneurial enthusiasm, the Modular Building Institute reports that its members are making significant progress.

* * *

LOOKING toward the future, a high-level committee formed in 2008 by the National Academies of Science and Engineering has recommended that the National Institute of Standards and Technology (NIST) "should work with industry leaders to bring together a critical mass of construction industry stakeholders to develop a collaborative strategy for advancing the competitiveness and efficiency of the industry." And further: "The collaborative strategy should identify actions needed to fully implement and deploy interoperable technology applications, job-site efficiencies, off-site fabrication processes, demonstration installations and effective performance measures." Good. There's a touch of bureaucratic gobbledygook in that, but essentially the idea is worthy. NIST is a well-established federal agency that, among other achievements, has supported a network of business centers that help manufacturers adapt modern production techniques. If NIST, along with capable construction "stakeholders," can help the industry to "move ahead," that is something we all want to support.

I only wish that prospective leaders could reach Joe DePaola in his concrete subcontractors club in the sky and learn from him the lessons of the two-day cycle. Joe knew that a construction job is much like a ballet, with graceful movement and timing being critical to success.

WHATEVER the future holds for the construction industry, I will not be part of it. Nor will KBF, at least as I've known it. The company has had a pretty good run, fifty-seven years and counting.

SO, as I reach the conclusion of this chapter—in my book and in my life—let me return to that merry Sondheim song and see how it ends:

Goodness and badness, man in his madness,
This time it all turns out all right.
Tragedy tomorrow, comedy tonight.

Those first two lines seem to apply to the construction industry I have come to know and love. Goodness and badness. Yes. Man in his madness. It often seems that way. And then: it all turns out all right. That's nice.

Tragedy tomorrow? I had forgotten about that line. Well, that's how it goes. Yet this need not be regarded as totally grim news. Every student of classical drama knows that the great tragedians were not pessimists but rather champions of resolute spirit exhibited in the face of a challenging universe.

So, the show's introduction ends on an up note, and we wait for the next scene with cheerful anticipation.

Acknowledgments

IF I HAD KNOWN, years ago, that I was going to write this book, I would have kept a diary. Of course, memory is a useful guide, since it filters past experience, selecting events that have stayed with us, presumably for good reason. But memory is famous for its failures, and luckily I have had access to other sources of information. Old letters and assorted papers accumulated at home and in the office have suddenly morphed into precious research material. The files at Kreisler Borg Florman, although winnowed as they necessarily have been after more than fifty years, still contain gems if you know where to look. Virginia Crowley knows where everything is, and she capably organized the material I needed most. John Cricco, who retired in 1997 after more than four decades with the firm, proved to have total recall, regaling me with tales, both amusing and alarming, about events we shared and supplementing his memories with carefully preserved appointment calendars.

Then there are Bob Borg's collected mementos. Sadly, Bob died in December 2010, just as I was working on this manuscript. But I had long had access to his scrapbooks, a remarkable collection of newspaper clippings and photos. Admittedly, those cheer-filled records of groundbreakings, topping-out parties, and dedication ceremonies, plus notices of industry awards and staff promotions, don't give a full picture of our life as general contractors. Bob was not blind to the difficulties we encountered, but he liked to dwell on the positives. The materials he saved give testimony to his optimistic nature and the pleasure he derived from his profession. Bob and I worked together harmoniously for many years. He was a good partner.

WHEN it came to the broader scope of my enterprise, currents of change in the New York City construction industry, I required help outside of my immediate circle. Here I was fortunate to enlist Scott Lewis, a researcher who has a thorough knowledge of the field and access to any odd bits of information, historical or financial, about which an author can possibly think to ask. Scott's friends at McGraw-Hill Construction Research and Analytics were quick to clarify terms and figures that seemed obscure to an amateur, and Gary J. Tulacz, senior editor of *Engineering News-Record,* was helpful in answering questions relating to his publication's numerous statistical tables and charts. Incidentally, *ENR* can appropriately claim to be "the bible of the industry," and editor-in-chief Jan Tuchman, along with her staff, deserves the thanks of all who seek to keep informed about our tumultuous corner of the cosmos.

When I was first embarking on this writing project, I was introduced to Robert Leicht, then a graduate research assistant at Penn State specializing in the construction industry. I recruited him to provide background information, all of which proved extremely helpful.

WORK on a book may begin with the recollection of experiences and the gathering of information. But this only brings one to the threshold. For me, writing has always been a solitary occupation, followed, sometimes belatedly, by the search for appraisal and assistance. In this instance the primary editorial review was undertaken by Judy, my wife and love. She entered the scene too late to be blamed for the conceptual whole and just in time to discard superfluous adjectives and remedy a number of awkward phrases. She also persuaded me to eliminate autobiographical material that had little to do with my work or my industry. This is a personal book, but its principal theme is construction. The story of my wonderful family—to whom I have dedicated the book—will have to be recorded elsewhere. I must note, however, that my son, Jonathan, undertook invaluable last-minute editing of the manuscript, and my son, David, who helped edit a couple of my earlier works, this time led the way, with imagination and good humor, in thinking up a title.

THIS brings me at last to Tom Dunne. And when I say "at last" I mean it in the sense of grand finale, major importance. Since 1974, when we signed the contract for *The Existential Pleasures of Engineering,* Tom has been editor, publisher, and good friend. After *Existential,* we worked together on three more books devoted to the theme of engineering and technology in the general culture, then a novel, and now a cross between a memoir and a study of our nation's most turbulent industry. That makes this the sixth collaboration over a period approaching four decades—the seventh if we count the second edition of *Existential*—and every step of the way Tom has provided editorial guidance, encouragement, and support. And, perhaps most important, a merry spirit. He wouldn't want me to overwrite, here or anywhere else, so I will simply express admiration, affection, and thanks.

I can't conclude, however, without taking grateful note of Tom's superefficient, ever-pleasant assistant, Margaret Smith, and of the wonderful Katie Gilligan, the editor who picks up all the pieces at the end and somehow makes the seemingly chaotic publishing process turn out just fine.

Index

DCA. *See* Department of Cultural Affairs
DDC. *See* Department of Design and
 Construction
de Acutis, Mario, 96–97
Death of a Salesman (Miller), 170
Death Wish (film), 308–9
debris, 265–66, 283
DeCicco, Frank, 199
Defoe, Daniel, 262
Dekind, Danny, 237–38, 240
DeMatteis, 85
DeMeo, Al, 161
Democratic National Convention of 1980,
 134
den Doolard, A., 312–13
DePaola, Joseph, 55–56, 96–97, 103,
 105–6, 108, 115, 176, 191, 193,
 195, 320
Department of Buildings, 144, 159
 bribery and, 205–6
 construction accidents and, 262–63
 corruption in, 187
 Lucchese crime family and, 207
Department of Commerce, 98
Department of Cultural Affairs (DCA),
 153
Department of Design and Construction
 (DDC), 83, 153, 282, 285–86
Department of Housing and Urban
 Development (HUD)
 Housing for the Elderly Program,
 140
 Model Cities Program, 231, 234–36
 Operation Breakthrough, 319
 Section 202, 82, 84, 90
Department of Housing Preservation and
 Development (HPD), 163, 171
Department of Labor, 249
Department of Transportation, 178
Depression, 65, 184
design engineering, 41, 160, 276–77
Design for Play (Dattner), 158
deus ex machina, 96
developers, 136, 165
Devoren, Peter, 289

Dewey, Thomas E., 198
Diamond, Jared, 107
Dic Concrete, 96–97, 103, 106, 176,
 195
dictation, 54
Dic-Underhill, 106, 191, 195
Diesel Construction Company, 57
DiNapoli, Louis, 193
Dinkins, David, 227–28
Dirkson, Everett, 80
DiRubbo, Leo, 286
discounting, 52
discrimination, 223–24, 256–57
diversity, 111
Doctors Without Borders, 258
Doe Fund, 173
Dolphins Stadium, 174
Doran, Phillip, 199
Dorr-Oliver Company, 69–70
Downtown Athletic Club, 35
Dukakis, Michael, 134
Duke, Milton, 162
Dun & Bradstreet, 177
Durocher, Leo, 53

E. W. Howell, 85
earth-fill dams, 16–17
East Midtown Plaza, 268–69
East Side Airlines Terminal, 125
École Polytechnique, 20
ecumenical training center, 67
efficiency, 317
Eisenberg, Susan, 249–51
Eisenhower, Dwight D., 225
Eken, 36
El Nuevo Mundo Tenants Association,
 234–35
Elghanayan, Fred, 167–68
Elghanayan, Henry, 167
Elghanayan, Nourallah, 167
Elghanayan, Tom, 167
Elgin National Industries, 48
Eliot, T. S., 306
Empire State Building, 179, 280
employment, 5, 226

Henegan Construction, 85
Henoch, Robert, 202
Herbert Construction Co., 139, 214–15
Hewett, Bob, 114
Higginbotham, J. C., 224
Hiroshima, 14
Hispanics, 235–36
HJD. *See* Hospital for Joint Diseases
    Orthopaedic Institute
Hochtief AG, 51
Hoffman, Dustin, 59
Hoffman, Linda, 139–40, 158, 252
Holden, Kenneth, 282–83
"The Hollow Men" (Eliot), 306
Hong Ning, 312
Hope, Bob, 98
Horn, Stacy, 219–20
Horowitz, Louis J., 36, 39
Hospital for Joint Diseases Orthopaedic
    Institute (HJD), 126
Housing and Development Administration
    (HDA), 141–43, 161–63
Housing and Home Finance Agency, 141
HPD. *See* Department of Housing
    Preservation and Development
HRH, 83, 85, 120–21, 144–45
HUD. *See* Department of Housing and
    Urban Development
Hughes, Howard, 98
Hugo, Victor, 221
humanities, 24–25
Hunter Roberts, 85
Hurricane Katrina, 133
Hyatt Regency of Kansas City, 276–77
hydropower, 46

Idlewild Airport, 26
inflation, 80
injuries, 269–73
The Innocents Abroad (Twain), 78
inspectors, 26
    corruption and, 206–7
    first encounter with, 42–43
    intimidation of, 1–2
    Morelli and, 119

Institute of Medicine, 76
insurance, workers' compensation, 272
insurance claims, 64, 270, 272–73
interior office construction, 215–16
interiors projects, 68
interviews, 66
intimidation, 1–2
Italian Americans, 111, 188
Italian Historical Society in America, 188
Italy, 33

Jacobs Engineering, 85
Javits, Jacob, 188
Javits Convention Center, 83
JC Penney Company, 212–13
Jefferson, Thomas, 19–20
Jereski, Bernie, 176
Jewish Community Center of Harrison, 67
Jewish Guild for the Blind, 144–46, 310
Jim Crow laws, 225
Jimmy (uncle), 34
Johnson, Lyndon B., 100, 136, 225–26,
    230
Johnson, Philip, 152
Johnson Wax headquarters, 151
Joint Board of Fur, Leather and Machine
    Workers Union, 141
Jones, J. Raymond, 143
Joseph, Peter, 171
Joseph P. Blitz, Inc., 51
Judaism, 111–12
Justice Department, 226–27

Kahan, Richard A., 228
KBF. *See* Kreisler Borg Florman
KBR, 85
Keating, Kenneth, 188
Kefauver Committee on Organized
    Crime, 185
Kelly, Raymond W., 236
Kelly's Stable, 224
Kennedy, John F., 136, 226
Kennedy, Robert F., 186, 307
kickbacks, 3, 210, 212, 217. *See also*
    corruption

New York Telephone Company, 68
New York Times, 48, 156, 158, 168, 186, 198, 206, 211, 213, 261, 267–68, 286
New York Times Book Review, 288–89
New York Times Magazine, 236
New York University (NYU), 25, 255
   Medical Center, 126
   Real Estate Institute, 178
   School of Continuing and Professional Studies, 238
Newark Star-Ledger, 197
newsreels, 9
Nike missile system, 68
9/11 attacks, 279–80
   cleanup, 285–87
   engineers and, 283–84
NIST. *See* National Institute of Standards and Technology
Nixon, Richard M., 136, 226
nonprofit groups, 82
Norman Winston House, 97–98
NOW. *See* National Organization for Women
Nowak, John, 114
Nuclear Development Corporation, 62
Nunez, Joshua, 238
nursing homes, 158–59
NYU. *See* New York University

Obama, Barack, 227
O'Brien, Joseph, 202
Occupational Safety and Health Act of 1970, 272
Occupational Safety and Health Administration (OSHA), 44, 208–9, 255, 263
On the Waterfront (film), 186
1 Penn Plaza, 179
one-family houses, 26
O'Neill, Brian, 201
Operation Breakthrough, 319
organized crime, 2, 185–86, 202–3. *See also* Mafia
Osborn project, 291–95

OSHA. *See* Occupational Safety and Health Administration
overhead, 79, 90
Owl's Head Wastewater Treatment Plant, 43–44
ownership, 44

PaineWebber, 136
Pan Am Building, 57
Paraguana Peninsula, 29–32
Paramount Pictures, 308
partnership, 59, 73–74
Passeri, Al, 77
Passeri, Mario, 77
Paulist Fathers, 42
PCL, 85
Pearl Harbor Day, 10–11
Peekskill Hospital, 81
Pei, I. M., 152
Pentagon Papers, 198
people skills, 76
performance-and-payment bonds, 104
Perini Corp., 85
Perkins Eastman, 291, 294
Permanent Mission of the USSR, 145
permits, 3
Perotta, Sandy, 284
Peter Cooper Village, 51
Peterkin, John B., 125
Phelan, Frank, 176, 193
Philadelphia Stock Exchange, 180
philanthropy, 167
Phillips, Andrea, 254
Pirraglia, Michael, 302
Pittelman, Carole, 175–76, 252–53
Plato, 25
Pocantico Hills, 36
political contacts, 133–34
politicians, 134–36, 210–11
Polo Grounds, 224
Polshek, James, 152–54
Polshek Partnership, 153, 177
Polytechnic Institute of Brooklyn, 110
Pools Unlimited, 110
Port Authority, 283